Verbos
Ingleses
GUÍA PRÁCTICA

LAROUSSE

Verbos Ingleses
GUÍA PRÁCTICA

LAROUSSE

NI UNA FOTOCOPIA MÁS

Verbos ingleses

D. R. © MCMXCVII, por Ediciones Larousse, S. A. de C. V.
          Renacimiento núm. 180, México, D. F. 02400

ISBN 970-607-650-6
     978-970-607-650-2

PRIMERA EDICIÓN - Trigésima segunda reimpresión

Impreso en México — Printed in Mexico

Introducción

Verbos ingleses. Guía práctica es un libro de referencia indispensable para todos aquellos que estén interesados en profundizar en el conocimiento de la lengua inglesa.

Como bien sabemos, el aprendizaje de una lengua extranjera supone, por una parte, el conocimiento de sus reglas gramaticales, y por otra, el dominio de una parte considerable de su vocabulario. En *Verbos ingleses* encontramos reunidos ambos aspectos: una guía práctica para comprender los modos, tiempos, usos y significados de los verbos ingleses complementada por un amplio repertorio con más de **2.000 frases verbales del inglés de HOY** y sus correspondientes equivalencias al español. Al final del texto se ofrece un índice exhaustivo que simplifica la consulta a los usuarios.

ÍNDICE

ÍNDICE

1 GLOSARIO DE TERMINOS GRAMATICALES

ACTIVA De las dos voces del sistema verbal la voz activa es la forma más común, como en *Pedro la atiende*. Su forma opuesta es la voz pasiva (*ella es atendida por Pedro*).

AUXILIAR Los auxiliares se utilizan para formar los tiempos compuestos de otros verbos, por ejemplo en **he has gone** (*se ha ido*), **has** y *ha* son los verbos auxiliares.

COLOQUIAL El lenguaje coloquial es el lenguaje corriente de hoy en día, el que utilizamos al hablar, pero no cuando escribimos cartas oficiales, contratos etc.

COMPLEMENTO DIRECTO Existen dos clases de complemento: **complemento directo y complemento indirecto**. En la oración «*He escrito una carta a mi hermano*» tenemos dos complementos. «*Una carta*» es el complemento directo (lo que he escrito) mientras que «*mi hermano*» es el complemento indirecto (a quien he escrito). En la oración «*He visto a mi hermano el sábado*» el complemento directo es «*mi hermano*».

CONDICIONAL Modo verbal que expresa lo que alguien haría o lo que pasaría si se cumpliese una condición, por ejemplo: *Se **habría roto** si te hubieses sentado encima.*

CONJUGACIÓN La conjugación de un verbo es el conjunto de formas de que se compone, según sus diferentes tiempos y modos.

CONTINUO Ver FORMA CONTINUA

FORMA BASE Ver INFINITIVO

FORMA CONTINUA La forma continua de un verbo se forma con **to be + participio presente**, como en los siguientes ejemplos: *I am thinking, he has been writing all day, will she be staying with us?* También recibe el nombre de «forma progresiva».

GERUNDIO Al gerundio podemos llamarlo «verbo sustantivado». En inglés tiene la misma forma que el **participio presente** del verbo, es decir: forma base + **-ing**. Por ejemplo: **Skiing is fun** (*El esquí es divertido*), **I'm fed up with waiting** (*estoy harto de esperar*).

IMPERATIVO Este modo es el que se utiliza cuando queremos dar una orden (p.e. *¡Vete!, ¡Cállate!*).

INDICATIVO Es el modo más utilizado. Describe una acción o un estado, como en *quiero, ha venido, intentamos*. Se opone al subjuntivo, al condicional y al imperativo.

INFINITIVO

El infinitivo en inglés es la forma base del verbo, la que se encuentra en los diccionarios, vaya o no precedida de **to**: **to eat** o **eat**. (La forma base no va precedida de **to**.)

INTERROGATIVO

Las palabras interrogativas se utilizan para hacer preguntas o interrogaciones, p.e. «¿*quién?*», «¿*por qué?*». La forma interrogativa de un verbo o una oración es la forma que se utiliza para hacer preguntas, por ejemplo: ¿*le conoce?, ¿tengo que hacerlo?, ¿pueden esperar un poco?*

MODAL

Los auxiliares modales en inglés son: **can/could, may/might, must/had to, shall/should, will/would** además de **ought to, used to, dare** y **need**. Una de sus características es que construyen la forma interrogativa sin necesidad de utilizar el auxiliar **do**.

MODO

El modo representa la actitud del hablante respecto a la acción de que habla. Ver INDICATIVO, SUBJUNTIVO, CONDICIONAL, IMPERATIVO

PARTICIPIO PASADO

En castellano son las formas *tomado, comido, vivido* etc. El participio pasado inglés es la forma que se utiliza después de *have*, como en: *I have **eaten**, I have **said**, you have **tried**.*

PARTICIPIO PRESENTE

El participio presente en inglés es la forma verbal terminada en **-ing**.

PASIVA

Un verbo está en voz pasiva, y no en voz activa, cuando el sujeto no hace la acción, sino que la «padece», es decir, recae sobre él: *los abonos son vendidos en taquilla*. En inglés la voz pasiva se forma con el verbo **to be** y el participio pasado del verbo, por ejemplo: ***he was rewarded** = fue recompensado*.

PERSONA

En todos los tiempos tenemos tres personas de singular (1ª = yo; 2ª = tú; 3ª = él/ella) y tres personas de plural (1ª = nosotros-as; 2ª =vosotros-as; 3ª = ellos/ellas).

PRONOMBRE

Un pronombre es una palabra que sustituye a un nombre. Existen diferentes clases. Los pronombres personales son: *yo, tú, él, ella, nosotros, nosotras, ellos, ellas, mí, ti*, etc. Los pronombres demostrativos son: *éste, ése, aquél, ésta* etc.

PROPOSICIÓN

Una proposición es un grupo de palabras entre las que al menos se incluye un sujeto y un verbo: *canta* es una proposición (en este sentido equivale a oración). Hay veces que varias proposiciones se unen, formando una oración compuesta (*canta cuando se ducha y está contento*).

PROPOSICIÓN SUBORDINADA	Una proposición subordinada es aquella que depende de otra. Por ejemplo en *dijo que vendría*, «*que vendría*» es una proposición subordinada.
REFLEXIVO	Los verbos reflexivos expresan acciones que hace el sujeto y que recaen sobre él mismo (p.e. *me visto*).
SUBJUNTIVO	Ejemplos: *necesito que vengas, ¡viva el rey!* El subjuntivo tiene un uso muy limitado en inglés.
SUJETO	El sujeto de un verbo es el nombre o pronombre que realiza la acción. En las oraciones «*como chocolate*» y «*Pedro tiene dos gatos*» los sujetos son «*yo*» (se sobreentiende) y «*Pedro*».
TIEMPO	El tiempo de un verbo indica cuándo tiene lugar la acción. Puede ser en el presente, en el pasado o en el futuro.
TIEMPO COMPUESTO	Los tiempos compuestos son aquellos que se forman con más de un elemento. En inglés se forman con ayuda de un **auxiliar** y del participio **presente** o **pasado** del verbo conjugado. Por ejemplo: *I am reading, I have gone.*
VERBO	El verbo es una palabra que describe una acción (*cantar, andar*). También puede describir un estado (*ser, parecer, estar, esperar*).
VERBO CON PARTÍCULA	Ejemplos de verbos con partícula son *ask for* o *run up*. Su significado generalmente difiere de lo que se espera cuando se tiene en cuenta las partes de las que se compone. Veamos algunos ejemplos: «*He goes in for skiing in a big way*» «*Le encanta hacer esquí*» (es muy diferente de: «*He goes in for a medical next week*» «*Le van a hacer un examen médico la semana que viene*») o «*He ran up an enormous bill*» «*Le ha supuesto una factura enorme*» (es diferente de: «*He ran up the road*» «*Subió la carretera corriendo*»).
VOZ	Existen dos voces: la voz activa y la voz pasiva. Ver ACTIVA y PASIVA

2   LAS FORMAS VERBALES: CONCEPTOS BÁSICOS

Los conceptos básicos son:

-forma base del verbo o infinitivo

-participio presente

-participio pasado

1) La **forma base del verbo** o **infinitivo** es la forma del verbo que aparece en el índice y en el diccionario de verbos con partícula que componen la segunda parte de este libro. Esta forma puede emplearse con y sin **to**. **Watch** es un infinitivo en las siguientes oraciones:

Do you want to watch?
¿Quieres mirar?

I can't watch.
No puedo mirar.

2) El **participio presente** es la forma verbal que termina en **-ing**:

Is anyone watching?
¿Está mirando alguien?

They were watching us.
Nos estaban mirando.

Observe que, como ocurre en el último ejemplo, el participio presente se utiliza para formar otros tiempos además del presente.

En lo que se refiere a la formación del participio presente ver el capítulo 5.

3) Existen dos clases de **participio pasado**. En el caso de los verbos regulares el participio pasado tiene la misma forma que el pasado, es decir: forma base + **-(e)d**:

watch - watched

dance - danced

Para aclaraciones referentes a la ortografía de esta forma verbal ver el capítulo 5.

Los participios pasados de los verbos irregulares aparecen listados alfabéticamente en la página 13. Aquí tenemos algunos ejemplos:

go - went

teach - taught

stand - stood

3   LOS AUXILIARES

A los verbos **be, do** y **have** se les llama verbos auxiliares.

Además de estos verbos hay otros auxiliares, los llamados auxiliares «modales» o «defectivos» (ver pág. 31). La diferencia fundamental que distingue a los verbos auxiliares **be, do** y **have** es que también pueden funcionar como verbos normales con significado completo, en ese caso equivalen a **ser/estar, hacer** y **tener** respectivamente.

Los auxiliares se utilizan para formar algunos tiempos:

> **What ARE you doing?**
> ¿Qué estás haciendo? (en este momento)

> **What DO you do?**
> ¿Qué haces? (habitualmente)

> **What HAVE you done?**
> ¿Qué has hecho?

Las formas de presente y pasado de estos auxiliares son las siguientes:

be
presente

	singular	plural
1ª	**I am**	**we are**
2ª	**you are**	**you are**
3ª	**he/she/it is**	**they are**

pasado

	singular	plural
1ª	**I was**	**we were**
2ª	**you were**	**you were**
3ª	**he/she/it was**	**they were**

do
presente

	singular	plural
1ª	**I do**	**we do**
2ª	**you do**	**you do**
3ª	**he/she/it does**	**they do**

pasado

	singular	plural
1ª	**I did**	**we did**
2ª	**you did**	**you did**
3ª	**he/she/it did**	**they did**

have
presente

	singular	*plural*
1ª	I have	we have
2ª	you have	you have
3ª	he/she/it has	they have

pasado

	singular	*plural*
1ª	I had	we had
2ª	you had	you had
3ª	he/she/it had	they had

4   LOS TIEMPOS

En inglés, la mayoría de los verbos tienen la misma forma para todas las personas en el mismo tiempo. Por ejemplo tenemos:

> **I/you/he/she/it/we/they went**

La gran excepción la constituye la tercera persona del singular del presente, a la que se añade la terminación **-s** o **-es** (ver los verbos modelo en el capítulo 5). Así tenemos:

	singular	*plural*
1ª	**I watch**	**we watch**
2ª	**you watch**	**you watch**
3ª	**he/she/it watches**	**they watch**

Los diferentes tiempos verbales se construyen de la forma que indicamos más abajo (las indicaciones sobre el uso de los tiempos aparece en los capítulos 16-18; sobre la formación de la voz pasiva ver el capítulo 6):

infinitivo	**(to) watch**
infinitivo continuo	**(to) be watching [be** + participio presente]
infinitivo compuesto	**(to) have watched [have** + participio pasado]
infinitivo compuesto continuo	**(to) have been watching**
presente simple	**I/you/he etc. watch(es)**
presente continuo	**am/are/is watching**
futuro simple[*]	**will watch**
futuro continuo[*]	**will be watching**
pasado simple	**I watched**
pasado continuo	**was/were watching**
presente perfecto	**have/has watched**
presente perfecto continuo	**have/has been watching**
pasado perfecto	**had watched**
pasado perfecto continuo	**had been watching**
futuro compuesto	**will have watched**
futuro compuesto continuo	**will have been watching**
condicional presente	**would watch**
condicional presente continuo	**would be watching**
condicional compuesto	**would have watched**
condicional compuesto continuo	**would have been watching**

[*]Algunos gramáticos consideran que en inglés el «futuro» no es un tiempo verbal completo, y lo clasifican más bien como un modo.

5   LOS VERBOS MODELO

En este capítulo proponemos una clasificación de los verbos en diferentes modelos, en función de las alteraciones ortográficas que en ellos se producen. Los verbos que aparecen en el índice del presente libro tienen un código que remite a un verbo modelo.

P1

	añadir
«he/she/it» en presente	**-s**
participio presente	**-ing**
participio pasado	**-ed**

Por ejemplo:

look : looks - looking - looked

P2

	añadir
«he/she/it» en presente	**-es**
participio presente	**-ing**
participio pasado	**-ed**

Por ejemplo:

watch : watches - watching - watched

NOTA: La terminación **-es** es común a los verbos que terminan en **-s, -x, -z, -ch** y **-sh**.

P3

	añadir
«he/she/it» en presente	**-s**
participio presente	**-ing**
participio pasado	**-d**

Por ejemplo:

agree : agrees - agreeing - agreed

P4

	quitar	*añadir*
«he/she/it» en presente		**-s**
participio presente	**-e** final	**-ing**
participio pasado		**-d**

Por ejemplo:

hate : hates - hating - hated

P5

	añadir
«he/she/it» en presente	**-s**
participio presente	doblar la consonante final **-ing**
participio pasado	doblar la consonante final **-ed**

Por ejemplo:

grab : grabs - grabbing - grabbed
occur : occurs - occurring - occurred

NOTA: Esta duplicación de consonante tiene lugar cuando le antecede una vocal breve tónica, como en los ejemplos que acabamos de ver. Pero no se produciría en el siguiente caso:

keep : keeps - keeping

ya que la vocal es larga. Tampoco en el siguiente:

vomit : vomits - vomiting - vomited

pues la vocal es átona.

En inglés BRITANICO en algunos casos se dobla esta consonante incluso cuando la vocal final es átona, como en los siguientes ejemplos:

travel : travels - travelling - travelled

kidnap : kidnaps - kidnapping - kidnapped

Pero en inglés AMERICANO estas formas tienen solamente una consonante:

travel - traveling - traveled

kidnap - kidnaping - kidnaped

En el índice final indicamos los verbos que se construyen sobre el modelo americano con la abreviatura *(Am.)*.

P6

	cambiar	añadir
«he/she/it» en presente	la y final en **ies**	
participio presente		**-ing**
participio pasado	la y en **ied**	

Por ejemplo:

accompany : accompanies - accompanying - accompanied

cry : cries - crying - cried

P7

	cambiar	añadir
«he/she/it» en presente		**-s**
participio presente	la **ie** final en **y**	**-ing**
participio pasado		**-d**

Por ejemplo:

die : dies - dying - died

P8

	cambiar	añadir
«he/she/it» en presente		**-s**
participio presente	la **c** final en **ck**	**-ing**
participio pasado	la **c** final en **ck**	**-ed**

Por ejemplo:

picnic : picnics - picnicking - picnicked

P9

Este código se utiliza para señalar los verbos cuyo participio pasado es irregular (ver pág. 13):

choose : chooses - choosing - chosen

Esta clase de verbos llevan dos códigos. En el caso de **choose** tendremos los códigos siguientes: P4P9. El P9 significa que se trata de un verbo irregular, y que sus formas, al ser irregulares, no se someten a alteraciones ortográficas precisas. Para las restantes formas se acopla al modelo P4.

P10

	añadir
«he/she/it» en presente	**-ses**
participio presente	**-sing**
participio pasado	**-sed**

Una forma rara:

non-plus : non-plusses - non-plussing - non-plussed

6   LA VOZ PASIVA

Fijémonos en este ejemplo:

I follow
Sigo

El verbo **follow** tiene un sentido activo, y el sujeto **I** realiza la acción de «seguir». Pero en:

I am followed
Soy seguido

el verbo **am followed** tiene un sentido pasivo, y el sujeto **I** es sobre el que recae la acción.

1) La voz pasiva se forma con el verbo **be** + participio pasado. Así del verbo **hide** tendremos las siguientes formas:

infinitivo	**(to) be hidden**
infinitivo compuesto	**(to) have been hidden**
infinitivo compuesto continuo	**(to) be being hidden**
presente simple	**are/is hidden**
presente continuo	**am/are/is being hidden**
futuro simple	**will be hidden**
futuro simple continuo	**will be being hidden**
pasado simple	**was/were hidden**
pasado continuo	**was/were being hidden**
presente perfecto	**have/has been hidden**
presente perfecto continuo	**have/has been being hidden**
pasado perfecto	**had been hidden**
pasado perfecto continuo	**had been being hidden**
futuro compuesto	**will have been hidden**
condicional presente	**would be hidden**
condicional presente continuo	**would be being hidden**
condicional pasado	**would have been hidden**
condicional pasado continuo	**would have been being hidden**

Ejemplos:

It was hidden under some old papers.
Estaba escondido bajo unos papeles viejos.

It had deliberately been hidden by his assistant.
Había sido escondido deliberadamente por su ayudante.

It was thought to have been hidden by the Romans.
Se pensaba que había sido escondido por los romanos.

He objected to this information being hidden away at the bottom of the form.
Se negó a que esta información se ocultase al final del formulario.

If he were a suspect, he would be being asked a lot of questions by now.
Si fuera sospechoso, ya estaría siendo interrogado.

If he had made any comment, it would almost certainly have been ignored.
Si hubiese hecho cualquier comentario con toda seguridad se le habría hecho caso omiso.

2)   Fíjese en esta oración en voz activa:

They sent him the wrong letter.
Le mandaron la carta que no era.

En voz pasiva tendría dos posibilidades:

The wrong letter was sent to him.
He was sent the wrong letter.
Se le mandó la carta que no era.

3)   A menudo pueden utilizarse verbos intransitivos con un significado pasivo:

It opens at the front.
Se abre por delante.

The sentence reads better like this.
Esta oración suena mejor de esta forma.

This material won't wash very well.
Este tejido no se lava muy bien.

7 LISTA DE VERBOS IRREGULARES

Indicamos con un asterisco (*) los americanismos. Entre paréntesis aparecen las formas poco corrientes, arcaicas o literarias. La traducción que se hace de cada verbo no es la única y es el significado que tiene con mayor frecuencia.

infinitivo		*pretérito*	*participio pasado*
abide	(soportar)	(abode)[1]	abided
arise	(surgir)	arose	arisen
awake	(despertarse)	awoke, awaked	awoken
bear	(llevar)	bore	borne[2]
beat	(golpear)	beat	beaten[3]
become	(hacerse)	became	become
befall	(llegar)	befell	befallen
beget	(engendrar)	begot	begotten
begin	(empezar)	began	begun
behold	(advertir)	beheld	beheld
bend	(doblar)	bent	bent[4]
bereave	(privar)	bereaved	bereft[5]
beseech	(implorar)	besought	besought
bestride	(cabalgar)	bestrode	bestridden
bet	(apostar)	bet, betted	bet, betted
bid	(ofrecer)	bade	bidden
bind	(unir)	bound	bound
bite	(morder)	bit	bitten
bleed	(sangrar)	bled	bled
blow	(soplar)	blew	blown
break	(romper)	broke	broken[6]
breed	(criar)	bred	bred
bring	(traer)	brought	brought
broadcast	(retransmitir)	broadcast	broadcast
build	(construir)	built	built
burn	(quemar)	burnt, burned	burnt, burned
burst	(estallar)	burst	burst
buy	(comprar)	bought	bought
cast	(tirar)	cast	cast
catch	(coger)	caught	caught
chide	(regañar)	chid, chided	chid, (chidden), chided
choose	(elegir)	chose	chosen
cleave	(hender)	clove, cleft	cloven, cleft[7]
cleave	(adherirse)	cleaved, (clave)	cleaved
cling	(agarrarse)	clung	clung
clothe	(vestir)	clothed, (clad)	clothed, (clad)
come	(venir)	came	come
cost	(costar)	cost	cost
creep	(arrastrarse)	crept	crept
crow	(cacarear)	crowed, (crew)	crowed
cut	(cortar)	cut	cut
dare	(atreverse)	dared, (durst)	dared, (durst)
deal	(tratar)	dealt	dealt
dig	(cavar)	dug	dug
dive	(zambullirse)	dived, dove*	dived
draw	(dibujar, tirar)	drew	drawn
dream	(soñar)	dreamt, dreamed	dreamt, dreamed
drink	(beber)	drank	drunk[8]

infinitivo		pretérito	participio pasado
drive	(conducir)	drove	driven
dwell	(habitar)	dwelt, dwelled	dwelt, dwelled
eat	(comer)	ate	eaten
fall	(caer)	fell	fallen
feed	(alimentar)	fed	fed
feel	(sentir)	felt	felt
fight	(luchar)	fought	fought
find	(encontrar)	found	found
fit	(sentar)	fit*, fitted	fit*, fitted
flee	(huir)	fled	fled
fling	(lanzar)	flung	flung
fly	(volar)	flew	flown
forbear	(abstenerse)	forbore	forborne
forbid	(prohibir)	forbad(e)	forbidden
forget	(olvidar)	forgot	forgotten
forgive	(perdonar)	forgave	forgiven
forsake	(abandonar)	forsook	forsaken
freeze	(congelar)	froze	frozen
get	(conseguir)	got	got, gotten*[9]
gild	(dorar)	gilt, gilded	gilt, gilded[10]
gird	(rodear)	girt, girded	girt, girded[10]
give	(dar)	gave	given
go	(ir)	went	gone
grind	(moler)	ground	ground
grow	(crecer)	grew	grown
hang	(colgar)	hung, hanged[11]	hung, hanged[11]
hear	(oír)	heard	heard
heave	(alzar)	hove, heaved[12]	hove, heaved[12]
hew	(tallar)	hewed	hewn, hewed
hide	(esconder)	hid	hidden
hit	(golpear)	hit	hit
hold	(mantener)	held	held
hurt	(dañar)	hurt	hurt
keep	(mantener)	kept	kept
kneel	(arrodillarse)	knelt, kneeled	knelt, kneeled
knit	(hacer punto)	knit, knitted[13]	knit, knitted[13]
know	(saber, conocer)	knew	known
lay	(poner, extender)	laid	laid
lead	(guiar)	led	led
lean	(apoyarse)	leant, leaned	leant, leaned
leap	(saltar)	leapt, leaped	leapt, leaped
learn	(aprender)	learnt, learned	learnt, learned
leave	(abandonar, partir)	left	left
lend	(prestar)	lent	lent
let	(dejar)	let	let
lie	(yacer)	lay	lain
light	(encender)	lit, lighted	lit, lighted[14]
lose	(perder)	lost	lost
make	(hacer)	made	made
mean	(significar)	meant	meant
meet	(encontrar)	met	met
melt	(derretirse)	melted	melted, molten[15]
mow	(segar)	mowed	mown, mowed
pay	(pagar)	paid	paid

infinitivo		pretérito	participio pasado
plead	(implorar)	pled*, pleaded	pled*, pleaded[16]
put	(poner)	put	put
quit	(dejar)	quit, (quitted)	quit, (quitted)[17]
read	(leer)	read	read
rend	(rajar)	rent	rent
rid	(librar)	rid, (ridded)	rid
ride	(montar a)	rode	ridden
ring	(sonar)	rang	rung
rise	(alzarse)	rose	risen
run	(correr)	ran	run
saw	(serrar)	sawed	sawn, sawed
say	(decir)	said	said
see	(ver)	saw	seen
seek	(buscar)	sought	sought
sell	(vender)	sold	sold
send	(enviar)	sent	sent
set	(colocar)	set	set
sew	(coser)	sewed	sewn, sewed
shake	(sacudir)	shook	shaken
shear	(esquilar, podar)	sheared	shorn, sheared[18]
shed	(despojarse)	shed	shed
shine	(brillar)	shone[19]	shone[19]
shoe	(calzar)	shod, shoed	shod, shoed[20]
shoot	(disparar)	shot	shot
show	(mostrar)	showed	shown, showed
shrink	(encoger)	shrank, shrunk	shrunk, shrunken[21]
shut	(cerrar)	shut	shut
sing	(cantar)	sang	sung
sink	(hundir)	sank	sunk, sunken[22]
sit	(sentarse)	sat	sat
slay	(matar)	slew	slain
sleep	(dormir)	slept	slept
slide	(deslizarse)	slid	slid
sling	(colgar)	slung	slung
slink	(escabullirse)	slunk	slunk
slit	(partir)	slit	slit
smell	(oler)	smelt, smelled	smelt, smelled
smite	(golpear)	smote	smitten[23]
sneak	(colarse)	snuck*, sneaked	snuck*, sneaked
sow	(sembrar)	sowed	sown, sowed
speak	(hablar)	spoke	spoken
speed	(ir de prisa)	sped, speeded	sped, speeded
spell	(deletrear)	spelt, spelled	spelt, spelled
spend	(gastar)	spent	spent
spill	(derramar)	spilt, spilled	spilt, spilled
spin	(girar)	spun	spun
spit	(escupir)	spat, spit*	spat, spit*
split	(dividirse)	split	split
spoil	(estropear)	spoilt, spoiled	spoilt, spoiled
spread	(extender)	spread	spread
spring	(saltar)	sprang	sprung
stand	(estar de pie)	stood	stood
steal	(robar)	stole	stolen
stick	(fijar)	stuck	stuck
sting	(picar)	stung	stung

infinitivo		pretérito	participio pasado
stink	(apestar)	stank	stunk
strew	(esparcir)	strewed	strewn, strewed
stride	(ir a zancadas)	strode	striden
strike	(golpear)	struck	struck, stricken[24]
string	(enristrar)	strung	strung
strive	(esforzarse)	strove	striven
swear	(jurar)	swore	sworn
sweat	(sudar)	sweat*, sweated	sweat*, sweated
sweep	(barrer)	swept	swept
swell	(inflarse)	swelled	swollen, swelled[25]
swim	(nadar)	swam	swum
swing	(balancearse)	swung	swung
take	(tomar)	took	taken
teach	(enseñar)	taught	taught
tear	(desgarrar)	tore	torn
tell	(contar)	told	told
think	(pensar)	thought	thought
thrive	(prosperar)	thrived, (throve)	thrived, (throve)
throw	(tirar)	threw	thrown
thrust	(empujar)	thrust	thrust
tread	(pisar)	trod	trodden
understand	(comprender)	understood	understood
undertake	(emprender)	undertook	undertaken
wake	(despertarse)	woke, waked	woken, waked
wear	(vestir)	wore	worn
weave	(tejer)	wove[26]	woven[26]
weep	(llorar)	wept	wept
wet	(mojar)	wet*, wetted[27]	wet*, wetted[27]
win	(ganar)	won	won
wind	(enrollar)	wound	wound
wring	(retorcer)	wrung	wrung
write	(escribir)	wrote	written

(1) Regular en la construcción **abide by** «cumplir con»: **They abided by the rules**.

(2) Pero en la voz pasiva o como adjetivo es **born** (= nacido): **He was born in France./A born gentleman**.

(3) Fíjese en esta expresión coloquial: **This has me beat./You have me beat there**. El significado es «*No me entra en la cabeza./Me has pillado (poniéndome en una situación difícil)*». También es frecuente **beat** con el significado de «muy fatigado, muerto»: **I am (dead) beat**.

(4) Tenga en cuenta esta expresión: **on one's bended knees** (*de rodillas*).

(5) Pero **bereaved** cuando significa «la consternada/desconsolada familia», como en el siguiente ejemplo: **The bereaved received no compensation** (*La desconsolada familia no recibió ningún tipo de compensación*). Compare: **He was bereft of speech** (*perdió la palabra*).

(6) Pero es **broke** cuando se trata de un adjetivo (= «arruinado»): **I'm broke**.

(7) **Cleft** sólo se utiliza cuando significa «partido en dos».
Observe las expresiones **cleft palate** (*fisura palatina*) y **(to be caught) in a cleft stick** (*(estar) entre la espada y la pared*), pero **cloven foot/hoof** (*pezuña hendida*).

(8) Cuando funciona como adjetivo precediendo al nombre a veces se utiliza **drunken** (= borracho), p.e. **a lot of drunken people** = *un montón de gente ebria* y **siempre deberá** emplearse delante de los nombres que se refieran a objetos inanimados: **one of his usual drunken parties** = una de sus habituales fiestas para beber).

(9) Pero en inglés americano también se dice **have got to** con el sentido de «tener que, deber»: **a man has got to do what a man has got to do**, *un hombre debe hacer lo que debe hacer*. Compare con: **she has gotten into a terrible mess**, *se ha metido en un jaleo terrible*.

(10) Las formas **gilt** y **girt** del participio pasado se emplean con bastante frecuencia en la función de adjetivo antepuesto al nombre: **gilt mirrors** *espejos dorados*, **a flower-girt grave** una tumba rodeada de flores (pero siempre se dice **gilded youth**, *la juventud dorada*, en el que **gilded** viene a significar «rico y feliz»).

(11) Es regular cuando significa «ahorcar».

(12) **Hove** se emplea en el lenguaje de la navegación, como en la expresión **heave into sight: just then Mary hove into sight**, *justo en ese momento divisamos a Mary*.

(13) Es irregular cuando tiene el sentido de «unir» (**a close-knit family**, *una familia unida*), pero regular cuando lo que quiere decir es «hacer punto», y cuando hace referencia a los huesos, «soldarse».

(14) Cuando el participio pasado se emplea como adjetivo delante del nombre generalmente se prefiere **lighted** a **lit: a lighted match**, *una cerilla encendida* (sin embargo: **the match is lit, she has lit a match**, *la cerilla está encendida, ha encendido una cerilla*). En los nombres compuestos generalmente se emplea **lit: well-lit streets** *calles bien iluminadas*. En sentido figurado (con **up**) **lit** únicamente se emplea en pasado o participio pasado: **her face lit up when she saw me**, *se le iluminó la cara cuando me vio*.

(15) **Molten** sólo se emplea en función de adjetivo antepuesto a un nombre, y sólo cuando significa «fundido a alta temperatura», p.e.: **molten lead**, *plomo fundido* (pero **melted butter**, *mantequilla fundida*).

(16) En las variedades escocesa y americana se emplea **pled** en pasado y participio pasado.

(17) En inglés americano las formas regulares no se emplean, y cada vez son menos frecuentes en inglés británico.

(18) Cuando el participio pasado antecede a un nombre generalmente su forma es **shorn**(**newly-shorn lambs**, *corderos recién esquilados*) y siempre es así en la expresión (**to be**) **shorn of**, (estar) privado de: **shorn of his riches he was nothing**, *privado de sus riquezas no era nada*.

(19) Es regular cuando tiene el sentido de «lustrar, sacar brillo» en inglés americano.

(20) En función de adjetivo se emplea **shod: a well-shod foot**, *un pie bien calzado*.

(21) **Shrunken** se utiliza sólo cuando funciona como adjetivo: **shrunken limbs/ her face was shrunken**, *sus miembros estaban encogidos/tenía la cara arrugada.*

(22) **Sunken** sólo se emplea en función de adjetivo: **sunken eyes**, ojos hundidos.

(23) Es un verbo arcaico cuyo participio pasado, **smitten**, todavía se emplea como adjetivo: **he's completely smitten with her**, *está totalmente loco por ella.*

(24) **Stricken** sólo se utiliza en sentido figurado (**a stricken family/stricken with poverty**, *una familia afligida, destrozada por la pobreza*). Es muy corriente en los nombres compuestos con el significado de «destrozado por»: **poverty-stricken, fever-stricken, horror-stricken** (también **horror-struck**), pero siempre se dice **thunderstruck**, *atónito.*
Una expresión americana es **the remark was stricken from the record**, *el comentario fue eliminado del acta.*

(25) **Swollen** es más corriente que **swelled** como verbo (**her face has swollen**, *se le ha hinchado la cara*) y como adjetivo (**her face is swollen/a swollen face**). **A swollen head**, *un engreído*, se utiliza para los que tienen un alto concepto de sí mismos, pero en inglés americano es **a swelled head**.

(26) Pero es regular cuando significa «abrirse paso, zigzaguear»: **the motorbike weaved elegantly through the traffic**, *la moto zigzagueó elegantemente a través del tráfico.*

(27) En inglés británico es irregular cuando tiene el sentido de «orinarse en»: **he wet his bed again last night**, *volvió a orinarse en la cama esta noche.*

8 LAS CONTRACCIONES

Las formas contractas son muy corrientes en el inglés hablado de hoy en día, así como en el inglés escrito de carácter no oficial:

BE

I am	I'm
you are	you're
he/she/it is	he's/she's/it's
we/they are	we're/they're

I am not	I'm not
you are not	you're not, you aren't
he/she/it is not	he's/she's/it's not, he/she/it isn't
we/they are not	we/they aren't

am I not?	aren't I?
are you not?	aren't you?
is he/she/it not?	isn't he/she/it?
are we/they not?	aren't we/they?

DO

I/you/we/they do not	I/you/we/they don't
he/she/it does not	he/she/it doesn't

do I/you/we/they not?	don't I/you/we/they?
does he/she/it not?	doesn't he/she/it?

HAVE

I have	I've
you/we/they have	you've/we've/they've
he/she/it has	he's/she's/it's (más usual en las formas del presente perfecto, como en: I've seen, etc.)

I/you/we/they have not	I/you/we/they haven't
he/she/it has not	he/she/it hasn't

have I/you/we/they not?	haven't I/you/we/they?
has he/she/it not?	hasn't he/she/it?

I/he/she/it was not	I/he/she/it wasn't
you/we/they were not	you/we/they weren't

I etc. did not	I etc. didn't
I/you etc. will	I'll/you'll etc.
I/he etc. will not	I/he etc. won't
I shall	I'll
I shall not	I shan't
I/you etc. would*	I'd/you'd etc.
I/you etc. would not*	I/you etc. wouldn't
I/he etc. would have*	I'd've/he'd've etc.
I/he etc. would not have*	I/he etc. wouldn't have

*De la misma forma con **should** en primera persona.

Las contracciones no sólo se utilizan con los pronombres personales:

That'll be the day!
Mummy's just gone out.

Ver también los Auxiliares Modales, página 31.

9   LA INTERROGACIÓN

1) Cuando en la oración no aparece ningún otro auxiliar (**be, have** o **will**) se forma la interrogación con el auxiliar **do**:

Do you like whisky?
¿Le gusta el güisqui?

How do you spell it?
¿Cómo se escribe?

Doesn't she expect you home?
¿No te espera en casa?

Did you talk to him?
¿Le hablaste?

Didn't I tell you so?
¿No te lo dije?

2) Si se utiliza otro auxiliar lo que se hace es invertir el orden de sujeto-verbo:

He is Welsh.
Es galés.

Is he Welsh?
¿Es galés?

They're going home tomorrow.
Mañana vuelven a casa.

Are they going home tomorrow?
¿Vuelven a casa mañana?

Daphne will be there too.
Daphne también estará allí.

Will Daphne be there too?
¿Estará Daphne también allí?

I can't understand.
No puedo entender.

Why can't I understand?
¿Por qué no puedo entender?

3) Si el sujeto es un pronombre interrogativo no se utilizará **do**:

Who made that noise?
¿Quién ha hecho ese ruido?

What happened?
¿Qué pasó?

4) Las «question tags» (= ¿verdad?):

a) A una afirmación le sigue una «question tag» negativa y viceversa:

You can see it, can't you?
¿Lo ves, verdad?

You can't see it, can you?
¿No lo ves, verdad?

Si la «question tag» no se utiliza para hacer una pregunta real, sino que sirve para recalcar la oración principal, a la oración afirmativa le seguirá una «question tag» afirmativa:

So, you've seen a ghost, have you?
Así que has visto un fantasma, ¿verdad?
(incredulidad, sarcasmo)

He's got married again, has he?
Se ha casado otra vez, ¿verdad? (sorpresa, interés)

Observe que la «question tag» concuerda con el tiempo verbal de la oración principal:

You want to meet him, don't you?
¿Quieres conocerle, verdad?

You wanted to meet him, didn't you?
¿Querías conocerle, verdad?

You'll want to meet him, won't you?
¿Querrás conocerle, verdad?

b) Si la proposición que precede a la «question tag» va regida por un auxiliar, será éste el que se utilice para formarla:

He has been here before, hasn't he?
¿Ya ha estado aquí antes, verdad?

They aren't stopping, are they?
¿No se paran, verdad?

You will sign it, won't you?
¿Lo firmarás, verdad?

c) Si, por el contrario, la proposición que precede a la «question tag» no va regida por ningún auxiliar, se utilizará **do** para formarla:

He lives in France, doesn't he?
¿Vive en Francia, verdad?

She left yesterday, didn't she?
¿Se fue ayer, verdad?

d) Si la «question tag» sigue a un imperativo se utilizará un auxiliar (sobre todo **will/would**). En este caso la «question tag» sirve para suavizar el tono de la oración, para evitar que resulte un mandato brusco:

Leave the cat alone, will you?
¡Deja tranquilo al gato, anda!

Take this to Mrs Brown, would you?
¿Llevas esto a Mrs Brown?

La forma negativa **won't** indica una invitación:

Help yourselves to drinks, won't you?
Servíos algo de beber, ¿vale?

10 LA FORMA NEGATIVA

1) Cuando no hay ningún auxiliar (**be, will** etc.) se utiliza **not** detrás de **do** (ver también Las contracciones, pág. 19):

I like it.
Me gusta.

I do not (don't) like it.
No me gusta.

She agrees with them.
Está de acuerdo con ellos.

She does not (doesn't) agree with them.
No está de acuerdo con ellos.

I expected him to say that.
Esperaba que dijera eso.

I didn't expect him to say that.
No me esperaba que dijera eso.

2) Si se utiliza cualquier auxiliar, se negará directamente con **not**:

I will (I'll) take them with me.
Me los llevaré.

I will not (won't) take them with me.
No me los llevaré.

They are just what I'm looking for.
Son precisamente lo que estoy buscando.

They are not really what I'm looking for.
(*contracción = **they aren't/they're not***)
No son precisamente lo que estoy buscando.

3) **Not** se utiliza para negar infinitivos y gerundios:

To be or not to be
Ser o no ser

Please try not to be stupid.
Por favor, intenta no ser tan tonto.

It would have been better not to have mentioned it at all.
Habría sido mejor no hablar de ello en absoluto.

He's worried about not having enough money.
Está preocupado por si no tiene bastante dinero.

Ver también El imperativo, pág. 24.

11 EL IMPERATIVO

1) La forma de imperativo corresponde al verbo en infinitivo (sin **to**):

Stop that!
¡Para ya!

Well, just look at him!
¡Pero... mírale!

Somebody do something!
¡Que alguien haga algo!

Have another.
Toma otro.

Try one of mine.
Prueba uno de los míos.

2) Para hacer una sugerencia o propuesta en primera persona del plural se emplea **let's** + infinitivo sin **to**:

Let's leave it at that for today.
Dejémoslo ahí por hoy.

Let's just agree to differ.
Aceptemos que no somos de la misma opinión.

3) La prohibición o imperativo negativo:

Para expresar prohibición u orden negativa se coloca **do not** o **don't** delante del infinitivo. En inglés hablado, y también escrito cuando carece de carácter oficial, **don't** es la forma preponderante, a no ser que quiera hacerse especial hincapié:

Don't listen to what he says.
No escuches lo que te dice.

Please don't feel you have to accept.
Por favor, no pienses que tienes que aceptar.

Look, I've told you before, do not put your hands on the hotplate!
Mira, te lo he dicho antes, no pongas las manos en la placa.

Cuando se utiliza **let's**, el **not** se sitúa entre **let's** y el verbo. También se puede utilizar **don't let's**:

Let's not go just yet.
Don't let's go just yet.
Quedémonos algo más. (literal: «No nos vayamos ya».)

4) **Do not** se utiliza con bastante frecuencia en los carteles de aviso:

Do not feed the animals.
No dé de comer a los animales.

5) Para reforzar un imperativo puede emplearse el auxiliar **do**:

Oh, do be quiet!
¡Anda, cállate!

12 PARA EXPRESAR CONDICIÓN

La oración:

If you don't hurry, you'll miss your train.
Si no te das prisa perderás el tren.

es una oración condicional. La condición aparece expresada en la proposición subordinada (introducida por **if**) que se puede colocar delante o detrás de la proposición principal (**you'll miss your train**).

La forma verbal varía dependiendo de la **referencia temporal** y del **grado de probabilidad** de que la condición se realice.

1) Referencia temporal de presente o futuro:

a) Gran probabilidad de que se realice:
Los verbos de la proposición subordinada (que comienza por **if**) aparecen en presente o en presente perfecto. El verbo de la proposición principal aparece con la estructura **will** + infinitivo (a veces **shall** + infinitivo en primera persona):

If I see her, I'll tell her.
Si la veo se lo diré.

If you have finished that one, I'll give you another.
Si has terminado esa, te daré otra.

Hay tres grandes excepciones:

* Si el verbo de la proposición principal también está en presente será de esperar que la condición exprese una consecuencia lógica, que ocurre ya sea automáticamente o habitualmente. En este caso **if** significa **whenever** (siempre que):

If the sun shines, people look happier.
Cuando el sol brilla, la gente parece más feliz.

If you're happy, then I'm happy.
Si eres feliz, yo soy feliz.

* Cuando en la proposición que empieza por **if** se utiliza **will** el hablante hace alusión a la voluntad o intención de que algo se cumpla:

If you will kindly look this way, I'll try to explain the painter's approach.
Si es tan amable de fijarse intentaré explicarle el enfoque del pintor.

Well, if you will mix your drinks, what can you expect!
¿Claro, si te empeñas en mezclar bebidas, qué es lo que esperas?

Cuando se utiliza esta estructura para pedir algo podemos hacer que la oración suene más cortés utilizando **would**:

If you would be kind enough to look this way...
Si fuera tan amable de fijarse...

* Cuando en la proposición que empieza por **if** se emplea **should** (no importa con qué persona verbal), se sobreentiende que la condición es menos probable. A estas proposiciones con **should** a menudo les sigue un imperativo, como ocurre en los dos primeros ejemplos:

If you should see him, ask him to ring me.
Si le vieras, dile que me llame.

If they should not be there, you will have to manage by yourself.
Si no estuvieran tendrás que arreglártelas tú solo.

En un estilo más cuidado podría omitirse **if** y comenzar la oración con la proposición subordinada con **should**:

Should the matter arise again, telephone me at once.
En caso de que volviera a surgir el problema, llámame por teléfono de inmediato.

b) Posibilidad remota o irreal:

En este caso hay muchos obstáculos para que se cumpla la condición o simplemente esperamos que no se cumpla. El verbo de la proposición subordinada aparece en pasado, mientras que en la principal aparece la estructura **would** (o **should** para la primera persona) + infinitivo:

If I saw her, I would (I'd) tell her.
Si la viera se lo diría.

Este tipo de oración no expresa necesariamente una posibilidad poco probable o irreal. Con frecuencia apenas hay diferencia con la construcción que vimos anteriormente en el punto 1-a:

If you tried harder, you would pass the exam. (= If you try harder, you will pass the exam.)
Si te esforzaras más, aprobarías el examen.

El uso del pasado puede dar a la oración un matiz más «amistoso» y educado.

2) Referencia al pasado:

a) En este caso lo que se expresa en la proposición que empieza por **if**, es decir, la condición, no se ha producido. El verbo de esta proposición está en pasado perfecto y en la principal aparece la estructura **would** (o **should** para la primera persona) + infinitivo perfecto:

If I had seen her, I would have told her.
Si la hubiera visto se lo habría dicho.

If you had finished that one, I would have given you another one.
Si hubieras acabado esa te habría dado otra.

If I had known that, I would have done something about it.
Si lo hubiera sabido habría hecho algo.

En un estilo ligeramente más cuidado puede omitirse **if** y hacer que la proposición subordinada empiece por **had**:

Had I seen her, I would/should have told her.
Si la hubiera visto se lo habría dicho.

b) Excepciones:

* Si la proposición principal hace referencia a la no realización en el presente de una condición del pasado también puede utilizarse **would** + infinitivo:

If I had studied harder, I would be an engineer today.
(= if I had studied harder, I would have been an engineer today)
Si hubiera estudiado más, ahora sería ingeniero.

* Utilizaremos el pasado en las dos proposiciones si, como ocurría en el punto a-1, se sobreentiende un resultado automático o habitual (**if** = when(ever), siempre que):

If people had influenza in those days, they died.
En aquellos días cuando la gente cogía la gripe moría.

* Si se tiene esperanza de que la condición se cumpla, las restricciones mencionadas sobre la concordancia de los tiempos no se tienen en cuenta. En este caso if a menudo significa «teniendo en cuenta que», «ya que»:

If he was rude to you, why did you not walk out?
Si se puso grosero contigo, ¿por qué no te fuiste?

If he was rude to you, why have you still kept in touch?
Si se puso grosero contigo, ¿por qué has mantenido el contacto con él?

If he was rude to you, why do you still keep in touch?
Si se puso grosero contigo, ¿por qué mantienes contacto con él?

13 EL GERUNDIO Y EL INFINITIVO

El gerundio, también llamado verbo sustantivado, tiene la misma forma que el participio presente (terminación **-ing**), pero su uso es diferente. Puede utilizarse:

1) Como un nombre:

Driving is fun.
Conducir es divertido.

Smoking is not good for you.
Fumar no es bueno para la salud.

I love reading.
Me encanta leer.

2) Como un verbo, seguido de un complemento directo o un atributo:

Writing this letter took me ages.
Escribir esta carta me ha llevado muchísimo tiempo.

Being left-handed has never been a problem.
Ser zurdo nunca ha sido un problema.

The thought of Douglas doing that is absurd.
La idea de que Douglas haga eso es absurda.

3) Función verbal, modificado por un adverbio:

It's a question of precisely defining our needs.
Se trata de definir nuestras necesidades con exactitud.

4) Con un adjetivo posesivo:

El uso del gerundio acompañado de un adjetivo posesivo (**my, his** etc.) es más corriente en el lenguaje escrito (formal) que en el lenguaje hablado:

We were surprised about you/your not being chosen.
Nos sorprendió que no fueras elegido.

5) Comparación del gerundio y el infinitivo:

A veces se puede emplear indistintamente uno u otro después del verbo:

I can't stand seeing him upset.
I can't stand to see him upset.
No soporto verle triste.

Pero a veces hay una diferencia importante:

We stopped having our rest at 3 o'clock. (= ended it)
Dejamos de descansar a las tres.

We stopped to have our rest at 3 o'clock. (= started it)
Paramos para descansar a las tres.

Aquí tiene una lista de verbos de uso frecuente a los que generalmente sigue sólo el infinitivo:

demand	exigir, pedir
expect	esperar
hope	esperar
want	querer
wish	desear

Y ahora otros verbos muy utilizados a los que generalmente sólo sigue el gerundio:

avoid	evitar
consider	considerar
dislike	no gustarle a uno
enjoy	disfrutar
finish	terminar
keep	mantener
practise	practicar
risk	arriesgar

6) El «split infinitive»:

El infinitivo recibe este nombre cuando se interpone un adverbio entre el infinitivo y el **to** que le precede:

They then decided to definitely leave.
Entonces decidieron marcharse definitivamente.

Esta forma tiene muchos detractores, quienes mantienen que es propia de un estilo inadecuado, y se prefiere:

They then decided definitely to leave.

14 EL SUBJUNTIVO

Las formas del subjuntivo se reconocen por la omisión de la -s en la tercera persona del singular, además del uso de **be** en vez de **is** y de **were** en vez de **was**. Este modo ño es en absoluto tan corriente en inglés como en castellano. Usos principales:

1) En modismos que expresan deseo:

Long live the King!
¡Viva el rey!

God rest his soul.
Que Dios le tenga en paz.

Heaven be praised.
Alabado sea Dios.

2) En la expresión **if need be** (= «si fuera necesario»):

Well, if need be, you could always hire a car.
Bueno, si fuera necesario siempre puedes alquilar un coche.

3) En las proposiciones del tipo de las siguientes:

It is vital that he understand this.
Es de vital importancia que lo comprenda.

They recommended she sell the house.
Le recomendaron que vendiera la casa.

We propose that this new ruling be adopted.
Proponemos que se adopte esta nueva ley.

El uso del subjuntivo se limita a un uso muy formal. En el lenguaje hablado es más frecuente en inglés americano que en inglés británico.

4) **If I was/were:**

Compare los siguientes ejemplos:

(a) **If I was in the wrong, it wasn't intentional.**
   Si hice mal, fue sin querer.

(b) **If I were in the wrong, I would admit it.**
   Si lo hiciera mal lo admitiría.

En el ejemplo (a) el hablante no tiene ninguna duda de que lo hizo mal, pero deja claro que no fue de forma malinteñcionada. Por el contrario, en el ejemplo (b) el hablante no acepta hacer nada mal, sin embargo puede haber algún tipo de duda, por eso utiliza el subjuntivo-**were**.

En la oración (b) también se podría utilizar **was**, y tendría el mismo sentido, pero en este caso se trataría de un lenguaje más coloquial, menos formal.

15 LOS AUXILIARES MODALES

1) CAN-COULD

Las formas contractas negativas son **can't-couldn't**. La forma negativa no contracta del presente es **cannot**.

a) Se utilizan para expresar capacidad (= **be able to**):

Can machines «think»?
¿Pueden «pensar» las máquinas?

I can explain that.
Puedo explicarlo.

When I was a student I could explain that sort of thing easily.
Cuando era estudiante podía explicar fácilmente ese tipo de cosas.

Para los demás tiempos se emplean las formas de **be able to** (en el último ejemplo que hemos visto también sería posible):

I used to be able to explain that sort of thing easily.
Yo podía explicar fácilmente ese tipo de cosas.

I'll be able to tell you the answer tomorrow.
Podré darte respuesta mañana.

I've never been able to understand her.
Nunca he podido entenderla.

Tenga en cuenta que en una proposición condicional **could** + infinitivo hace referencia al presente o al futuro. Compárelo con **would** en el capítulo 12 (Para expresar condición):

You could do a lot better if you'd only try.
Podrías hacerlo mucho mejor con solo intentarlo.

b) Para expresar permiso:

Can/Could I have a look at your photos?
¿Puedo echar un vistazo a tus fotos?

Observe que al igual que **can, could** puede hacer referencia tanto al presente como al futuro. La única diferencia es que **could** es un tanto más cortés o vacilante. Por ejemplo un niño nunca diría:

Could I go out and play?
¿Podría salir a jugar?

A veces **could** se emplea para expresar permiso en el pasado cuando el contexto no deja lugar a dudas de que se trata de algo pasado:

For some reason we couldn't smoke in the lounge yesterday, but today we can.
Por alguna razón ayer no podíamos fumar en el salón, pero hoy sí podemos.

Para los demás tiempos se emplean las formas de **be allowed to** (en el último ejemplo que hemos visto también sería posible):

We weren't allowed to see him, he was so ill.
No pudimos (no nos permitieron) verle, estaba muy enfermo.

Will they be allowed to change the rules?
¿Se les permitirá/Podrán cambiar las normas?

c) Para expresar posibilidad:

That can't be right.
Eso no puede ser verdad.

What shall I do? - You can always talk to a lawyer/you could talk to a lawyer.
¿Qué debo hacer? - Siempre puedes hablar con un abogado/Podrías hablar con un abogado.

En este caso es evidente que **could** no hace referencia al pasado, sino al presente o al futuro. Para hacer referencia al pasado debe emplearse **could** seguido del infinitivo pasado:

You could have talked to a lawyer.
Podrías haber hablado con un abogado.

I know I could have, but I didn't want to.
Ya sé que podía haberlo hecho, pero no quise.

* **Could** y **may** pueden utilizarse indistintamente algunas veces cuando expresan posibilidad:

You could/may be right.
Podrías llevar razón./Puede que lleves razón.

Pero a veces existe   una diferencia importante entre **can** y **may** en lo que se refiere a la expresión de la posibilidad:

(a) **Your comments can be overheard.**
Pueden oír tus comentarios.

(b) **Your comments may be overheard.**
Podrían oír tus comentarios.

En (a) la posibilidad reside en el hecho de que se hacen en voz alta, por ejemplo, independientemente de que haya alguien cerca y las oiga en realidad. Mientras que (b) simplemente se hace referencia a la posibilidad de que de una forma u otra puedan ser oídos.

En la forma negativa también podemos observar la diferencia:

Don't worry, he can't have heard us.
No te preocupes, no puede habernos oído. (es imposible que nos haya oído)

Because of all the noise, he may not have heard us.
Con todo este ruido puede que no nos haya oído.

d) Para hacer sugerencias sólo se utiliza **could**:

You could have talked to a lawyer.
Podrías haber hablado con un abogado.

They could always sell their second house if they need money.
Siempre pueden vender su segunda casa si necesitan dinero.

e) A menudo se emplea **could** para expresar reproche o enfado:

You could have told me I had paint on my face!
¡Podrías haberme dicho que tenía pintura en la cara!

2) MAY-MIGHT

La forma negativa contracta **mayn't** como expresión del permiso negativo, es decir, la prohibición, desaparece progresivamente y se ve reemplazada por **may not** o **must not/mustn't**. La forma negativa contracta de **might** es **mightn't**.

a) Para expresar permiso:

May I open a window? - No, you may not!
¿Puedo abrir una ventana? - ¡No, no puedes!

El uso de **may** es ligeramente más cortés que el de **can**. El uso de **might** para pedir permiso resulta extremadamente cortés:

I wonder if I might have another of those cakes.
Me pregunto si podría tomar otro de esos pasteles.

Might I suggest we stop there for today?
¿Podría sugerir que nos detuviéramos aquí por hoy?

Observe que **might** hace referencia al presente y al futuro, y raramente hace referencia al pasado cuando se utiliza en una proposición principal. Compare los siguientes ejemplos:

He then asked if he might smoke (**might** en la proposición subordinada).
Entonces preguntó si podía fumar.

He then asked if he was allowed to smoke.
Entonces preguntó si podía fumar.

y

He wasn't allowed to smoke.
No podía fumar (no le estaba permitido hacerlo).

En el último ejemplo no puede utilizarse **might**. En su lugar se recurre a las formas de **be allowed to**.

b) Para expresar posibilidad:

It may/might still be possible.
Todavía puede ser posible.

They may/might change their minds.
Puede que cambien de opinión./Podrían cambiar de opinión.

It mayn't/mightn't be necessary after all.
Después de todo puede que no sea necesario.

She may/might have left a note upstairs.
Puede que haya dejado arriba una nota.

c) Para expresar sorpresa (generalmente se utiliza **might**):

And who may/might you be?
¿Pero quién te crees que eres?

And what might that be supposed to mean?
¿Y qué querría decir eso?

d) Para expresar sugerencias (solamente **might**):

They might at least apologize.
Al menos podrían disculparse.

You might like to try one of these cigars.
Quizá te apetezca probar uno de estos puros.

Fíjese que este uso constituye a veces prácticamente una orden:

You might take this down the road to your Gran.
Podrías llevarle esto a la abuela.

You might like to read the next chapter for Monday.
Bien podrían leer/Lean el siguiente capítulo para el lunes.

e) Para expresar reproche (solamente **might**):

You might have told me he was deaf!
¡Podrías haberme dicho que era sordo!

They might have written back to us at least!
¡Al menos podrían habernos contestado!

f) Para expresar deseo:

May you have a very happy retirement.
Le deseo que tenga una jubilación muy feliz.

May all your dreams come true!
¡Ojalá que todos tus sueños se hagan realidad!

May/Might you be forgiven for telling such lies!
¡Que Dios te perdone por decir esas mentiras!

Este uso generalmente queda reservado a expresiones hechas y
consagradas por la tradición o consideradas como pertenecientes a un
estilo bastante pomposo y literario.

3) MUST-HAD TO

La forma contracta negativa es **mustn't** (en lo referente a **have** ver la pág. 19).

a) Para expresar obligación:

We have no choice, we must do what he wants.
No tenemos elección. tenemos que hacer lo que quiere.

Must you go already?
¿Tienes que irte ya?

También puede emplearse **have to**, o en un lenguaje más coloquial **have got to**:

We have no choice, we have (got) to do what he says.
No tenemos elección, tenemos que hacer lo que dice.

Do you have to go already?/Have you got to go already?
¿Tienes que irte ya?

A menudo el significado es el mismo, pero en ciertos casos cuando se sobreentiende que existe una obligación proveniente del exterior (p.e. cuando alguien le manda que haga algo) se prefiere utilizar **have to**:

I have to be there for my interview at 10 o'clock.
Tengo que estar allí para mi entrevista a las diez.

Para el pasado y el futuro se emplea **have to**:

We had to do what he wanted.
Tuvimos que hacer lo que quería.

I'll have to finish it tomorrow.
Tendré que terminarlo mañana.

b) La forma negativa:

1) **Must not** se emplea para expresar prohibición:

You mustn't drink and drive.
No debes beber y conducir.

2) **Don't have to** o **haven't got to** se emplean para indicar una ausencia de obligación:

We don't have to drive all night, we could always stop off at a hotel.
No tenemos por qué conducir toda la noche, siempre podemos hacer parada en un hotel.

En lo que se refiere al pasado del apartado 1) se utiliza **be allowed to**:

When we were children we weren't allowed to...
Cuando éramos niños no nos dejaban...

El pasado del apartado 2) se ajusta a la conjugación de **have**:

You didn't have to buy one, you could have used mine.
No tenías por qué comprar uno, podías haber utilizando el mío.

c) Para expresar probabilidad:

Hello, you must be Susan.
Hola, usted debe ser Susan.

That must be my mistake.
Ese debe haber sido un fallo mío.

She must have been surprised to see you.
Debe haberse sorprendido de verte.

A menudo se emplea **have to** con este mismo significado:

You have to be kidding!
¡Debes estar de broma!

e igualmente con **have got to**, sobre todo en inglés británico:

Well, if she said so, it's got to be true. (it's = it has)
Bueno, si ella lo dice, será verdad.

4) OUGHT TO

La forma contracta negativa es **oughtn't to**. A diferencia de lo que ocurre con los demás auxiliares modales, el infinitivo que sigue a **ought** lleva **to**.

a) Para expresar obligación:

Ought to tiene el mismo significado que **should** cuando expresa obligación:

You oughtn't even to think things like that.
Ni siquiera deberías pensar cosas así.

And he ought to know!
¡Y él debería saberlo!

Con este significado **ought to** es menos fuerte que **must**. Compare los siguientes ejemplos:

I must/have to avoid fatty foods. (obligación estricta o necesidad)
Tengo que evitar las comidas grasas.

I ought to avoid fatty foods. (obligación menos estricta)
Debería evitar las comidas grasas.

Must o **have (got) to** normalmente sustituyen a **ought to** en la interrogación:

Must you/Do you have to/Have you got to visit your mother every Sunday?
¿Tienes que visitar a tu madre todos los domingos?

b) Para expresar probabilidad:

She ought to be halfway to Rome by now.
En este momento debe estar a medio camino de Roma.

£50? - That ought to be enough.
¿Cincuenta libras? - Eso debe ser bastante.

5) SHALL-SHOULD

Las formas contractas negativas son **shan't-shouldn't**. En lo que se refiere a su uso en oraciones condicionales ver la pág. 25. Para su utilización en la expresión del futuro ver pág. 47.

a) Para expresar obligación, a menudo moral (solamente **should**):

You should take more exercise.
Deberías hacer más ejercicio.

You shouldn't talk to her like that.
No deberías hablarle así.

What do you think I should do?
¿Qué piensas que debería hacer?

Something was obviously not quite as it should be.
Había algo raro.

With a new fuse fitted it should work.
Con un nuevo fusible debería funcionar.

b) Para expresar probabilidad (**should** solamente):

It's after ten, they should be in Paris by now.
Ya son más de las diez, debe estar ya en París.

If doing one took you two hours, then three shouldn't take longer than six hours, should it?
Si hacer una te llevó dos horas, tres no deberían llevarte más de seis horas, ¿verdad?

Is it there? - Well, it should be, because that's where I left it.
¿Está ahí? - Bueno, debería estar, porque ahí es donde lo dejé.

c) Para expresar lo mismo que **would** de una forma ligeramente más cortés (**should** solamente):

I should just like to say that...
Solo me gustaría decir que...

I should hardly call him a great innovative mind, but...
Yo no diría que tiene gran espíritu innovador, pero...

d) Para expresar sorpresa, o incluso enfado:

There was a knock at the door, and who should it be but...
Llamaron a la puerta y ¿quién te creerás que era?

Where's the money gone? - How should I know?
¿Dónde está el dinero? - ¿Y cómo lo voy a saber yo?

e) **Shall** se utiliza en el lenguaje legal y oficial:

These sums shall be payable monthly.
Estas cantidades se podrán pagar mensualmente.

As shall be stipulated by the contract.
Como estipule el contrato.

The bearings shall have a diameter of no less than...
Los cojinetes tendrán un diámetro no inferior a...

6) WILL-WOULD

Las formas negativas contractas son **won't-wouldn't**. Lo relativo a su uso en oraciones condicionales se encuentra en la página 25. En lo que se refiere al futuro consultar pág. 47.

a) **Will** se utiliza para insistir en una capacidad, una tendencia natural o inherente, o sobre un comportamiento característico:

Concrete will not normally float.
El hormigón normalmente no flota.

The paint will normally last for two to three years.
La pintura generalmente resiste dos o tres años.

The tank will hold about 50 litres.
El tanque tiene una capacidad de cincuenta litros.

Leave him alone and he'll play for hours.
Si le dejas se pasará horas jugando.

They will keep getting the address wrong!
¡Se empeñan en escribir mal la dirección!

The car won't start on damp mornings.
Las mañanas húmedas no hay quien arranque el coche.

Would se utiliza en estos casos para hacer referencia al pasado:

Let him alone and he would play for hours.
Si le dejabas solo se pasaba horas jugando.

They would insist on calling me «Jacko».
Se empeñaban en llamarme «Jacko».

I lost it. - You would! That's typical of you!
Lo perdí. - ¡No me extraña, siempre te pasa!

b) Para dar órdenes o para reforzar una afirmación:

You will do as you are told!
¡Harás lo que se te mande!

He will (damn well) do as he's told!
¡Hará lo que le digan!

Will you stop that right now!
¡Quieres dejarlo ya!

I will not tolerate this!
¡No voy a tolerar esto!

c) Para apelar (con tono un tanto ceremonioso) a la memoria o el conocimiento de alguien:

You will remember the point at which we left off last week's seminar.
Recordarán el punto en que interrumpimos el seminario de la semana pasada.

As you will all doubtless be aware, there have been rumours recently about...
Como sin lugar a dudas todos ustedes sabrán, últimamente han corrido rumores de que...

d) Para hacer suposiciones:

There's someone at the door. - That'll be Graham.
Alguien llama a la puerta. - Será Graham.

How old is he now? - He'll be about 45.
¿Cuántos años tiene ahora? - Tendrá unos 45.

e) Para hacer propuestas o invitaciones:

Will you have another cup? - Thank you, I will.
¿Quieres otra taza? - Sí, gracias.

Won't you try one of these?
¿No quiere probar uno de estos?

f) Para formular peticiones:

Will/Would you move your car, please?
¿Le importaría mover el coche, por favor?

La utilización de **would** es más cortés, menos directa.

OTROS AUXILIARES

7) USED TO

Used to (para expresar una costumbre en el pasado) puede considerarse como una especie de auxiliar, pues el uso de **do** es opcional:

He used not to smoke so much.
He didn't use to smoke so much.
(Antes) no fumaba tanto.

A veces equivale al imperfecto español:

Did you use to know him?
Used you to know him?
¿Le conocías?

De los dos ejemplos mencionados la primera forma es la más corriente en inglés hablado.

8) DARE-NEED

Estos verbos pueden funcionar como verbos léxicos normales o como auxiliares modales. Cuando son auxiliares no toman la **-s** en la tercera persona del singular del presente; no se emplea **do** para formar la negativa o la interrogativa, y si les sigue un infinitivo, éste no va precedido de **to**.

a) Como verbos léxicos normales:

I don't dare to say anything.
No me atrevo a decir nada.

Would/Do you dare to ask him?
¿Te atreves a preguntarle?

You don't need to ask first.
No necesitas preguntar.

Do I need to sign it?
¿Tengo que firmarlo?

b) Como auxiliares modales:

I daren't say anything.   **Dare you ask him?**
No me atrevo a decir nada.   ¿Te atreves a preguntarle?

You needn't ask first.   **Need I sign it?**
Es que no necesitas preguntar.   ¿Tengo que firmarlo?

* **Dare** también puede funcionar como verbo léxico en las formas interrogativa y negativa (es decir, con **do**) y al mismo tiempo ir seguido por un infinitivo sin **to**, como los auxiliares:

I don't dare say anything.
No me atrevo a decir nada.

* En las proposiciones principales que no son interrogativas ni negativas **need** siempre funciona como verbo léxico normal:

I need to go to the toilet.
Tengo que ir al lavabo.

9) HAVE, GET

Have o **get** pueden utilizarse como verbos causativos, como ilustran los siguientes ejemplos:

We're going to have/get the car resprayed.
Vamos a pintar de nuevo el coche. (es decir, nos lo van a hacer)

I can't do it myself, but I can have/get it done for you.
No puedo hacerlo yo, pero puedo hacer que te lo hagan.

El locutor no es el que realiza la acción, sino que otro se la hace.

Cuando **have/get** van seguidos por un infinitivo en voz activa el **to** después de **have** desaparece, pero se mantiene detrás de **get**:

I'll have the porter bring them up for you.
I'll get the porter to bring them up for you.
Haré que las suba el mozo.

16 PARA EXPRESAR TIEMPO PRESENTE

1) El presente simple se emplea:

a) Para acontecimientos habituales o generales o para verdades universales:

I have a shower in the mornings.
Me ducho por las mañanas.

She works for an insurance company.
Trabaja para una compañía de seguros.

Where do you buy your shoes?
¿Dónde te compras los zapatos?

Where do you come from?
¿De dónde eres?

What do I do when the computer bleeps at me?
¿Qué hago cuando el ordenador me dé un pitido?

The earth goes round the sun.
La tierra gira alrededor del sol.

b) Con verbos que expresan un estado anímico, así como los que expresan deseo, desagrado, punto de vista o los que hacen referencia a los sentidos (gusto, olfato, tacto, vista y oído):

I (dis)like/love/hate/want that girl.
Me (dis)gusta/Amo/Odio/Quiero a esa chica

I believe/suppose/think/imagine he's right.
Creo/Supongo/Pienso/Imagino que tiene razón.

We hear/see/feel/perceive the world around us.
Oímos/Vemos/Sentimos/Percibimos el mundo en torno nuestro.

Do I smell gas?
¿Huele a gas?

2) El presente continuo se emplea:

a) Para expresar acontecimientos en curso, que se desarrollan en el momento en que hablamos:

What are you doing up there?
¿Qué haces ahí arriba?

I'm trying to find my old passport I left here.
Estoy intentando encontrar mi viejo pasaporte que dejé aquí.

At the moment it's being used as a bedroom.
En este momento lo están utilizando como dormitorio.

What are you thinking about?
¿En qué estás pensando?

b) Para expresar una actitud (de descontento, enojo, sorpresa o hilaridad) ante un hecho:

He's always mixing our names up (contrariedad, hilaridad).
Siempre confunde nuestros nombres.

He's always losing his car keys.
Siempre está perdiendo las llaves del coche.

You're always saying that!
¡Siempre estás diciendo eso!

You're not going out looking like that!
¡No vas a salir así!

3) Diferencia entre el presente simple y el presente continuo:

I live in London (simple).
Vivo en Londres.

I'm living in London (continuo).
(En la actualidad) vivo en Londres.

En la segunda oración se sobreentiende que el hablante no vive en Londres de forma permanente, sino que lo hace temporalmente. La primera oración describe un hecho establecido.

I have a shower every morning. (simple)
Me ducho todas las mañanas.

I'm having a shower every morning (these days). (continuo)
(En la actualidad) me ducho todas las mañanas.

En el segundo ejemplo se señala que ducharse diariamente por las mañanas es algo eventual, algo que se está haciendo por el momento (pero que puede que cese). En la primera oración, que contiene un presente simple, no se hace restricción temporal alguna.

She works for an insurance company.
Trabaja para una compañía de seguros.

She's working for an insurance company.
Está trabajando para una compañía de seguros.

En este caso la diferencia entre el ejemplo inglés y el castellano es paralela. La primera oración hace referencia a una situación estable, mientras que en la segunda hay un matiz de eventualidad o temporalidad.

Hay casos en que no hay diferencia entre el presente simple y el presente continuo:

How are you feeling this morning?
How do you feel this morning?
¿Qué tal te sientes esta mañana?

17 PARA EXPRESAR TIEMPO PASADO

1) El pasado simple:

Se emplea para referirnos a hechos o estados que se realizaron o tuvieron lugar en el pasado:

He got up and left the room.
Se levantó y salió de la habitación.

Broken again? - I only fixed it yesterday!
¿Otra vez roto? - ¡Lo arreglé justo ayer!

In what year did the Rolling Stones first have a hit?
¿En qué año tuvieron su primer éxito los Rolling Stones?

2) Used to/would:

Estas dos formas se emplean para expresar acontecimientos habituales en el pasado:

We always used to have fish on Fridays.
Siempre comíamos pescado los viernes.

On Fridays we would have fish.
Los viernes tomábamos pescado.

3) El pasado continuo:

Este tiempo hace hincapié en el carácter de continuidad, de duración de una acción o de un hecho:

I was living in Germany when that happened.
Cuando eso ocurrió yo estaba viviendo en Alemania.

Sorry, could you say that again? - I wasn't listening.
Lo siento, ¿podría repetirlo? - No estaba escuchando.

What were you doing out in the garden last night?
¿Qué hacía en el jardín ayer por la noche?

I was having supper when he came home.
Yo estaba cenando cuando él llegó a casa.

El pasado simple y el pasado continuo a menudo se emplean juntos en una oración para poner en relación de forma conveniente dos hechos que ocurrieron en el pasado. En el último ejemplo tenemos un hecho puntual (**he came home**), que se opone a otro hecho que tiene cierta duración, y que ya estaba transcurriendo cuando se produce el hecho puntual (**I was having lunch**). Compare este ejemplo con el anterior.

I had supper when he was coming home.
Cené cuando él volvía a casa.

Esta oración es muy diferente. El hecho que tiene cierta duración, o mayor duración, es **he was coming home. I had supper** hace referencia a algo que ocurrió en un momento preciso que se incluye en el trasfondo de la otra acción. Compare los dos ejemplos anteriores con el siguiente:

I was having supper while he was coming home.
Estaba cenando mientras que él volvía a casa.

En esta oración el hablante no nos presenta una acción como escenario de la otra, sino que las dos se desarrollan de forma paralela.

4) El presente perfecto:

a) El presente perfecto se emplea para estados o acontecimientos del pasado que tienen una relación con el presente:

I've read nearly all of Somerset Maugham's books.
He leído casi todos los libros de Somerset Maugham.

I have never read any of Somerset Maugham's books.
Nunca he leído los libros de Somerset Maugham.

En estos dos ejemplos se hace referencia a lo que se ha leído hasta ahora de las obras de Somerset Maugham.

Compare los ejemplos anteriores con el siguiente:

I read one of Maugham's novels on holiday last year.
Leí una de las novelas de Maugham durante las vacaciones del año pasado.

Esta oración describe un hecho realizado en su totalidad en el pasado.

Veamos algunos otros ejemplos en los que se comparan los dos tiempos:

Have you seen him this morning? (se dice si todavía estamos en la mañana).

Did you see him this morning? (se dice por la tarde o por la noche)
¿Le has visto esta mañana?

b) Podemos emplear el aspecto continuo para resaltar la duración de una acción o de un estado de cosas:

What have you been reading recently?
¿Qué has estado leyendo últimamente?

We haven't seen you for ages. Where have you been keeping yourself?
Hace siglos que no te vemos. ¿Dónde has estado metido?

What have you been saying to him to make him cry?
¿Qué le has estado diciendo para que llore?

I've been meaning to ask you something, doctor.
Quería hacerle una pregunta, doctor.

No obstante, a veces la diferencia entre el presente perfecto simple y el presente perfecto continuo es mínima:

I've been living here for 15 years (continuo).
I've lived here for 15 years (simple).
Vivo aquí desde hace quince años.

Observe que el empleo de **since** sirve para indicar un momento preciso en el pasado:

I've been living here since 1972.
I've lived here since 1972.
Vivo aquí desde hace quince años.

La diferencia de uso entre el presente perfecto simple y el continuo a veces es muy sutil:

I've been waiting for you here a whole hour!
¡He estado esperándote desde hace ya una hora!

I've waited for you for three whole hours!
¡Te estoy esperando desde hace ya tres horas!

El segundo ejemplo no se lo diríamos a la persona que esperamos si acaba de llegar; sí que podríamos decírselo por teléfono, dando a entender que estamos esperando pero vamos a dejar de hacerlo de inmediato. El primer ejemplo sí podríamos decírselo a la persona en cualquiera de las dos situaciones.

5) El pasado perfecto:

a) Este tiempo se emplea para describir una acción o un estado de cosas del pasado que se desarrolla con anterioridad a otros acontecimientos del pasado. Pone en relación un momento del pasado con otro anterior:

The fire had already been put out when they got there.
El incendio ya había sido extinguido cuando llegaron allí.

He searched the directory but the file had been erased the day before.
Buscó en el archivo, pero el documento había sido borrado el día anterior.

Had you heard of him before you came here?
¿Habías oído hablar de él antes de venir aquí?

They hadn't left anything in the fridge, so I went out to eat.
No habían dejado nada en la nevera, así que salí a comer.

También puede emplearse para indicar el cese de un estado de cosas (especialmente estados de ánimo, etc.):

I had hoped to speak to him this morning.
Esperaba hablar con él esta mañana.

Al utilizar este tiempo se indica que ahora la probabilidad de hablarle es escasa o nula.

b) Para hacer hincapié en la duración se utiliza el pasado perfecto continuo:

I'd been wanting to ask that question myself.
Yo también quería hacer esa pregunta.

Had you been waiting long before they arrived?
¿Esperaste mucho antes de que llegaran?

El uso del pasado perfecto en las proposiciones que expresan condición se explica en la página 26.

18 PARA EXPRESAR TIEMPO FUTURO

1) **Will** *y* **shall**

a) Cuando el hablante hace referencia al futuro de la primera persona puede emplear **will** o **shall**. Estas dos formas se contraen en **'ll**. No obstante el uso de **shall** está restringido a Gran Bretaña generalmente:

I will/I'll/I shall let you know as soon as I can.
Te informaré tan pronto como pueda.

We won't/shan't need that many.
No necesitaremos tanto.

b) Para las otras personas se emplea **will**:

You'll be sorry.
¡Lo lamentarás!

Lunch will take about another ten minutes.
El almuerzo estará dentro de aproximadamente diez minutos.

They'll just have to wait.
Sólo tendrán que esperar.

c) Si el locutor quiere expresar una intención en segunda o tercera persona (por ejemplo una promesa o una amenaza) a veces se utiliza **shall**, aunque es menos corriente que **will**:

You shall be treated just like the others.
Se te tratará como a los demás.

They shall pay for this!
¡Me las pagarán por esto!

Si la intención o la voluntad no es la del hablante, se empleará **will('ll)**:

He will/He'll do it, I'm sure.
Lo hará, estoy seguro-a.

d) **Shall** se emplea para hacer propuestas, sugerencias:

Shall we make a start?
¿Empezamos?

e) **Will** puede utilizarse para hacer una petición:

Will you come with me, please?
¿Me acompaña, por favor?

f) Para proponer hacer algo o para afirmar algo referente a un futuro inmediato:

En los ejemplos siguientes se prefiere **will** a **shall** (aunque la forma contracta es, con diferencia, la más utilizada):

That's OK, I'll do it.
Vale, lo hago/haré yo.

I'll have a beer, please.
Tomaré una cerveza, por favor.

That's the door bell. - OK, I'll get it.
Alguien llama. - Vale, yo abro.

2) El futuro simple y el futuro continuo:

a) **Will** y **shall** cuando van seguidos de la forma continua se utilizan para hacer hincapié en la continuidad de una acción:

What will (what'll) you be doing this time next year?
¿Qué estarás haciendo en esta época el año que viene?

b) Compare los ejemplos siguientes:

Will you speak to him about it? (simple)
¿Le hablarás de eso?

Will you be speaking to him about it? (continuo)
¿Piensas hablarle de eso?

El uso de la forma continua en el segundo ejemplo indica que el hablante no hace una petición o una demanda (como ocurre en el primer ejemplo) sino que pregunta por una posible intención de «hablar con alguien» (**speak to him about it**) a la persona a quien se dirige.

3) **Be going to:**

a) A menudo se emplea de la misma forma que **will**:

Will it ever stop raining?
Is it ever going to stop raining?
¿Parará de llover alguna vez?

b) **Be going to** es más corriente que **will** o **shall** cuando se trata de expresar una intención:

I'm going to take them to court.
Voy a llevarles a juicio.

They're going to buy a new car.
Van a comprar un coche nuevo.

Pero si la oración es más larga, e incluye otros grupos adverbiales y otras proposiciones, también podremos emplear **will**:

Listen, what we'll do is this, we'll make him think that we've left, then we'll come back in through the back door and ...
Escucha, vamos a hacer lo siguiente, le hacemos pensar que nos hemos ido, después volvemos por la puerta trasera y ...

c) **Be going to** se prefiere a **will** cuando las razones que justifican las previsiones tienen una relación directa con el presente:

I know what he's going to say (because it's written all over his face).
Sé lo que va a decir (Lo lleva escrito en la cara).

4) El presente simple:

a) Este tiempo se emplea para hacer referencia al futuro cuando se hace referencia a un plan establecido:

When does the race start?
¿Cuándo empieza la carrera?

The match kicks off at 2.30.
El partido empieza a las dos y media.

Como hemos visto en el segundo ejemplo, es de uso corriente emplear el presente simple con un adverbio de tiempo:

We go on holiday tomorrow.
Mañana nos vamos de vacaciones.

The plane leaves at 7.30.
El avión sale a las siete y media.

b) El presente simple generalmente se utiliza en proposiciones temporales y condicionales:

You'll be surprised when you see her.
Te sorprenderás cuando la veas.

If the sun shines, I'll be truly amazed.
Si el sol brilla, estaré realmente sorprendido.

No confunda las proposiciones de esta clase que comienzan por **when** e **if** con las proposiciones del estilo interrogativo indirecto:

Does he know when they're arriving? (when are they arriving?)
¿Sabe cuándo llegan? (¿cuándo llegan?)

I don't know if he'll agree (will he agree?)
No sé si estará de acuerdo (¿estará de acuerdo?)

5) El presente continuo:

a) El presente continuo se utiliza a menudo de forma parecida a **be going to** para expresar una intención:

I'm putting you in charge of exports (= I'm going to put you in charge of exports)
Te voy a poner a cargo de las exportaciones.

What are you doing for your holidays? (= What are you going to do for your holidays?)
¿Qué vas a hacer en vacaciones?

Pero observe la ligera diferencia que hay entre los dos ejemplos siguientes:

I'm taking him to court.
Le llevo a juicio.

I'm going to take him to court.
Voy a llevarle a juicio.

El primer ejemplo es más preciso que el segundo, menos sujeto a cambios.

El segundo ejemplo da cuenta de un hecho menos fijo.

b) El presente continuo también puede utilizarse para hablar de algo previsto para el futuro, de forma parecida a **will**+ infinitivo continuo o al presente simple:

He's giving a concert tomorrow.
Mañana dará un concierto.

c) Puede emplearse de la misma forma que el presente simple para hacer referencia a acontecimientos planificados en el futuro:

When are they coming?
¿Cuándo vienen?

They're arriving at Heathrow at midnight.
Llegarán a Heathrow a medianoche.

6) **Be to:**

Be to se emplea frecuentemente para hacer referencia a planes concretos, en particular planes que han organizado para nosotros otras personas, la suerte, o el destino.

All the guests are to be present by 7.30.
Todos los invitados se presentarán antes de las siete y media.

I'm to report to a Mr Glover on Tuesday.
Tengo que presentarme a un tal Sr. Glover el martes.

Are we ever to meet again, I wonder?
Me pregunto si nos veremos de nuevo alguna vez.

7) **Be about to:**

Esta forma se utiliza para expresar un futuro inmediato:

Please take your seats, the play is about to begin.
Por favor tomen asiento, la obra está a punto de empezar.

En inglés americano esta forma también puede emplearse para expresar una intención de futuro:

I'm not about to sign a contract like that!
No estoy dispuesto a firmar semejante contrato.

En inglés británico la tendencia es utilizar **be going to** en casos como éste.

8) El futuro perfecto:

a) El futuro perfecto se emplea para hacer referencia a una acción que habrá terminado/sido terminada en el futuro:

By the time you get there, we will have finished dinner.
Para cuando llegues allí ya habremos terminado de cenar.

b) También se utiliza el futuro perfecto continuo para expresar suposiciones:

I expect you'll have been wondering why I asked you here.
Me imagino que se estará preguntando por qué he pedido que viniera.

19 PARTÍCULAS VERBALES

En este capítulo nos ocuparemos de las partículas que pueden acompañar a los verbos. Cada partícula aparece acompañada de la explicación sobre sus principales usos, generalmente en forma de breve definición. Para cada uno de los usos se ofrecen varios ejemplos.

ABOUT

1 Indica movimiento en todas direcciones, a veces con una idea de desorden, de confusión:

I felt about for the light switch. The pain of his wounds made him lash about. (*sacudirse*) I was rushing about trying to get ready when the phone rang. People milled about in the streets. I wish you would stop fussing about.

2 Indica inactividad, ociosidad:

I hate standing about at street corners, so make sure you're on time. She always keeps me hanging about when we arrange to meet.

3 En torno a, alrededor de:

Make sure there's nobody about before you force the window. He looked about for a taxi. There's a lot of hay fever about at this time of year.

4 Sobre un cierto tema:

What do you think about his latest film? They know a lot about antiques. Are his books known about over here? What's he rambling on about now? (*contar*).

ACROSS

1 De un lado a otro:

We walked across the railway lines.

2 Al otro lado:

Always help old ladies across busy roads. I'm just popping across for a newspaper.

3 Indica un esfuerzo intelectual, esfuerzo dedicado a la comprensión:

He finds it hard to put his ideas across. How can I get it across to them that it's important to keep copies of all their files?

AFTER

1 Detrás de, siguiendo a:

The boy was running after his ball and just dashed out into the road. There she is at the corner — send someone after her.

2 En busca de:

The police are after him.

3 Sobre un tema:

Nurse, if anyone calls to enquire after Mr Thompson, tell them he's resting comfortably.

4 Indica un lazo o parecido entre miembros de una familia:

My niece takes after me. He's called after his grandfather.

AGAINST

1 Hacia:

The cat startled me, brushing against me in the dark hall.

2 En contra de:

I'm against capital punishment. She always kicked against the idea of marriage.

3 Indica algún tipo de protección:

Fluoride is said to guard against tooth decay.

4 Indica algo perjudicial para alguien:

Will the fact that he has a previous conviction go against him?

AHEAD

1 Delante de:

The favourite has got ahead now and looks likely to win. Look straight ahead, please.

2 Indica el movimiento hacia la realización, el progreso:

You will never get ahead unless you are conscientious. Why do you think you have kept ahead of the competition all these years? The project is moving ahead, nicely.

3 En el futuro:

Looking ahead to the next budget... It is essential to plan ahead.

ALONG

1 A lo largo de:

He walked along the street in a daze. The road runs along the river bank.

2 Indica una acción en curso, en progreso:

We were driving along when suddenly... We were tearing along at a hundred miles an hour. Things are coming along nicely. How's she coming along at school? The work is just chugging along at a pretty slow pace. How do old age pensioners manage to rub along on so little money? (*arreglárselas*)

3 Indica salida, partida:

I'll have to be hurrying along if I want to catch my train. I'll be getting along now then. The police told the crowd to move along. She told the children to run along and play.

4 Acompañamiento:

Why not bring your sister along? He's going to have to drag his little brother along.

5 Hacia un sitio no muy lejano, que a menudo se encuentra en la misma calle.

My mother sent me along to see how you were.

APART

1 Indica una separación:

The two fighters had to be dragged apart. I saw them draw apart as I entered the room. I can't get these two pieces apart.

2 En trozos, en partes diferentes, en completo desorden:

He says it just came apart in his hands. The police pulled the flat apart looking for drugs.

3 Aparte, a un lado:

The doctor drew the parents apart. Joking apart, what do you really think?

4 Indica una distinción del resto, una no inclusión en un grupo:

What sets her apart from all the other children in my class is... He stands apart from the others because of his very placid temperament.

AROUND (ver también ROUND)

1 En diferentes sitios, en torno a uno:

You have to search around for that kind of information. I'm hunting around for a pen that works.

2 En los alrededores:

He's around somewhere, have you looked in the kitchen? Where's that umbrella? It must be lying around.

3 Indica que no se tiene nada que hacer:

How much longer do we have to wait around before he arrives?

ASIDE

1 A un lado:

Please step aside and let us pass. They moved the old wardrobe aside to reveal...

2 Con el fin de crear cierta intimidad, aparte:

The teacher called him aside to ask how his father was. He drew her aside for a moment.

3 Indica que se deja algo a un lado para volver más tarde a ello:

Leaving that question aside for the moment... Could you lay that aside and work on this instead? I have some money put aside if you need it.

AT

1 En un lugar preciso:

I called at your mother's this morning but she wasn't in (*ir a casa de alguien*). This train will call at Preston and Carlisle (*poner en comunicación*). How many stations did you stop at?

2 En una dirección, hacia:

The explorers worked their way through the jungle, chopping at the undergrowth with their machetes. Don't clutch at my hand like that! The birds were picking at the crumbs. He hinted at the possibility of a promotion.

AWAY

1 Indica una partida o una ausencia:

I'm sorry but he has been called away on some important business. He drove away in a taxi. He ran away into the crowd.

2 Indica un alejamiento:

The child backed away from the dog. Something must be done to get her away from their influence. Why do you move away whenever I touch you?

3 Indica que se continúa con algo durante cierto tiempo:

Let the mixture boil away for five minutes. Teenagers chewing away at gum... She's pegging away at her maths (*trabajarse algo*). Well, keep asking away until you get an answer. There he was, snoring away on the sofa. They just sat there giggling away. She was in the bath, singing away. He lay groaning away on the ground.

4 Para librarse de algo, para quitar algo:

I want you to brush those leaves away from the path. Maybe someone with a van could take the wardrobe away. She rubbed the dirt away from the window. If you don't want it, throw it away.

5 Para poner a salvo o apartar algo:

Lock it away where it'll be safe. He keeps it stored away in the attic. I wouldn't be surprised if he had salted away a fair bit in this time.

6 Hasta desaparecer:

The water has all boiled away. He is wasting away with grief. The water gradually trickled away down the slope. He slowly rubbed the old paint away.

7 Agotar algo:

He has drunk his entire wages away.

8 Indica el principio de una acción:

Could I ask some questions? Sure, fire away.

BACK

1 Hacia atrás:

She flung back her hair. Move your men back, Lieutenant. Thinking back

2 Para dar la idea de retorno:

Flood waters are receding and people are beginning to filter back to their homes. It's so cold I think I'll head back. She's being moved back to Personnel Department. I'll send it back to you in the post. She asked her secretary to read the letter back (*volver a leerla en voz alta, para textos que han sido dictados*).

3 De nuevo, otra vez:

We've bought back our old house. Could you play that bit back? (*rebobinar y volver a poner una grabación*)

4 Indica la idea de retirada:

The intense heat forced them back. The plant will die back in autumn but give you a lovely show again in summer.

5 Indica que disminuye la marcha etc.:

Rein your horse back or you'll be in trouble. The pilot throttled the engines back and came in to land.

6 Indica que se reduce algo de golpe:

This old rose bush needs to be chopped back. We'll have to cut back on our expenses. We trimmed back the hedge a bit.

7 Indica que se reprime o se contiene algo:

I forced back my tears. What are you keeping back from us?

BEHIND

1 Detrás:

The wall they were hiding behind gave way. His wife always walks behind.

2 Con retraso:

The landlady says we're getting behind with the rent. If you're slipping behind with the payments/your work... You're dropping badly behind with your work.

3 Indica que algo o alguien se queda:

Do you mind being left behind to look after the children? That's OK, you go on ahead, I'll stay behind.

BY

1 Indica movimiento, paso:

We had to push by a lot of people. The cars raced by. Time goes by so fast, doesn't it?

2 Indica a qué se hace referencia:

My mother swears by castor oil. Which theory do you go by?

3 Indica que se hace una visita o una parada rápida:

I've just dropped by for a minute. Come by some time. I'll pop by to see you one day. We stopped by at the art gallery on the way home.

DOWN

1 Indica movimiento de arriba hacia abajo:

The sun blazed down on their bare heads. Call Tom down for tea (*es decir, dile que baje*). She dropped down from the tree. Pass me down that big plate from the top shelf.

2 Indica un movimiento hacia el suelo o hacia abajo:

I bent down to pick up the old man's stick. The hurricane blew down hundreds of mature trees. He drew her down beside him on the couch. Draw the blinds down.

3 Indica que se toma nota, para hacer uso de algo más tarde:

Could someone write down the main points? I've got it down in my notebook. I could see him scribbling something down.

4 Indica que se finaliza algo:

The audience hooted the proposal down. It was voted down. They all shouted the speaker down.

5 Indica que se fija algo:

We have to chain the garden furniture down or it would vanish overnight. Screw the lid down properly. They tied him down on the ground. Glue it down.

6 Indica que se para un vehículo:

We waved a taxi down.

7 Indica la transmisión de una generación a otra:

The necklace has been passed down from mother to daughter for centuries. An old folksong which has come down through the centuries.

8 Indica una reducción o disminución:

All the prices in the shop have been marked down. Thin the sauce down with a little milk if necessary. You're going too fast, slow down. The pilot eased down on the throttle.

9 Indica que algo no funciona como debería:

The computer is down again. She broke down and wept.

10 Indica una sanción impuesta por una autoridad:

The police are clamping down on licence-dodgers. The teacher really came down on me for not having learnt the dates properly. The court is going to hand down its sentence tomorrow.

11 Indica el consumo de bebidas o alimentos:

If you don't force some food down, you'll collapse. The dog gobbled it all down in a second. She absolutely wolfed her dinner down. Come on now, drink this down.

FOR

1 Indica el propósito, el objetivo:

With all this overtime she's doing, she must be bucking for promotion. She felt in her bag for the keys. Stop fishing for compliments! The qualities looked for in candidates are...

2 Indica que se está a favor de algo:

He argued strongly for a return to the traditional methods of teaching grammar. The points of view argued for in this paper.

FORTH

1 Hacia adelante, sobre todo cuando se trata de hacer frente a algo:

The Saracens sallied forth to engage the infidel in hand to hand combat (*uso anticuado*). He sallied forth to face the waiting fans (*uso humorístico*).

2 Da idea de nacimiento, de surgimiento:

Mary brought forth a son (*empleo anticuado, bíblico*). The tree puts forth the most gloriously scented blossom.

3 Indica que la persona que habla lo lleva haciendo ya un largo rato, y además indica un cierto tono pomposo:

He is always holding forth about something. She spouted forth about the benefits of free enterprise.

FORWARD

1 Hacia adelante, todo recto:

Please come forward one by one as I call your names. The cat edged forward to the corner of the lawn where the bird was sitting. Bring your chair forward.

2 Hablando del futuro, anticipando acontecimientos:

We're really looking forward to seeing them again. That's something I am definitely not looking forward to. Looking forward to hearing from you (*expresión utilizada al final de una carta formal*).

3 Adelantar, cuando se trata de fechas:

The chairman has decided to bring the board meeting forward a week.

4 Para algo que se propone o que se sugiere:

Does anyone have any other suggestions they wish to bring forward? The theory that he puts forward in his book.

FROM

1 De, procedencia:

We'll be flying from Heathrow. Where did you fly from? Where did you spring from? (*¿De dónde has salido?*) Where do babies come from? They come from Ghana (*es decir, son de Gana*). They will be coming from Ghana next week (*en este caso vienen de Gana*).

HOME

1 En casa, donde se vive:

Who is taking you home? I'll see you home safely. Go home.

2 Indica que se pone algo en su sitio o que se mete lo más profundo posible:

Make sure you hammer the nails home. Is the plug pushed home properly?

3 Indica que se hace a alguien comprender o apreciar algo:

Did you drive it home to them that they must be back by midnight? The recent accident brought home to them very forcefully the need for insurance. That comment really hit home (*tuvo efecto*).

IN

1 Indica un movimiento del exterior al interior:

We opened the door and the cat just wandered in. There's no need to burst in like that. We crept in so as not to disturb you. Don't stand so close to the edge of the pool — you might fall in.

2 Indica la localización en un lugar:

I think it was a bad idea to leave that bit in the letter. You shouldn't have left it in. I'm going to the bank to pay these cheques in. The car's pretty full, but we could squeeze one more in.

3 Indica que se está encerrado o que algo está cerrado:

When the police arrived, they found he had barricaded himself in. Women at home with children often feel fenced in. Help! I'm locked in! The old doorway was bricked in.

4 Indica que algo se añade a otra cosa:

Fold in the flour. Rake in some fertilizer. These extra ideas which the director of the film built in are not found in the original novel. A new character was then written in to the series.

5 Indica que se acerca algo o que nos aproximamos a algo:

Members of the orchestra eventually began to filter in. The train pulled in to the station. As I looked out of the window, I saw a car drive in.

6 Indica la realización de una cosa:

Fill in this form. The artist then drew in the remaining features.

7 En casa, propia o de otra persona:

I'm staying in this evening to wash my hair. You've bought in enough tins to last a lifetime. Let's invite the people next door in for a drink.

8 Indica la entrega de algo o alguien:

The wanted man handed himself in to the police. Give your essays in tomorrow. When do you need this work in by?

9 Indica que se termina o se para algo:

I'm jacking my job in. Pack that noise in! The engine's packed in.

10 Indica que algo queda totalmente destruido:

They had to beat the door in since nobody had a key. The roof fell in, showering the firemen with debris.

11 Indica que algo disminuye o se recorta:

> I asked my dressmaker to take the sleeves in. Pull the rope in a bit to get rid of the slack. Hold your stomach in.

INTO

1 Indica un movimiento de fuera a adentro:

> Don't just barge into the room, knock first. I could see into the room and there was nobody there. The operator cut into our conversation. The Fraud Squad is enquiring into the affair.

2 Indica que se utiliza parte de algo, generalmente por necesidad:

> We're going to have to break into our savings to pay for the repairs to the roof. It cuts into our time too much.

3 Indica un contacto físico:

> If you looked where you were going, you wouldn't keep barging into people. Some idiot running for a train cannoned into me.

OFF

1 Indica que se quita a alguien o algo:

> Don't bite it off, use the scissors. It took ages to scrape the old paint off. He was taken off in a police car. We're going to have to force the lid off.

2 Da una idea de partida:

> The car slowly moved off. The boys rushed off when they saw the policeman approaching. Don't hurry off, stay and have some tea. He just wandered off down the road and I never saw him again.

3 Indica el principio de algo, el punto de partida:

> Let me start off by saying... Who's going to lead off with the first question?

4 Indica que se abandona un medio de transporte:

> As the bus slowed, he jumped off. The doors opened and everyone got off. Come on, hop off and let me have a go on your bike. She doesn't like riding because she keeps falling off.

5 Indica que se apaga algo:

> Put the lights off, please. He choked off my screams with a gag.

6 Indica que la calidad de algo ha bajado:

> Don't touch the soup until it has cooled off a bit. This meat has gone off. Attendances have fallen off.

7 Para enfatizar el significado de un verbo:

The scriptwriters have decided to kill this character off. The detective was bought off. Most of the land has been sold off.

8 Indica un permiso (para no ir al trabajo):

Can I have next week off, please? They gave him a couple of days off.

9 Indica que algo ha quedado inutilizable, inaccesible:

The street has been barricaded off because of a gas leak. For reasons of safety, that part of the road has been closed off. They have divided some of the rooms off in an attempt to save on heating costs. This part has been partitioned off from the rest of the room. The rubbish dump has been walled off.

ON

1 Indica la continuación de una acción:

Read on to the end of the chapter. They just chatted on for hours. She worked on into the night. I think I'll work on a little longer. He ran on despite the cries for him to stop. Shall we stroll on then? They climbed on until the light failed. He slept on in spite of the noise around him.

2 Indica que se pone algo a alguien:

He whipped a dressing gown on and went to answer the door. The police clapped handcuffs on the thief. What did he have on? It was too small, I couldn't get it on.

3 Indica que algo está funcionando:

Do you know that you've left the headlights on? Turn the TV on, would you?

4 Indica que algo se utiliza como base:

What do the animals feed (up)on in winter? All cars should run on unleaded petrol. What sort of fuel does it run on? She thrives (up)on hard work. That wasn't something I'd planned on.

5 En cualquier medio de transporte:

The train stopped and everybody got on. They couldn't get any more passengers on. How many passengers are allowed on?

6 Indica algo que se ajusta:

The lid hooks on. Where does this bit fit on? He latches on to anyone who looks rich.

7 Indica aceptación:

It seemed like an excellent idea and we seized (up)on it immediately.

8 Indica que se hace avanzar:

The jockey's having to whip the horse on. The crowd is clapping her on as she reaches the last mile. He wanted to look in the car showroom, but I hurried him on.

9 Indica que algo está planeado o previsto:

I've got something on every night next week. What's on TV tonight?

10 Da la idea de transmisión de una persona a otra:

She handed your book on to me. Could you pass the news on?

OUT

1 Indica que se sale de un sitio:

They bolted out of the door. She drove out of the garage. He said a few words and then hurried out. I'm popping out to the library.

2 Indica una privación o una exclusión:

That tree will have to come down, it's blocking out all the sun. I've thrown out that old jacket of yours. Deal me out of this game — it's about time I went home. Heavy floods have driven thousands of people out of their homes. Go and get him out of bed. They have a habit of freezing out people they don't like. I feel a bit left out.

3 Indica que se parte, se sale:

The train had only just pulled out when... He walked out on his wife and kids. I've had enough of this relationship, I'm getting out.

4 Indica una distribución.

We need volunteers to hand out leaflets. Who's going to deal out the cards?

5 Indica que algo se estira o se extiende:

He held out his hand in a pleading gesture. Reach out your glass. You can pull the elastic out to twice its length.

6 Indica que algo se quita, se retira:

Is it time to take the cake out (*fuera del horno*)? Don't push me out of the way. A lot of pages have been ripped out. We had a bit of an argument about it but I finally screwed some money out of him.

7 Indica que se quiere resolver o se consigue resolver un problema:

I couldn't get the equation to work out. Things just didn't pan out between us. It all came out right in the end.

8 Indica que se sale de una situación difícil o que se intenta:

How did you get out of doing your homework? I wish I could wriggle out of this visit to my in-laws.

9 Indica un ruido fuerte:

Stop barking out orders like a sergeant-major. The loudspeakers were blaring out the candidate's message. She cried out in pain. Speak out clearly, please.

11 Fuera, no en casa:

The soldiers camped out in the fields. It was such a beautiful night we said the children could sleep out. I've been invited out for lunch. Is he in or is he out?

12 Indica que algo se alarga:

I left the dress to be let out at the seams. Your essay needs to be fleshed out. The speech was rounded out with some statistics on the company's performance in the last year.

OVER

1 De un lado a otro, a través:

She walked over the railway bridge. He saw me on the other pavement and hurried over. Hey, move over, there's room for two in this bed! I'll fly over and see you. They plan to bring witnesses over from France to testify.

2 Recorriendo una corta distancia:

I'll drive over and see you soon. Our neighbours are having us over for dinner on Saturday night.

3 Indica que se pasa de una cosa a otra:

We've switched over to another paper. I don't like this programme, could you change over?

4 Indica que se da la vuelta a algo:

He folded over the letter so that I couldn't see the signature. Fork the ground over thoroughly before planting.

5 Indica que se transmite un sentimiento, una impresión etc.:

It is very difficult to get over to men how women feel about rape. They need to find a better way of putting their company image over. They come over as being rather arrogant. How did they come over to you?

6 Por encima de:

He bent over the balcony for a better look. He shuddered at the thought of the threat hanging over him.

7 Indica la idea de cubrir:

Skies are expected to cloud over later in the day. The lake rarely freezes over. The door was papered over many years ago. The beautiful old floorboards have been carpeted over. The horrible realization that I was not alone crept over me.

8 Indica que se hace que algo dure más o que sobre algo:

The film has proved so popular that it is being held over for another two weeks. There's quite a lot left over.

9 Indica que se hace algo por completo, o que se finaliza:

The party was over by midnight. Just check over the names on the guest list. Be sure to read your essay over before handing it in.

10 Indica que algo se sale de sus límites:

The milk has boiled over. The river flooded over into the streets. The water was all spilling over.

11 Indica que se es derribado, que se cae:

She was knocked over by a bus. She tumbled over. Over he went with a crash!

PAST

Indica el paso, ya sea del tiempo, o pasar delante de un sitio:

He brushed past me in the street. We had just gone past the shop when... Cars raced past. Time just flies past. He just casually strolled on past.

ROUND (sobre todo en inglés británico)

1 Indica un movimiento circular:

Thoughts were spinning round in her head. You must hand your sweets round.

2 En forma de círculo:

A crowd gathered round to watch. They all crowded round.

3 Indica que se hace el recorrido de algo:

We went round the art gallery. Would you like to see round the house? Were you able to see round? I'll phone round and see if anyone else knows about it. Could you ask round?

4 Indica que se cambia algo de lugar:

I've been bumping into things ever since your mother changed all the furniture round. He turned the car round and went home.

5 Por casa, cuando se trata de personas que viven o trabajan relativamente cerca:

Could you call round tomorrow morning, doctor? They always go out when their son has some of his friends round. Drop round some time. Let's invite them round.

THROUGH

1　A través de, indica el paso por un sitio:

We arrived at Ipswich and just drove straight through. The door was thrown open and the policeman came bursting through, gun at the ready. He looked through me as if I didn't exist. We're not stopping here, just passing through.

2　Irrupción en:

The crowd broke through the barriers. The sun is expected to break through sometime this morning. Supplies are filtering through. You're wearing your jumper through at the elbows. The soles of my boots are almost worn through.

3　Indica éxito:

She brought all of us through the exam. His teachers pushed him through. We'll just have to muddle through without her. He was very ill, but he's pulled through now. Against all the odds, they fought through.

4　Indica que algo se hace completamente, de principio a fin:

They went through everyone's hand luggage. Will you read through my speech and give me your opinion? I'll be up all night wading through this paperwork. Have these bags been looked through yet? It has to be read through twice. It had obviously been checked through in some detail. The plan hasn't been properly thought through.

5　Indica el final:

I'm through with men! Let me know when you get through with what you're doing.

TO

1　Indica movimiento hacia un lugar:

Name the foreign countries you've travelled to.

2　Indica que se vuelve a la consciencia:

When do you think he'll come to?

3　Indica relación:

What do you say to this suggestion? Who are you talking to? Has your letter been replied to yet? Are you being attended to, madam?

4　Indica que algo se cierra:

Could you push the door to a little?

TOGETHER

Conjunto:

We always gathered together for morning prayers. Let's collect some of the neighbours together and talk about it. You must keep the group together and not let people wander off on their own. What were just vague ideas are coming together into a definite proposal. He's really got it together (*lograr cumplir sus ambiciones*).

TOWARDS (toward en inglés americano)

1 En dirección hacia:

He started walking towards the bridge. My husband wants a holiday in Spain but I'm leaning towards France.

2 Dando a:

The castle looks towards the sea. The street which it looks towards.

3 Respecto a:

How does she really feel towards him?

4 Indica que se hace o se utiliza algo con un propósito:

I'd like to start saving towards my retirement. Put that money towards a new car.

UNDER

1 Bajo, debajo de:

When the sirens sounded, we always used to get under the table. Fold the edges under. The sides of the carpet are folded back and tacked under with staples.

2 En virtud de, bajo:

Under the terms of the new law... That information comes under the Official Secrets Act. Who do you work under?

3 Indica represión, mantenimiento de algo en un estado de orden aparente:

A military government held the country under for many years. The government is doing its best to keep the rebels under.

4 Indica pertenencia a una categoría o clasificación:

I'm looking for books on garden design. - What subject do they come under in the catalogue? What should I look under? - Vegetables or fruit?

UP

1 Indica movimiento hacia arriba:

Hand that hammer up so I don't have to get off the step ladder. Pass the suitcases up. The climbers struggled slowly on up. Bet you can't lift that up. She hitched up her skirt and started to run. I'll just finish pinning up the hem of this dress. Hold your head up.

2 En una planta superior:

Carry this tray up to your father. Do you know where his room is or do you want me to see you up? Let's invite our neighbours up for coffee.

3 Indica que algo se alza o se endereza:

I jumped up to protest. They all stood up. The old man sat up in bed with a start. Don't slouch, straighten up your shoulders.

4 Indica que algo se aproxima:

Old age has crept up. The manager of the shop rushed up to ask if he could be of assistance. He wandered up to us.

5 Indica la mejoría de un estado:

Business is looking up. The weather has cleared up.

6 Indica la subida de un precio, cantidad, volumen etc.:

This has forced house prices up. Turn the television up, I must be going deaf. He's souping up the engine of his car. The fire blazed up, catching them by surprise. Let me plump up your pillows. Why did they do the pub up? - I liked the old-style décor they had before.

7 Indica que se junta o busca algo:

She bundled up her clothes and beat a hasty retreat. I'm going to have to gen up on the latest fashions. He wants me to hunt up his ancestors. Where can I pick up a taxi? Do you think you can rake up enough money for the deposit? Where did you dig up that story?

8 Indica apoyo:

A street of shored-up buildings. What's it held up by? Can anyone back up your story?

9 Indica el fin de una acción:

That wraps up our programme for this week. She bust up the marriage, not him. Come on, drink up. They ate up and went.

10 Indica que se hace algo a fondo o completamente:

She's in big trouble for smashing up the company car. You've fouled our plans up. Should actors black up or not to play Othello (*teñirse la cara de negro*)? It helps soften the material up. Tighten this screw up. The mixture has hardened up sufficiently for us to use it now.

11 Indica que se termina por llegar a algo tras una serie de acciones:

We ended up in the pub of course. We're going to land up in hospital if you don't slow down.

12 Indica que algo está cerrado, oculto al exterior:

He'll be locked up for several years. Why don't you talk about your problems instead of bottling things up? They've bricked the old doorway up.

13 Indica que algo está hecho pedazos:

Chop the meat up for me. I hate the noise the waste disposal unit makes as it crunches everything up. Slice it up into smaller pieces.

14 Indica que se saca algo:

You owe me money, so pay up. He has been coughing up a lot of phlegm.

UPON

A veces equivale a «on» (ver ON), pero de uso más culto.

WITH

1 Compañía:

Who did you stay with? Who did he come with? Their kids have nobody to play with.

2 Indica lo que se utiliza:

What was it painted with? You can have the ones I've finished with.

20 CLASES DE VERBOS CON PARTÍCULA

En el diccionario de verbos con partícula que aparece en la segunda parte de esta obra los verbos se dividen en las siguientes clases:

vi, vic, vtsep, vtss, vtssc

*Es importante tener en cuenta que el carácter transitivo o intransitivo de un verbo no se corresponde necesariamente en los dos idiomas. Como podrá comprobarse en muchos casos.

VI (verbo intransitivo)

get off - **He got off at Victoria Station.**
Se bajó en la Estación Victoria.

listen in - **Do you mind if I listen in while you talk?**
¿Le importa si escucho mientras que habla?

VIC (verbo intransitivo con complemento)

Estos son verbos intransitivos a los que acompaña una partícula que a veces puede o debe ir seguida de un complemento:

join in : They all joined in the chorus (el complemento **the chorus** puede omitirse).
Todos se unieron (al coro).

come across - **Where did you come across that word?** (el complemento **word** es necesario)
¿Dónde has visto esa palabra?

Esta construcción a veces parece corresponderse con la de un verbo transitivo, p.e. en el segundo ejemplo, y a veces incluso puede darse una forma pasiva:

A type of virus which had never been come across before.
Una clase de virus con el que nunca nos habíamos encontrado.

VTSEP (verbo transitivo con partícula separable)

Se pueden separar las dos partes del verbo:

dig up - **They're digging the road up. = They're digging up the road.**
Están de obras en la carretera.

Existe forma pasiva:

The road is being dug up again.
De nuevo está la carretera en obras.

Si el complemento del verbo es un pronombre personal HAY QUE separar las dos partes del verbo:

look up - **I'll look him up when I'm in Paris.**
Iré a verle cuando esté en París.

VTSEP*

Cuando el código lleve el asterisco (*) indicará que se trata de verbos transitivos con partícula separable a la que se puede posponer un complemento:

knock over -   **She knocked the coffee over.** (vtsep)
                     She knocked the coffee over the carpet. (vtsep*)
                     Derramó el café encima de la alfombra.

(Nota: Los complementos como **£10** en la oración «**They've put the price up £10**", «*Han subido el precio diez libras*» no se incluyen en esta categoría; el asterisco a veces sólo hará referencia a tan sólo uno de los significados del verbo.)

VTSS (verbo transitivo con partícula siempre separable)

take back -   **The old song really took Grandpa back.**
                    Esta vieja canción realmente transportó al abuelo al pasado.

El complemento NO puede situarse detrás de la partícula. El uso de la voz pasiva es posible:

Grandpa was really taken back by the old song.
El abuelo realmente se vio transportado al pasado al oir la vieja canción.

VTSSC (verbo transitivo con partícula siempre separable y con complemento)

La partícula siempre debe separarse del verbo Y HAY QUE colocar un complemento después del verbo y después de la partícula:

let in for - Do you realize what you could be letting yourself in for?
¿Te das cuenta en lo que te estás metiendo?

He's let me in for a lot of extra work.
Me ha creado una gran cantidad de trabajo suplementario.

DICCIONARIO DE VERBOS CON PARTÍCULA

En el diccionario de verbos con partícula hemos utilizado las siguientes abreviaturas:

Am.	inglés americano
Br.	inglés británico
Fam.	estilo familiar
Fig.	sentido figurado
Pop.	estilo popular

Las abreviaturas referentes a la clasificación de los verbos son:

vi	verbo intransitivo
vic	verbo intransitivo con complemento
vtsep(*)	verbo transitivo con partícula separable
vtss	verbo transitivo con partícula siempre separable
vtssc	verbo transitivo con partícula siempre separable y con complemento

Consultar la explicación de esta clasificación en las páginas 70-71.

A

abide by VIC *(cumplir, acatar)* You'll have to abide by the rules.

account for VIC **(a)** *(dar cuenta de)* How did they account for their absence? - There's no accounting for taste I suppose, but have you seen what they ve done with their front room? **(b)** *(localizar)* The firemen did not need to enter the building since all the occupants were accounted for. **(c)** *(destruir, liquidar)* In recent action, the rebels have accounted for a great many government troops. -Those two will account for as many sweets as all the other kids put together. **(d)** *(ser la causa de)* Shoplifting accounts for most of the store's losses.

act (up)on VIC **(a)** *(actuar sobre)* Rust is caused by salt acting on metal. **(b)** *(seguir un consejo etc.)* Acting on her lawyer's advice, she has decided not to sue.

act out VTSEP *(realizar, llevar a cabo)* He treats his patients for neuroses by having them act out their fantasies.

act up VI *(comportarse mal)* That child acts up every time her mother goes out without her. *(funcionar mal)* The photocopier is acting up again.

add in VTSEP* *(añadir)* Add in a little salt and the mixture is complete.

add on VTSEP* *(añadir)* We're thinking about adding on a conservatory. -Should we add something on as a tip?

add up 1 VI **(a)** *(sumar)* I'd have thought that at your age you could add up by now! **(b)** *(tener explicación)* It's all beginning to add up. -It's a mystery, it just doesn't add up. **2** VTSEP *(sumar, añadir a un cálculo)* If you add all the figures up, the total is surprisingly large.

add up to VIC **(a)** *(ascender a)* How much does it all add up to? **(b)** *(alcanzar; la suma de varias acciones o hechos)* Is that all you've done? - It doesn't add up to much, does it? -If you put all the facts together it adds up to quite an interesting case.

adhere to VIC *(adherirse a)* I don't adhere to that philosophy at all.

admit to VIC *(confesar, admitir)* He admitted to a slight feeling of apprehension.

agree on VIC *(ponerse de acuerdo en algo, decidir)* They cannot agree on a name for the baby. -Well, that's agreed on then.

agree to VIC *(aceptar)* She felt she could not agree to my terms. -They agreed to their son taking the job.

agree with VIC **(a)** *(estar de acuerdo con, aprobar)* I am afraid I cannot agree with you. -She doesn't agree with all this psychoanalytic treatment for child molesters. **(b)** *(sentar bien)* Seafood doesn't agree with me.

allow for VIC *(tener en cuenta, contar con)* When calculating how much material you'll need, always allow for some wastage. -I suppose I should allow for his inexperience. -Has that been allowed for in your figures?

allow out VTSEP *(dar permiso para salir)* The curfew meant that nobody was allowed out after dark. - Some prisoners are allowed out at weekends.

angle for VIC *(buscar, ir tras algo)* He was angling for promotion so he developed a sudden interest in the boss's daughter. -Never angle for compliments.

answer back 1 VI **(a)** *(responder de malos modos)* Don't answer back, young man! **(b)** *(replicar)* She's the boss, so I can't answer back. **2** VTSEP *(responder a alguien de malos modos)* That child will answer anyone back.

answer for VIC **(a)** *(responder de)* If he keeps on at me like this, I won't answer for my actions. **(b)** *(ser responsable de)* The people who elected him have a great deal to answer for.

answer to VIC **(a)** *(responder ante)* If you lay one finger on him, you'll have me to answer to. -Who do you answer to in your job? **(b)** *(responder a, ajustarse a)* A woman answering to the description has been seen in the area.

argue away 1 VTSEP *(quitar importancia a)* You cannot argue the facts away - ozone depletion is a serious problem. **2** VI *(discutir sin parar)* They've been arguing away all morning.

argue for/against VIC *(discutir a favor de/en contra de)* The speakers will argue for and against unilateral disarmament.

argue out VTSEP *(discutirlo, llegar a un resultado discutiendo)* I'll leave you to argue it out between you.

ask after VIC *(preguntar por, interesarse por)* Let your father know I was asking after him.

ask around 1 VI *(preguntar, enterarse)* I'll ask around at work and see if anyone else is interested. **2** VTSEP *(invitar a casa de uno)* Why don't we ask them around for dinner one night?

ask back VTSEP *(invitar a casa de uno para terminar una salida)* Do you want to ask them back for a drink after the theatre?

ask in VTSEP *(invitar a casa de uno cuando la persona invitada está cerca)* I would ask you in for tea but my husband's not very well.

ask out VTSEP *(invitar a salir)* He's asked her out so many times she must be running out of excuses by now. -When he finally summoned up the courage to ask her out...

ask up VTSEP *(invitar a subir a casa de uno)* Don't get too excited if she asks you up for coffee — her mother lives with her!

attend to VIC **(a)** *(atender a alguien, ocuparse de algo)* Are you being attended to, Madam? -I'll attend to this. **(b)** *(atender, prestar atención)* Now attend to the experiment very closely: I'll be asking you questions later.

auction off VTSEP *(subastar)* They auctioned off all the family silver to raise some money.

average out 1 VTSEP *(hacer/calcular la media)* I've averaged out how much I spend a week, and it's frightening. **2** VI *(alcanzar un promedio)* Over a full year it averages out quite differently.

average out at VIC *(ser por término medio)* How much does that average out at a year?

B

babble away/on VI *(farfullar)* You were babbling away in your sleep last night. -I have no idea what you're babbling on about.

back down VI *(echarse atrás)* He takes pride in never backing down, however strong the opposition's case.

back on to VIC *(dar a... por la parte trasera)* The house backs on to a lane.

back out 1 VI **(a)** *(dar marcha atrás)* He backed out of the drive. **(b)** *(volverse atrás)* They can't back out from the deal now! **2** VTSEP *(sacar en marcha atrás)* I'm not very good at backing the car out — will you do it?

back up 1 VI *(retroceder para dejar sitio)* All the cars had to back up to let the ambulance past. **2** VTSEP **(a)** *(apoyar, basar)* He'll need to back up his claim to the estate with something stronger than that. -I doubt if the electors will back them up. **(b)** *(llevar en marcha atrás)* The driver had to back his lorry up all the way to the service station. **(c)** Am. *(inmovilizó)* The accident backed the traffic up all the way to the turnpike.

bail out VTSEP **(a)** *(poner en libertad bajo fianza)* Their lawyer bailed them out. **(b)** *(sacar de un apuro)* I'm not bailing you out again — you're on your own this time.

balance out 1 VI *(cuadrar)* The figures don't balance out. **2** VTSEP *(complementarse)* He cooks and she knows a lot about wine, so they balance each other out very nicely.

bale out 1 VI **(a)** *(saltar en paracaídas en caso de urgencia)* Dad never tires of telling how he had to bale out over the Channel during a dogfight. **(b)** *(achicar)* She's taking on a lot of water — start baling out. **2** VTSEP *(achicar)* We'll have to bale the water out first.

band together VI *(unirse)* If we band together, we can do something about this problem.

bandy about/around VTSEP* *(hacer uso excesivo de palabras etc.)* «Decentralization» is a word the government bandies about a lot. *(dar mucho bombo a algo)* The newspapers have been bandying that story around for weeks now.

bank (up)on VIC *(contar con)* Him turn up on time? - I wouldn't bank on it if I were you.

bargain for VIC *(esperarse)* If she marries him, she'll get more than she bargained for. -I didn't bargain for your kid brother coming as well.

bash about VTSEP Fam. (*zurrar)* Her husband bashes her about something awful. *(maltratar)* You can always rely on baggage handlers bashing your suitcases about.

bash on VI Fam. *(seguir adelante como sea)* The weather forecast was bad but they decided to bash on with their plans for a picnic.

battle on VI *(seguir luchando, a pesar de todas las dificultades etc.)* He has fallen very far behind the other runners but he's still battling on. -Just battle on as best you can in the circumstances.

bawl out VTSEP (a) *(vociferar)* Please don't bawl out my name. (b) *(echar la bronca)* The boss really bawled us out for that mistake.

bear down 1 VI (a) *(empujar; la mujer durante el parto)* If that obstetrics nurse had said «bear down, dear» one more time, I would have hit her.
(b) *(dirigirse hacia de forma amenazante, ir de frente contra)* The crew of the fishing boat jumped overboard as they saw the liner bearing down on them. -The boys scattered as the headmaster bore down on them. **2** VTSEP *(agobiar, pesar sobre)* The Third World is borne down by the burden of poverty.

bear out VTSEP *(confirmar, dar la razón)* Onlookers bore out her statement to the police. -He feels that the report bears him out in his estimates of radiation levels in the area.

bear up VI *(aguantar, no dejarse hundir)* Mother found it difficult to bear up when there was still no news after the second day. -Bear up! - Just one more day to the weekend.

bear (up)on VIC *(guardar relación)* I don't see how that bears on what I am supposed to be doing.

bear with VIC *(tener paciencia con)* The old lady asked the salesman to bear with her while she looked for her glasses.

beat back VTSEP *(rechazar, hacer retroceder)* They beat back the attackers three times but were eventually overrun.

beat down 1 VI *(caer con fuerza)* The rain was beating down so fast it was difficult to see the road. **2** VTSEP (a) *(regatear el precio)* I felt quite proud of myself for beating him down so much. (b) *(derribar, destruir)* The drunk threatened to beat the door down if they didn't open up. -Hailstorms have beaten down the county's entire barley crop.

beat off VTSEP *(dejar a un lado, rechazar)* The tourists tried unsuccessfully to beat off all the people trying to sell them things.

beat out VTSEP (a) *(apagar a golpes)* Desperate sheep-farmers were beating out the brush fires with their bare hands. (b) *(marcar)* She beat out the rhythm on the table. (c) *(desabollar)* The car door panel will have to be beaten out.

beat up VTSEP (a) *(dar una paliza)* Beating up old ladies is his speciality.
(b) *(batir)* Just beat up a few eggs for an omelette.

beaver away VI *Fam.* *(currar, apencar)* He's still beavering away at his studies.

belt out VTSEP *Fam.* *(cantar a voz en grito)* He really belted that song out.

belt up VI (a) *Pop.* *(cerrar el pico)* I wish you would belt up. (b) *(ponerse el cinturón de seguridad)* I'm not starting this car until you belt up.

bind over VTSEP *(obligar legalmente)* He's the kind of judge who will bind people over rather than send them to prison. -The drunk was bound over for three months to keep the peace.

black out 1 VI *(perder el conocimiento)* She was all right until she saw the blood and then she blacked out. **2** VTSEP (a) *(apagar las luces)* The impact of the scene is heightened when they black the stage out. (b) *(impedir la retransmisión de)* We regret that industrial action has blacked out this evening's programmes.

blast off VI *(despegar; naves espaciales)* The latest space shuttle blasted off at 5 am local time today.

blaze away VI (a) *(mantener el fuego)* The troops blazed away at the target. (b) *(flamear)* The fire is blazing away merrily in the grate.

blink at VIC *(hacer la vista gorda)* His wife doesn't blink at his bad behaviour.

blink away VTSEP *(ahogar, contener; el llanto)* I blinked my tears away.

block in VTSEP *(encerrar, bloquear; especialmente con un coche)* That man next door has blocked me in again.

block off VTSEP *(cortar)* The street will be blocked off until the wreckage is cleared.

block up VTSEP (a) *(atascar, tapar)* Don't throw the tea leaves down the sink or you'll block it up. -The worst thing about a cold is that your nose gets all blocked up. (b) *(bloquear, obstruir)* They've blocked up the entrance.

blossom out VI *(transformarse en algo positivo)* She's blossoming out into quite a beautiful young woman.

blot out VTSEP (a) *(tachar, borrar)* A word has been blotted out here. -You must try to remember and come to terms with the past, not blot it out. (b) *(ocultar)* The mist has blotted out the view.

blow in 1 VI (a) *(quedar destruido por una corriente o explosión)* All the windows blew in because of the explosion. (b) *(entrar a causa del viento)* Shut the door — the dust is blowing in. (c) *Fam. (presentarse, llegar por sorpresa)* When did you blow in? **2** VTSEP (a) *(destrozar por una corriente)* The blast blew all the windows in. (b) *(hacer entrar aire)* Blow some more air in.

blow off 1 VI *(salir volando)* Some of the roof tiles have blown off. **2** VTSEP (a) *(barrer; el viento)* The high winds blew the tiles off the roof. (b) *(saltar, hacer saltar)* The gunman threatened to blow their heads off.

blow out 1 VI (a) *(apagarse)* The candles have blown out. (b) *(reventar)* The rear tyre blew out. **2** VTSEP (a) *(apagar)* Be sure to blow the match out properly. (b) *(calmarse)* The storm soon blew itself out. (c) *(modismo)* to blow someone's brains out = «*saltarle a alguien la tapa de los sesos*».

blow over 1 VI (a) *(derrumbarse)* The garage must have blown over in high winds last night. (b) *(pasarse; discusiones, malos ratos)* It will soon blow over and you'll be friends again. -The storm will blow over soon. **2** VTSEP *(derribar; el viento)* Did the wind blow anything over?

blow up 1 VI (a) *(volar, explotar)* The ammunitions depot blew up. (b) *(encolerizarse)* Do you often blow up like that? (c) *(estallar, surgir; una discusión etc.)* The argument blew up out of nowhere. **2** VTSEP (a) *(volar, estallar)* Terrorists have blown up the presidential palace. (b) *(inflar, hinchar)* Do the tyres need blowing up? (c) *(aumentar documentos etc.)* I'd like this photograph blown up. (d) *(exagerar)* You're blowing this up out of all proportion.

bluff out VTSEP *(salir airoso de algo gracias a la inteligencia o la astucia)* When the police get here, we'll just have to bluff it out. -She can bluff her way out of anything.

board in/up VTSEP *(tapar, cerrar)* The windows and doors have all been boarded up to stop tramps getting in.

bog down VTSEP *generalmente en voz pasiva (estar atascado)* The car is bogged down in the mud. -The important thing is not to get bogged down in details.

boil down to VI *(reducirse a)* What his claim boils down to then is...

boil up 1 VTSEP *(hervir)* The doctor wants you to boil up some water. **2** VI *Fam. (hervir)* I could feel the anger boiling up inside me = «*Sentía cómo me hervía la sangre*».

bolt down 1 VTSEP *(bajar)* She bolted down the stairs and into the street. **2** VTSEP *(tragar, comer con rapidez)* Don't bolt your food down like that.

bone up on VIC *Fam. (empollar)* You'll have to bone up on your history if you want to pass that test next week.

book in 1 VI *(firmar en el libro de registros al llegar al hotel)* Do we have to book in at a certain time? **2.** VTSEP* *(hacer una reserva para)* I've booked them in to the best hotel in town.

book up 1 VI *(reservar)* Have you booked up for a holiday? **2** VTSEP *generalmente en voz pasiva (estar lleno)* The hotel is all booked up.

boot up 1 VTSEP *(arrancar, en informática)* Use this diskette to boot the computer up. **2** VI *(arrancar, un ordenador)* For some odd reason the computer is refusing to boot up.

bottle up VTSEP *(contener, reprimir los sentimientos)* It does no good to bottle your feelings up.

bottom out VI *Fam. (tocar fondo)* The government hopes that unemployment has finally bottomed out.

bow out VI *Fam. (coger permiso/vacaciones)* When the company introduced computers, old Mr Parsons decided the time had come to bow out.

bowl out VTSEP *(eliminar; en el cricket)* We bowled him out for ten.

bowl over VTSEP **(a)** *(derribar)* The old lady was bowled over by a boy on a bike. **(b)** *(desconcertar)* I was bowled over by winning first prize.

box in VTSEP **(a)** *(rodear)* The defence seem to have him boxed in. **(b)** *(empotrar)* We're boxing in the sink. **(c)** *(encerrar)* Don't you feel boxed in in such a small room?

branch off VI *(bifurcarse)* The road branches off to the left.

branch out VI *(extender actividades a)* The company intends to branch out into a new area of business.

brazen out VTSEP *(enfrentarse con insolencia) generalmente en la expresión «to brazen it out»* When they accused him of gate-crashing the party, he brazened it out and refused to admit he hadn't been invited.

break away VI **(a)** *(dar esquinazo a)* She broke away from the guards who were escorting her to hospital. **(b)** *(separarse)* When did you break away from your family? -It was the year France broke away from NATO. **(c)** *(derrumbarse, hundirse)* The merest touch and the surface breaks away.

break down 1 VI **(a)** *(averiarse)* The car broke down on the motorway. **(b)** *(fallar, no ser consistente)* That's where your argument breaks down. **(c)** *(fracasar)* Their marriage seems to be breaking down. -Talks between the two sides have broken down. **(c)** *(derrumbarse, por un ataque de nervios etc.)* I broke down in tears. **(d)** *(desglosarse, dividirse)* The compound breaks down into a number of components. **2** VTSEP **(a)** *(derribar)* The firemen had to break down the door to rescue the children. **(b)** *(vencer)* She was unable to break down her parents' opposition to her plans. **(c)** *(desglosar)* We really need to break the figures down a bit further.

break in 1 VI **(a)** *(interrumpir, cortar una conversación etc.)* I really must break in at this point. **(b)** *(entrar a la fuerza)* When did you realize that someone had broken in? **2** VTSEP **(a)** *(derribar)* The thieves broke the door in. **(b)** *(domar)* She's good at breaking in horses. **(c)** *(hacerse a los zapatos)* I hate having to break in new shoes.

break into VIC **(a)** *(entrar a la fuerza)* Thieves broke into a number of houses on the street last night. **(b)** *(utilizar parte de)* I'll have to break into my holiday money to pay for the repairs to my car. **(c)** *(interrumpir)* Why did you break into the conversation like that? **(d)** *(ponerse a...)* I broke into a cold sweat when I realized how high up I was. -He often breaks into song in the shower.

break off 1 VI **(a)** *(írsele a uno de)* It just broke off in my hand — honestly. **(b)** *(pararse, detenerse; dejar de hacer algo)* Can we break off for the rest of the day? -He broke off when the chairman entered the room. **2** VTSEP **(a)** *(partir, romper)* Break off two pieces of chocolate for you and your brother. **(b)** *(suspender)* Talks have been broken off. **(c)** *(cortar una relación amorosa)* It wouldn't surprise me if they broke it off soon. -They've broken off the engagement.

break out VI **(a)** *(estallar, surgir, expandirse)* Fires have broken out all over the city. **(b)** *(salirle a uno algo)* The baby is breaking out in a rash. **(c)** *(escaparse)* The prisoners broke out last night. **(d)** *(exclamar)* «I don't agree,» she broke out. **(e)** *(abrir; normalmente una botella)* Let's break out another bottle.

break up 1 VI **(a)** *(disolverse, deshacerse)* The ice on the river is breaking up at last. *(hacerse pedazos)* Their marriage is breaking up. *(expresión)* I just broke up = «me partí de risa». **(b)** *(acabar)* When did the party finally break up? -The schools will be breaking up for summer soon. **(c)** *(separarse, una pareja)* I've heard that they are breaking up. **2** VTSEP **(a)** *(desguazar, hacer añicos)* You'll have to break the earth up before you can plant anything. **(b)** *(parar)* The guard broke up the fight between the prisoners. **(c)** *(destruir)* It was his drinking that broke the marriage up.

bring about VTSEP *(ocasionar, causar)* What brought this about?

bring back VTSEP **(a)** *(llevar a casa)* Mum told me to bring you back for supper. **(b)** *(restablecer un estado)* A couple of days in bed will bring him back to normal. **(c)** *(reelegir)* It will be up to the electors whether to bring back the previous government. **(d)** *(recordar)* That song brings back memories.

bring down VTSEP **(a)** *(hacer que se venga abajo)* If that boy doesn't stop jumping up and down like that he's going to bring the house down about our ears. *(expresión)* Their jokes always bring the house down = «sus *chistes siempre se llevan la palma».* **(b)** *(derribar)* The spy plane was brought down by a missile. **(c)** *(hacer bajar)* The badly damaged plane was brought down with no loss of life. **(d)** *(hacer caer)* It was really the students who brought down the government. -He brought him down with a rugby tackle. **(e)** *(llamar la atención ante una autoridad)* Stop making so much noise or you'll bring the headmaster down on us. **(f)** *(bajar, reducir)* This new drug will bring his temperature down. -She would have brought the price down even further if you'd gone on bargaining.

bring in VTSEP **(a)** *(traer, al interior)* I've brought Mrs Jones in to see you. **(b)** *(introducir)* New tax legislation will be brought in next year. **(c)** *(hacer o pedir la intervención de)* The company is bringing consultants in to see if the problems can be solved. -This argument is between you two — why bring me in? **(d)** *(celebrar Año Nuevo)* to bring in the New Year. **(e)** *(ganar)* How much money is your eldest son bringing in? **(f)** *(pronunciar un veredicto etc.)* The jury brought in a verdict of not guilty.

bring off VTSEP* **(a)** *(rescatar)* The crew are being brought off the ship today. **(b)** *(lograr)* Did you bring the deal off?

bring on VTSEP **(a)** *(conducir, hacer entrar)* Please bring on our next contestant. **(b)** *(provocar, causar)* Damp days always bring on my arthritis. -What brought this on? **(c)** *(hacer surgir)* This mild weather will bring the roses on nicely. **(d)** *(expresión)* I brought it on myself = *«sólo yo tengo la culpa».*

bring out VTSEP **(a)** *(conducir al exterior, hacer salir)* They brought the man out under armed guard. **(b)** *(hacer que alguien muestre su personalidad)* His grand-daughter is about the only one who can bring him out (of himself). **(c)** *(sacar a la luz, publicar, dar a conocer)* The sun has brought out all the bulbs. -Disasters bring out the best — and worst — in people. -They're bringing out the new models very soon. **(d)** *(provocar; cuando se trata de alergias)* Strawberries bring her out in a rash.

bring round VTSEP **(a)** *(llevar a casa de alguien)* I'll bring him round to meet you some time. **(b)** *(convencer)* You'll never bring my dad round to that way of thinking. **(c)** *(reanimar)* They brought her round quite quickly after she fainted. **(d)** *(llevar hacia)* I finally managed to bring the conversation round to what I wanted to talk about.

bring up VTSEP **(a)** *(criar, educar)* We've brought four kids up. **(b)** *(plantear, poner sobre la mesa)* Madam Chairwoman, I wish to bring up the question of travel expenses. **(c)** *(vomitar)* Everything she swallows she brings up ten minutes later.

brown off VTSEP *Fam. (fastidiar)* I'm browned off with always having to do the dishes. -You're all looking a bit browned off — what's wrong? -He's very browned off with you because you didn't go to the party (= *está enfadado*).

brush aside VTSEP *(apartar, dejar a un lado)* The Minister brushed aside the reporters. -She won't listen — just brushes our objections aside.

brush up VTSEP **(a)** *(recoger con un cepillo)* I want all those crumbs brushed up off the floor. **(b)** *(refrescar conocimientos)* He'll have to brush up his French.

buck up 1 VI **(a)** *(darse prisa)* Buck up or we'll be late. **(b)** *(animarse)* I wish he would buck up a little. **2** VTSEP **(a)** *(subirle la moral a alguien)* The good news bucked me up no end. **(b)** *(modismo)* to buck up one's ideas = «*rectificarse, corregirse*».

bucket down VI *Fam. (llover a cántaros)* It's bucketing down.

buckle down/to VI *(ponerse a hacer algo)* I suppose I had better buckle down if I want to finish the housework this morning. -If you don't buckle down to your piano practice... -He buckled to and finished cleaning the car.

build on 1 VTSEP* *(añadir)* Next door are building on a conservatory. **2** VIC *(basarse en, continuar a partir de)* The company is building on its earlier success.

build up 1 VI *(aumentar)* Pressure on the government is building up. **2** VTSEP **(a)** *(reunir, juntar, acumular)* I wouldn't build my hopes up if I were you. -We're trying to build up our savings so we can buy a house soon. **(b)** *(crear)* His father built that company up from nothing. -You've built up quite a reputation for yourself. **(c)** *(fortalecer, entonar)* The children need some vitamins to build them up. **(d)** *generalmente en voz pasiva (urbanizar)* The area has become completely built up. **(e)** *(promonocionar)* The play has been so built up that it's impossible to get tickets for it.

bump into VIC **(a)** *(chocar con, darse con)* I was so engrossed in my thoughts that I bumped into a lamp post. **(b)** *(encontrar por casualidad)* He's always bumping into people he knows.

bump off VTSEP *Fam. (liquidarse a alguien)* His job was bumping people off for a fee.

bump up VTSEP *Fam. (subir)* They've bumped up the price of beer again.

bundle off VTSEP* *(llevar de urgencias)* The baby was bundled off to hospital in an ambulance.

bung up VTSEP *Fam. (taponar)* Who bunged the sink up? -I'm/My nose is all bunged up.

burn down 1 VI **(a)** *(ser arrasado por el fuego)* The theatre burned down. **(b)** *(disminuir; un fuego)* The fire is burning down. **2** VTSEP *(quemar, incendiar)* Vandals have burned down a number of derelict buildings in the area.

burn out 1 VI **(a)** *(apagarse)* The fire is burning out. *Fig.* **(b)** *(desaparecerle el entusiasmo a alguien)* Social workers frequently burn out at an early age. **2** VTSEP **(a)** *(hacer salir, por causa de un incendio)* They were burned out. **(b)** *(apagar)* The fire has burnt itself out.

burn up 1 VI *(consumirse)* The rocket burned up in the atmosphere. **2** VTSEP *(consumir, quemar)* Children burn up a lot of energy playing. -This stove burns up a lot of wood.

burst into VIC **(a)** *(irrumpir)* She burst into the room. **(b)** *(ponerse a, echar a)* He burst into tears. -Then they all burst into song.

burst out VI **(a)** *(echarse a)* I burst out laughing. **(b)** *(gritar)* «Where were you last night?» he burst out. **(c)** *(salir corriendo)* They all burst out of the room.

butt in VI *(meterse; en una conversación etc.)* We were just having a cosy chat when she butted in. -Is this a private argument or can anybody butt in?

buy into VIC *(comprar acciones de)* He has bought into his neighbour's business.

buy off VTSEP *Fam. (comprar a una persona)* The councillor was bought off with an all-expenses paid holiday in the south of France.

buy out VTSEP *(comprar la parte de otra persona)* All the other shareholders have been bought out.

buy up VTSEP **(a)** *(acaparar)* Look at all those parcels — she must have bought up the entire store! **(b)** *(comprar grandes cantidades)* Because of the threatened shortage, people have been buying up toilet paper.

buzz off VI *Fam. (largarse)* Tell that kid brother of yours to buzz off. -Just buzz off and leave me alone!

C

call back 1 VI **(a)** *(volver)* I'll call back later to see her. **(b)** *(volver a llamar por teléfono)* If you'd like to call back in an hour... **2** VTSEP **(a)** *(volver a llamar a alguien por teléfono)* He said he would call you back. **(b)** *(llamar a alguien para que venga)* I know she's on holiday but she'll have to be called back to deal with this. -I think the last pair should be called back for another audition.

call for VIC **(a)** *(exigir)* The Opposition is calling for her resignation. **(b)** *(pasar/ ir a recoger)* Would it be too much of a rush if I called for you at seven? **(c)** *(requerir)* This is the kind of job that calls for brains rather than brawn. -That's wonderful news - it calls for a celebration.

call in 1 VI **(a)** *(visitar)* The social worker is going to call in later. **(b)** *(llamar por teléfono)* Off-duty nurses called in and offered to help. -Prison officers are not actually on strike but a great many of them are calling in sick. **2** VTSEP **(a)** *(llamar a, pedir que venga)* They've finally decided to call the doctor in. **(b)** *(retirar de la circulación)* The bank has called in its loans.

call off VTSEP **(a)** *(anular, cancelar)* The meeting will have to be called off. -Does this mean we'll have to call our holiday off? -They've called it off *(el compromiso de boda)*. **(b)** *(quitar de encima)* Call your dog off!

call out 1 VI *(gritar, chillar)* Don't call out in the street like that. **2** VTSEP **(a)** *(nombrar a alguien, pedir a alguien que salga)* The master of ceremonies called out the names of the prizewinners. **(b)** *(llamar a alguien, pedir que venga)* Call out the guard! -I don't like calling the doctor out at this time of the night. **(c)** *(llamar a la huelga)* The men were called out (on strike) halfway through the morning shift.

call up VTSEP **(a)** *(llamar, hacer venir)* The situation looked dangerous and the lieutenant decided to call up reinforcements. **(b)** *(llamar a filas)* Dad was called up in 1940. **(c)** *(llamar por teléfono a alguien)* Please don't call me up at midnight. **(d)** *(evocar)* The speech called up thoughts of the past. -

call (up)on VIC **(a)** *(visitar a)* Gentlemen used to ask permission to call on young ladies. **(b)** *(exhortar, hacer un llamamiento)* The Opposition called on the Government to make its position clear.

calm down 1 VI *(relajarse, tranquilizarse)* Getting hysterical won't help, just calm down. -I want you all to calm down now, children. **2** VTSEP *(calmar)* Leave it to mum, she'll calm him down.

care for VIC **(a)** *(cuidar de, ocuparse de)* She has spent years caring for her invalid mother. **(b)** *(gustarle a uno algo o alguien)* You know I don't care for that kind of language. -I don't believe he ever cared for you or he wouldn't have treated you the way he did.

carry away VTSEP *(dejarse llevar por los sentimientos)* He let his enthusiasm carry him away. -She gets carried away by the sound of her own voice. - Take it easy, don't get carried away! *(no te exaltes)*

carry forward VTSEP **(a)** *(cambiar de fecha)* Can I carry my leave forward and have six weeks next summer? **(b)** *(pasar a otra página o columna; en contabilidad)* This amount should have been carried forward to the next page.

carry off VTSEP **(a)** *(llevarse)* She carried off the prizes for Latin and French. **(b)** *(salirle a uno)* It wasn't the easiest of speeches to make but you carried it off very well. **(c)** *(matar, llevarse; cuando se trata de enfermedades)* Tuberculosis carried off a great many people in the last century.

carry on 1 VI **(a)** *(continuar, seguir)* Just carry on with what you were doing. **(b)** *Fam. (hacer una escena, comportarse de malos modos)* He carried on just because his wife wanted an evening out. -What a way to carry on! **(c)** *Fam. (tener una aventura)* Have you been carrying on behind my back? **2** VTSEP **(a)** *(continuar con, proseguir)* Grandfather wants me to carry on the business after he dies. **(b)** *(mantener)* We have carried on a correspondence for years.

carry out VTSEP **(a)** *(sacar)* They had to carry him out since he couldn't walk. **(b)** *(mantener, cumplir)* Never make a promise that you cannot carry out. **(c)** *(realizar)* The coastguard is carrying out a search for the missing crew members.

carry through VTSEP *(llevar a cabo)* The plan has to be carried through to the last detail.

carve out VTSEP **(a)** *(tallar, esculpir)* He has now carved out twenty or so statues. **(b)** *Fig. (abrirse)* The company plans to carve out its own niche in the market.

carve up VTSEP **(a)** *(cortar, trinchar)* Ask the butcher to carve the meat up for you. **(b)** *(dividir, repartir)* They just carved up the land among themselves with no regard for the native inhabitants. **(c)** *Fam. (adelantar de forma peligrosa a alguien por carretera)* Did you see how that fool carved me up?

cash in 1 VTSEP *(hacer efectivo)* Are you going to cash in your premium bonds? **2** VIC *(sacar provecho)* She's cashing in on the fact that her father knows a lot of influential people.

cast away VTSEP *(abandonar; estar abandonado tras un naufragio)* Robinson Crusoe was cast away on his desert island for a great many years.

cast back VTSEP *(echar hacia atrás; en el tiempo)* If you cast your mind back a week, you will recall that...

cast off 1 VTSEP **(a)** *(cerrar el punto; al tejer)* Cast off the remaining stitches. **(b)** *(soltar amarras de)* We cast the launch off at dawn. **2** VI **(a)** *(cerrar; al tejer)* Cast off when only four stitches remain. **(b)** *(soltar amarras)* They will cast off shortly.

cast on 1 VI *(hacer el punto)* I usually cast on with my thumb. **2** VTSEP *(hacer/ echar el punto (de))* Cast on 80 stitches. -Have you cast the sleeve on yet?

catch at VIC *(echar mano de, intentar coger)* She caught at his sleeve and asked for help.

catch on VI **(a)** *(agarrar, imponerse; una moda)* I remember you saying that the Beatles would never catch on. **(b)** *Fam. (coger = entender)* She's so naive she didn't catch on.

catch out VTSEP **(a)** *(coger a alguien en una mentira, pillar)* The police caught him out by asking for a description of the programme he said he was watching. **(b)** *(eliminar; en cricket)* He was caught out very early on.

catch up 1 VI **(a)** *(ganar terreno)* The runners behind are catching up. **(b)** *(ponerse al día, recuperarse de)* I wish I could catch up with my work/ sleep. **2** VTSEP **(a)** *(alcanzar, ponerse a la altura de)* You go ahead and I'll catch you up. **(b)** *(quedar atrapado)* They were caught up in a traffic jam for hours.

cave in VI *(derrumbarse, venirse abajo)* The walls and roof caved in under the force of the blast.

centre on VIC *(centrarse en, tener como tema principal)* The play centres on the idea of survivor guilt.

chain up VTSEP *(encadenar)* I hope he chains that brute of a dog up at night. -In those days people could be chained up in prison for years.

chalk up VTSEP *Fam.* **(a)** *(apuntarse)* The team chalked up another win today. **(b)** *(apuntar, tener en cuenta)* Chalk it up, will you, and I'll pay next week. **(c)** *(modismo)* She'll just have to chalk it up to experience = «tendrá que atribuírselo a la experiencia».

chance on VIC *(ir a dar con; por casualidad)* I chanced on this piece of Meissen in a grubby little second-hand shop.

change down VI **(a)** *(cambiar de marcha; automóvil)* Traffic lights coming up — change down.

change over VI **(a)** *(pasarse a)* Is it a good idea to change over entirely to electricity? **(b)** *(cambiarse)* Let's change over and you wash while I dry. *(cambiar de cadena; televisión)* As soon as opera or ballet comes on the TV, he changes over.

change up VI *(cambiar a una marcha superior; automóvil)* You have to change up faster than that.

chase up VTSEP *(encontrar algo con mucha dificultad)* We finally chased her up in the library. -Why not ask one of the big stores to chase up the pattern for you?

chat up VTSEP *Fam. (ligar con, tontear con)* He's just chatting you up. -I wish I could chat up men the way she does.

cheat on VIC **(a)** *(engañar a alguien)* Why didn't you tell me he was cheating on me? **(b)** *(engañar sobre algo)* It's not a good idea to cheat on your expenses.

check in 1 VI *(firmar el libro de registros al llegar a un hotel)* Have you checked in? **2** VTSEP **(a)** *(registrar la llegada de alguien)* They must be here — I checked them in myself. **(b)** *(hacer una reserva en)* She's quite high-powered, so check her into a four-star hotel.

check out 1 VI **(a)** *(irse de un hotel)* They checked out last night. **(b)** *Pop. (casar, pegar)* It doesn't check out. **2** VTSEP **(a)** *(informarse sobre, comprobar)* We've checked her out and she's who she says she is. **(b)** *(registrar la salida de)* The reception clerk will check you out.

check through VTSEP **(a)** *(examinar, rebuscar en)* They checked through everyone's hand luggage. **(b)** *(facturar por avión)* I have to change at Geneva, but can my bags be checked right through to London?

cheer on VTSEP *(animar)* He's there every Saturday to cheer his team on.

cheer up 1 VI *(animarse)* I hate it when people tell you to cheer up. **2** VTSEP **(a)** *(animar, reanimar)* A visit to the pub will cheer him up. **(b)** *(alegrar, dar vida)* The new curtains really do cheer the room up.

chew on VIC **(a)** *(masticar)* He chewed on his pipe stem for a bit and then said... **(b)** *(rumiar, meditar)* How much longer do you need to chew on it?

chew over VTSEP *(rumiar)* I have been chewing this little problem over in my mind, Watson, and...

chew up VTSEP **(a)** *(masticar bien)* Chew your food up well before swallowing. **(b)** *(estropear, destrozar)* Your machine has chewed up my bank card. -It's those heavy lorries that are chewing up the road.

chicken out VI *Fam.* **(a)** *(rajarse)* I arranged a blind date with Annabel for my brother but he chickened out at the last minute. -Don't chicken out on us. **(b)** *(escabullirse, librarse de)* He chickened out of his dental appointment.

chip in *Fam.* **1** VI **(a)** *(intervenir, dar su opinión)* If I can chip in for a moment... **(b)** *(participar en un gasto)* We've all chipped in for a present for her. **2** VTSEP *(poner, contribuir con)* How much is everyone else chipping in?

chip off 1 VI *(descascarillarse)* The paint is chipping off. **2** VTSEP* *(desportillar)* Be careful with those plates — I don't want any pieces chipped off. *(desportillar, descascarillar)* We slowly chipped off the old paintwork.

choke back VTSEP *(reprimir, contener)* Looking at these pictures, I find it hard to choke back my tears/anger.

choke up VTSEP *(taponar, bloquear)* The drain is all choked up with leaves.

chuck in/up VTSEP *Fam. (mandar a paseo)* You're surely not thinking of chucking up your job? -One day I'm going to chuck all this in and buy a farm. -He's chucked his latest girlfriend in.

chug along VI *Fam. (ir a paso de tortuga)* Dad always chugs along at about 35, even on the motorway.

clam up VI *(callarse)* Don't clam up on me, talk to me!

clamp down VI *(ponerse duro)* The police are clamping down this Christmas, so don't drink and drive.

clamp down on VIC *(ponerse duro con)* The authorities are clamping down on misleading advertising.

clean out VTSEP **(a)** *(limpiar y ordenar)* I'll clean out a few cupboards today, I think. **(b)** *Fam. (dejar sin un duro)* The casino cleaned him out. **(c)** *Fam. (arrasar con)* Someone has cleaned the shop out of sugar.

clean up 1 VTSEP **(a)** *(limpiar o lavar a fondo)* When are you going to clean this place up? It's a mess. -The kids need to be cleaned up before we go to your mother's. **(b)** *(limpiar; no dejar a un solo indeseable)* I like those old cowboy films where the sheriff says «I'm going to clean up this town.» **2** VI *Fam. (forrarse)* She really cleaned up at the roulette table.

clear away 1 VTSEP *(quitar, llevarse)* Workmen were clearing away the debris. -It's your turn to clear the dishes away. **2** VI *(desaparecer, esfumarse)* The clouds have all cleared away.

clear off 1 VTSEP* *(quitar de)* Clear all those papers off the table. **2** VI *(irse, largarse)* Clear off! -The boys cleared off when they saw the headmaster coming down the street.

clear up 1 VTSEP **(a)** *(aclarar)* I'd like to clear up a point or two. -We have some problems that need to be cleared up. **(b)** *(limpiar, hacer limpieza en)* I can't come out — I have to clear up my room. **(c)** *(curar)* The doctor said this cream would clear up the acne. **2** VI **(a)** *(despejarse, mejorar; al hablar del tiempo)* It's clearing up. **(b)** *(desaparecer)* Don't worry — that rash will soon clear up.

climb down VI **(a)** *(descender)* It took the climbers three hours to climb down. **(b)** *(dar su brazo a torcer)* She'll never climb down, however strong the arguments against her.

clock in 1 VI **(a)** *(hacer un tiempo de)* The last of the marathon runners clocked in at six hours. **(b)** *(fichar; en el trabajo)* I have to clock in. -You clocked in 10 minutes late. **2** VTSEP *(fichar por alguien)* Do you think just this once you could clock me in?

clock off 1 VI *(fichar la salida; en el trabajo)* When did you clock off? **2** VTSEP *(fichar la salida por alguien)* I'll clock you off if you like.

clock up VTSEP **(a)** *(lograr, realizar)* He clocked up a faster time than any of his rivals in the race. **(b)** *Fam. (llevarse)* The team has clocked up another victory.

close down 1 VI **(a)** *(cerrar definitivamente)* The factory is closing down next month. -We're closing down soon. **(b)** *(terminar; programas)* They closed the restaurant down because of health code violations.

close in 1 VI **(a)** *(acortarse)* The days are closing in. **(b)** *(aproximarse)* Winter is closing in. **(c)** *(rodear)* Government troops are said to be closing in on the rebels. **2** VTSEP *(cerrar, tapar)* They're thinking of closing the porch in.

close up 1 VI *(acercarse)* The photographer asked the people in the front line to close up so he could get them all into the photo. **2** VTSEP *(cerrar)* They must have gone away for some time — the house is all closed up. -The opening in the fence has been closed up to prevent similar tragedies in the future.

cloud up 1 VI **(a)** *(emcapotarse)* It's clouding up. **(b)** *(empañarse)* The mirror has clouded up. **2** VTSEP *(empañar)* The bathroom is poorly ventilated — steam always clouds the windows up.

club together VI *(juntarse; para hacer algo)* If we club together, we can get one big present instead of lots of small ones.

cobble together VTSEP *(hacer algo con prisas o sin cuidado)* My speech won't be very good I'm afraid — I cobbled it together on the train.

collect up VTSEP *(recoger)* I began to collect up my parcels.

comb through VIC *(repasar cada detalle)* I've combed through the entire book and haven't found any reference to him.

come across 1 VI *(resultar)* How did her story come across? -They come across as (being) rather nice people. **2** VIC *(encontrar por casualidad)* I came across this when I was tidying up — is it yours?

come across with VIC *Fam. (apoquinar)* If we don't come across with the money, they say they'll kill him.

come along VI **(a)** *(apresurarse)* Come along children, please! **(b)** *(avanzar, progresar)* My speech was coming along rather well until yesterday. **(c)** *(llegar)* Everything was peaceful until you came along. **(d)** *(ir también)* Can I come along?

come apart VI **(a)** *(romperse)* Honestly, I don't know how it happened — it just came apart in my hands. **(b)** *(estropearse)* She feels her life is coming apart at the seams.

come at VIC *(atacar, agredir)* The pair of them came at me with a baseball bat.

come away VI **(a)** *(irse)* Why not come away with me to Paris for the weekend? *(alejarse de)* Come away from that cat — it's got fleas. **(b)** *(soltarse)* The handle has come away from the knife.

come back VI **(a)** *(volver a la memoria)* I've forgotten her name but it will come back eventually. **(b)** *(recuperarse, volver a producirse)* We thought the fight was all over but he's coming back very strongly now. -Short hair is coming back. **(c)** *(salir con, replicar)* Then she came back with one of her usual cutting remarks.

come by 1 VIC **(a)** *(hacerse)* How did your brother come by all those bruises? **(b)** *(encontrarse)* I wonder where he came by all that money. **2** VI *(visitar)* I'll come by next week if that suits.

come down VI **(a)** *(reducirse, bajar)* Oil prices have been coming down. -Her temperature came down overnight. **(b)** *(rebajar)* He'll come down a few pounds if you bargain. **(c)** *(ser quitado de)* That disgusting poster is coming down right now — or else. **(d)** *(llegar hasta)* This is what we've come down to — selling the family silver. **(e)** *(reducirse a)* It all comes down to money. **(f)** *(llegar hasta)* The curtains should come right down to the floor. **(g)** *(serle legado a alguien)* The necklace came down to her from her great-aunt.

come down on VIC **(a)** *(echárse encima)* One mistake and he'll come down on you like a ton of bricks. **(b)** *(decidirse por, decantarse por)* He'll wait and see what happens and then come down on the winning side.

come down with VIC *(coger una enfermedad)* I always come down with a cold at this time of year.

come forward VI *(presentarse, comparecer)* The police have appealed for witnesses to come forward.

come in VI **(a)** *(llegar)* Our new stock will not come in until next week. **(b)** *(ingresar en caja)* I don't have much coming in at the moment — can you wait a bit? **(c)** *(tener que ver)* Where does she come in in all this? **(d)** *(venir, resultar)* An extra pair of hands always comes in useful. **(e)** *(conectar)* Are you receiving me? Come in, please.

come in for VIC *(recibir, obtener, encontrarse con)* The government is coming in for a lot of criticism over its latest proposals. -He came in for a lot of adverse publicity when he was younger.

come in on VIC *(entrar en, tomar parte en)* Why should we let him come in on the deal?

come into VIC **(a)** *(heredar)* She'll come into a tidy little sum when her great-uncle dies. **(b)** *(meterse en)* Wait a minute — when did I come into this crazy scheme? *(tener que ver)* Ability doesn't come into it — it's who you know that matters. **(c)** *(modismos)* to come into blossom = «*florecer*», to come into effect = «*entrar en vigor*». Could you explain how the car came into your possession, sir? = «¿*Señor, podría decirme como entró en posesión de este coche?*»

come of VIC **(a)** *(resultar de)* Nothing will come of it. -This is what comes of being too self-confident. **(b)** *(venir de)* The mare comes of good stock. **(c)** *(modismo)* She inherited a fortune when she came of age = «... *cuando alcanzó la mayoría de edad*».

come off 1 VI **(a)** *(soltarse, quitarse)* Could you fix my bike? The chain has come off. -I'm afraid the carpet is ruined — wine stains never come off. **(b)** *(celebrarse, tener lugar)* I shall be very surprised if that wedding ever comes off. **(c)** *(resultar)* Yet another attempt to beat the record that hasn't come off. **(d)** *(salir; de un accidente etc.)* Considering what he's done, he has come off very lightly. -It could have been a serious accident, but they all came off without a scratch. **(e)** *(salir; bien o mal parado)* We came off very badly in the debate on capital punishment. **(f)** *Pop. (correrse)* He did eventually come off but it was a long wait. **2** VIC **(a)** *(salir, irse; manchas etc.)* That kind of mark never comes off silk. **(b)** *(soltarse)* The handle has come off the knife. **(c)** *(abandonar)* They're threatening to come off the gold standard. **(d)** *(exclamación que expresa impaciencia, incredulidad: ¡Venga ya!)* Come off it — I've heard that line before.

come on VI **(a)** *(darse prisa)* Come on, or we'll miss the start. **(b)** *(darse, resultar; en el sentido de avanzar)* How's the work coming on? **(c)** *(empezar)* The rain came on about six. -I have a sore throat coming on. -When does that programme you want to watch come on? **(d)** *(entrar en escena, aparecer)* The character he plays doesn't come on until halfway through the first act. **(e)** *Pop. (hacerse)* She tried to come on like a *femme fatale* but soon gave it up. -He was coming on a bit too macho.

come out VI **(a)** *(salir, aparecer)* The magazine comes out on a Wednesday. -When do you expect your latest film to come out? Now that the sun has come out, maybe I'll get my washing dried. -Next door's roses always come out early. **(b)** *(darse a conocer)* The election results came out a few hours ago. -The truth will come out eventually. **(c)** *(hacer huelga)* Nurses all over the country have come out in protest. (d) *(salirle a uno; erupciones cutáneas)* The baby has come out in a rash. (e) *(salir bien; fotografías)* They're pleased that their holiday photographs have come out so well. (f) *(desaparecer; manchas etc.)* I've had this coat cleaned three times and the stain still hasn't come out. (g) *(salir del hospital, de la cárcel)* She'll be coming out soon. (h) *(salir; un cálculo)* Of course the equation hasn't come out — you copied the figures down wrongly. (i) *(declararse)* We've come out against the idea of moving. -The committee came out in her favour. (j) *(salir parado)* She came out of that looking rather silly, don't you think?

come out with VIC *(salir con, saltar con)* I'm always on the edge of my seat wondering what he'll come out with next. -She finally came out with what was bothering her.

come over 1 VI (a) *(dejarse convencer)* I doubt if I will ever come over to your way of thinking. (b) *(resultar, dar la impresión de)* He comes over as (being) a bit pompous, but in fact he's rather shy. (c) *(sentirse, encontrarse)* Granny says she came over all funny in the supermarket. **2** VIC *(sobrevenirle a uno un cambio de humor)* I don't know what's come over her — she's usually such a quiet little thing.

come round VI (a) *(reanimarse)* Give him time — he'll come round eventually. (b) *(dejarse convencer)* I'm sure they'll come round to our point of view in the end. (c) *(recobrar la consciencia)* Imagine that poor woman coming round and seeing all those faces staring at her. (c) *(repetirse con cierta frecuencia)* He swears birthdays come round more often after you're forty.

come through 1 VI (a) *(llegar, ser concedido; documentos oficiales)* He's very annoyed because his visa is taking so long to come through. (b) *(superar, sobrevivir)* It must have been a terrifying experience but they have come through all right. **2** VIC (a) *(salirle bien a uno algo)* Their daughter has come through her law exams with flying colours. (b) *(superar, salir de)* I am sure you will come through this ordeal. -Very few people came through the First World War unscarred either physically or mentally.

come to 1 VI *(recuperar la consciencia)* She came to in a hospital bed. **2** VIC (a) *(ascender a)* The bill came to much more than I could afford. *(llegar a)* That nephew of his will never come to anything. *(llegar a; sentido negativo)* Has it come to this, that we must leave a house our family has lived in for 400 years? (b) *(tratarse de)* When it comes to buying a car, find yourself a reputable dealer. (c) *(llegar a convertirse en)* If it comes to a malpractice suit, the surgeon is in trouble. -When does the case come to trial? *(modismo)* I do wish she would come to the point = «me gustaría que fuese al grano». (d) *(modismo)* Come to that, where were you last night? = «A propósito, ¿dónde estabas anoche?»

come up VI (a) *(salir; juicios etc.)* When does her case come up (for trial)? (b) *(surgir, mencionarse)* He beat a hasty retreat when the subject of fee-paying schools came up. (c) *(salir, ser puesto)* Do you think this question will come up in the exam? (d) *(estar dentro de poco)* Two other houses in our street are coming up for sale soon. (e) *(salir)* My number never comes up in the draw. -The bulbs are starting to come up. (f) *(surgir; un hecho, un imprevisto)* Call me if anything comes up that you can't handle.

come up against VIC *(encontrarse con; para obstáculos o situaciones difíciles)* You realize that you'll come up against some pretty strong opposition on this? -Who does she come up against in the next round?

come up to VIC **(a)** *(llegar a)* She's so tall that I only come up to her shoulder. -We're coming up to the halfway mark now. **(b)** *(responder a, estar a la altura de)* His latest play does not come up to expectations.

come up with VIC *(pensar, ocurrírsele a uno algo, salir con algo)* She's come up with a solution. -He keeps coming up with these awful jokes. -I'll let you know if I come up with anything that might help.

conk out VI *Fam.* **(a)** *(escacharrarse)* The radio has conked out on us. **(b)** *(irse; perder el conocimiento)* He's conked out — better send for a doctor.

cool down 1 VI **(a)** *(calmarse)* We'll talk about it once you've cooled down. **(b)** *(enfriarse)* It has cooled down quite a bit since yesterday. -Let the soup cool down a bit. -Things have cooled down between them. **2** VTSEP **(a)** *(calmar)* I'll try to cool her down but I don't think I'll have much success. **(b)** *(refrescar, aliviar)* How about a beer to cool you down after all that hard work?

cotton on VI *Fam.* *(coger = entender)* I never did cotton on.

cough up 1 VTSEP **(a)** *(escupir al toser)* If you can cough the phlegm up, you'll soon feel better. -People with tuberculosis cough up blood. **(b)** *Fam.* *(apoquinar)* I've got to cough up another £50. **2** VI *Fam.* *(soltar prenda)* He coughed up for the meal.

count in VTSEP *(contar a, incluir a)* Have you counted the neighbours in? - Anybody want to go out for lunch? - Count me in!

count on VIC *(contar con)* We can always count on you to be late. -He counted on me and I let him down.

count out VTSEP **(a)** *(contar)* If you want to know how much money you have, count it out. **(b)** *(dejar fuera de combate)* His opponent is on the canvas and being counted out. **(c)** *(excluir)* He's teetotal, so count him out of the pub crawl. *(no contar con)* A weekend camping out in the snow? - No thanks, count me out!

count up VTSEP *(sumar)* I've counted these figures up time and time again and get a different answer every time.

cover up 1 VI **(a)** *(disimular)* Don't try to cover up... I know it was you. The government was accused of covering up. **(b)** *(cubrirse; protegerse mutuamente)* The architects and builders are covering up for each other. **2** VTSEP **(a)** *(tapar)* That dress is much too low. - Cover yourself up a bit. **(b)** *(ocultar, disimular)* It's highly unlikely that he meant to cover things up.

crack down VI *(endurecer su postura)* In view of the increase in drunk driving, the police are going to crack down.

crack down on VIC *(ponerse duro con)* They're going to crack down on drunk drivers.

crack up VI **1 (a)** *(hacerse pedazos)* The ice on the pond is cracking up.

(b) *(venirse abajo)* If he doesn't take a holiday soon, he'll crack up. -Do you think their marriage is cracking up? -She cracked up under the pressure. **(c)** *(partirse de la risa)* I cracked up when he said that. **2** VTSEP *Fam. (modismo)* Some teachers of that university are not what they're cracked up to be = «*Algunos profesores de esa universidad no están a la altura de la fama que les precede.*»

cream off VTSEP *(seleccionar, coger la flor y nata)* The oldest universities cream off the best candidates.

cross off VTSEP* *(tachar)* Cross his hame off the list.

cross out VTSEP *(tachar, marcar)* Cross your mistakes out neatly, please.

cry off VI *(rajarse)* I hate it when people cry off at the last minute.

cry out VI **(a)** *(llorar de dolor)* The pain made her cry out. **(b)** *(pedir a gritos)* That room is just crying out for red velvet curtains.

cuddle up VI *(acurrucarse)* Cuddle up if you're cold. -The little girl cuddled up to her grandmother.

curl up VI **(a)** *(acomodarse, ponerse a gusto)* I like to curl up in bed with a good book. **(b)** *(enrollarse)* Hedgehogs curl up into a ball for protection.

cut across VIC **(a)** *(atajar)* We cut across the playing field. **(b)** *(ir en contra de)* Concern for the environment cuts across party lines.

cut back 1 VI *(hacer recortes, ahorrar)* We're definitely going to have to cut back. **2** VTSEP **(a)** *(podar)* Now is the time to cut your raspberries back. **(b)** *(reducir)* The company is cutting back production until the seamen's strike is over.

cut down 1 VTSEP **(a)** *(talar)* They're cutting down the trees that were damaged in the storm. **(b)** *(matar, abatir)* He was cut down by machine-gun fire. **2** VI *(restringir el consumo)* If you won't stop smoking then at least cut down.

cut in 1 VI **(a)** *(interrumpir)* The interviewer cut in to ask a question. **(b)** *(cerrar el paso)* That idiot will cause an accident cutting in in front of people like that. **2** VTSEP *(dejar participar a alguien)* Can you cut me in on one of your deals?

cut off VTSEP **(a)** *(*cortar)* They had to cut his clothes off in the emergency room. -Cut off his head! **(b)** *(aislar)* The town has been cut off by floods. -Don't you feel cut off living in the country? **(c)** *(cortar la electricidad, el teléfono)* We'd hardly said hello before we were cut off. -It's dreadful to think how many people have their electricity cut off because they can't afford to pay the bills. **(d)** *(desheredar)* The old man cut his son off without the proverbial penny.

cut out 1 VI *(pararse; un motor)* Will you have a look at the engine — it keeps cutting out. **2** VTSEP **(a)** *(recortar)* I cut this magazine article out for you. **(b)** *(cortar)* The worst bit is cutting the dress out. **(c)** *(prescindir de)* Cut out starchy food for a couple of weeks. **(d)** *Fam. (dejar)* I've told you already to cut out the silly jokes.

cut out for VTSSC *Fig. generalmente en voz pasiva (estar hecho para)* I'm not cut out for all these late nights.

cut up VTSEP **(a)** *(cortar)* Cut the meat up quite small. **(b)** *generalmente en voz* *pasiva (estar molesto, sentirse herido)* He was definitely a bit cut up for not being invited.

D

dash off 1 VI *(irse a toda prisa)* She was sorry she missed you, but she had to dash off. **2** VTSEP *(escribir a toda prisa)* I dashed off an answer yesterday. *(hacer en un santiamén)* He says he dashes these paintings off in his spare time.

deal with VIC **(a)** *(hacer tratos con)* Armament manufacturers will deal with anybody. **(b)** *(ocuparse de)* She dealt with that problem very well. -The case wasn't very professionally dealt with. **(c)** *(tratarse de)* The play deals with euthanasia.

die away VI *(desvanecerse, desaparecer)* The noise of the car engine died away.

die off VI *(morirse uno tras otro)* By the time he was in his twenties, his relatives had all died off. -Their livestock is dying off as the drought intensifies.

die out VI *(extinguirse)* Entire species are dying out as their habitat is destroyed.

dig in 1 VI **(a)** *(cavar trincheras)* The first thing the troops had to do when they got to the front was to dig in. **(b)** *Fam. (atacar el plato)* Dig in — there's lots more where that came from. **2** VTSEP *(revolver con la pala)* Before planting, dig in a couple of handfuls of fertilizer.

dig into VIC **(a)** *Fam. (atacar)* Dig into that pie as much as you like — I made two. **(b)** *(escarbar en)* They want us to dig into her past.

dig out VTSEP **(a)** *(desenterrar)* Dig out the roots. **(b)** *(encontrar excavando; en caso de hundimientos etc.)* They hope to have the remaining survivors dug out by nightfall. **(c)** *(descubrir, encontrar)* Have you dug those files out yet? -We want more information on the company's early days, so see what you can dig out.

dig up VTSEP **(a)** *(desenterrar)* This rose bush will have to be dug up and moved. **(b)** *(hallar)* We're hoping to dig up some items to show that there was a Roman encampment here. -I've dug something up that might prove he's been lying to us.

dip into VIC **(a)** *(meter rápidamente)* She dipped her toes into the bath water to test it. **(b)** *(echar mano a, coger parte de)* She doesn't want to dip into her savings if she can help it. **(c)** *(leer de vez en cuando, hojeando)* This is the kind of anthology to be dipped into rather than read all at once.

dish out VTSEP **(a)** *(servir)* Mum's dishing supper out now. **(b)** *(dar, repartir; cosas que preferimos que no nos den)* You're always dishing out advice.

dish up 1 VTSEP *(servir algo)* Somebody dish up the soup. **2** VI *(servir)* When will you be dishing up?

dispense with VIC *(prescindir de)* He called it «dispensing with my services» — I call it getting the sack.

dispose of VIC **(a)** *(deshacerse de)* Dispose of your waste paper here. **(b)** *Fam. (liquidarse a alguien)* We have to dispose of him before he talks. **(c)** *(librarse de)* So far she has disposed of six opponents who want to take the title away from her.

divide out VTSEP *(repartir)* They divided the food out.

divide up VTSEP *(repartir en, distribuir en)* Contestants will be divided up into groups of four.

do away with VIC **(a)** *(abolir)* They should do away with school: **(b)** *(matar, eliminar)* He has threatened to do away with himself.

do by VIC *Fam. (portarse con)* The company did very badly by its employees. -She did very well by her grand-daughter at Christmas. -He'll feel very hard done by if you don't at least send him a birthday card.

do down VTSEP **(a)** *(timar, engañar)* Why did you let the salesman do you down? **(b)** *(hablar mal de)* There's always someone ready to do you down.

do for VIC *Fam.* **(a)** *(matar)* If he keeps on treating her this way, she'll do for him. **(b)** *(agotar)* It was that last hill that did for me. **(c)** *(hacer la casa a)* Who does for you?

do in VTSEP *Fam.* **(a)** *(matar, liquidar)* Somebody on our street was done in last night. **(b)** *(agotar, dejar hecho trizas)* Christmas shopping always does me in.

do out VTSEP *(limpiar, hacer)* Will you do the kitchen out tomorrow please, Mrs Jones?

do out of VTSSC *Fam. (estafar)* He always maintained that he had been done out of his inheritance. -They did him out of his share of the money.

do over VTSEP **(a)** *(volver a decorar)* The whole house needs doing over. **(b)** *Fam. (dar una buena tunda)* The other gang did him over. **(c)** *Am. (rehacer)* The teacher said I had to do my project over.

do up 1 VI *(cerrarse, abrocharse)* Clothes that do up at the front pose fewer problems for people in wheelchairs. **2** VTSEP **(a)** *(cerrar, abrochar)* Do your buttons up. **(b)** *(envolver)* It seems a pity to open it when it's done up so nicely. **(c)** *(renovar)* They're doing up all the buildings on the street. **(d)** *(ponerse de tiros largos)* You've really done yourself up — what's the occasion?

do with VIC **(a)** *cuando se utiliza con «could» (necesitar)* You could do with a haircut. -What I could do with right now is a hot bath. **(b)** *(tener que ver con)* He has something to do with computers. -It sounds very fishy to me and you should have nothing to do with it. -That's got nothing to do with it! -It has to do with your mother, I'm afraid. -My business has nothing to do with you. **(c)** *(terminar con)* I've done with trying to help people. -He says it's all over — he's done with her. -If you've done with the hammer, put it back where it belongs.

do without 1 VIC *(prescindir de)* We can do without the sarcasm. **2** VI *(prescindir de ello)* If you don't find anything you like in here, then you'll have to do without.

double back 1 VI *(retroceder sobre sus pasos)* They felt they ought to double back since they didn't recognize any landmarks. **2** VTSEP *(doblar)* Double back the bedclothes and let the mattress air.

double over/up VI *(retorcerse)* The pain struck again and she doubled over. -The joke made me double up.

double up VI *(compartir cama/habitación)* With so many guests coming, some of them are going to have to double up. -Do you mind doubling up with me?

drag behind 1 VTSEP° *(arrastrar, llevar a rastras)* I made for the bus stop, dragging my cases behind me. **2** VI *(llevar a rastras; sentido figurado, es decir con retraso o dificultad)* You're dragging behind in maths.

drag in VTSEP **(a)** *(arrastrar hasta el interior)* The trunk is too heavy to lift — let's drag it in. **(b)** *Fam. (mencionar)* Why do you have to drag in the one mistake I made?

drag on VI *(eternizarse)* The play dragged on and on.

drag out VTSEP *(prolongar)* I had to drag my presentation out to fill the time allotted to me.

drag up VTSEP **(a)** *(subir a rastras)* Drag it up the stairs. **(b)** *Fam. (llevar, traer)* You dragged me up to London for this? **(c)** *(sacar a colación)* There's no need to drag up the past. **(d)** *Fam. (dejar que se críen solos)* Those children are being dragged up, not brought up. -Where were **you** dragged up?

draw alongside 1 VI *(ponerse al lado/a la misma altura)* Then this big Mercedes drew alongside... **2** VIC *(ponerse al lado de/a la misma altura que)* The Customs launch drew alongside the liner.

draw away 1 VI **(a)** *(partir)* We waved as the car drew away. **(b)** *(distanciarse, separarse)* The first half dozen runners are now beginning to draw away. **(c)** *(apartarse)* I can't help drawing away when he touches me. **2** VTSEP *(separar, alejar)* She drew us away from the other guests.

draw back 1 VI *(retroceder)* She drew back from the edge of the cliff. **2** VTSEP **(a)** *(atraer de nuevo a)* What drew you back to music? **(b)** *(abrir)* He drew back the curtains and light flooded into the room.

draw in 1 VI **(a)** *(llegar)* The train will be drawing in soon. -The car drew in to the drive. **(b)** *(acortarse; las noches y los días)* The days have started to draw in again. **2** VTSEP **(a)** *(traer)* Fresh air from outside is drawn in by these ventilators. **(b)** *(meter en, implicar en)* They were arguing again and I left because I didn't want to be drawn in.

draw on VI *(acercarse, aproximarse)* As summer drew on...

draw out 1 VI *(alargarse; las noches y los días)* After Christmas, the days start to draw out. **2** VTSEP **(a)** *(sacar)* She drew out a gun. *(sacar; dinero)* I've drawn out all my savings. **(b)** *(prolongar)* They drew the meeting out on purpose. **(c)** *(hacer hablar a alguien)* I managed to draw her out on her plans.

draw up 1 VI *(pararse; en coche)* He drew up with a squeal of brakes. **2** VTSEP **(a)** *(elaborar, preparar)* I think we should draw up a plan of action. **(b)** *(formular, redactar)* The old lady drew up a new will. **(c)** *(acercar)* Draw up a chair and join us.

dream away VTSEP *(pasarse soñando)* He'll dream his whole life away at this rate.

dream up VTSEP *(concebir, imaginarse)* They've dreamed up some scheme that they say will make us all rich.

dredge up VTSEP **(a)** *(dragar)* The barges are dredging up silt. **(b)** *(sacarse algo)*. Where did you dredge that old scandal up?

dress up 1 VI **(a)** *(arreglarse, ponerse ropa elegante)* For that special occasion when you want to dress up... **(b)** *(disfrazarse)* It's a Hallowe'en party and everybody has to dress up. **2** VTSEP **(a)** *(arreglarse, ponerse elegante)* She dressed herself up for the wedding. **(b)** *(disfrazar)* You could dress yourself up as Pierrot.

drink down VTSEP *(tragar)* Drink this down and you'll soon feel better.

drink in VTSEP **(a)** *(beber, tragar)* These plants will drink in as much water as you care to give them. *Fig.* **(b)** *(absorber)* I'm drinking in your every word.

drink up 1 VI *(bebérselo del todo)* Drink up and I'll get the next round. **2** VTSEP *(beber del todo)* Have you drunk up your tea?

drive at VIC *(querer decir)* I'm sorry, but I really don't see what you're driving at. -Did you think she was driving at something when she said she couldn't afford a holiday this year?

drive back 1 VI *(volver en coche)* Are you driving back or taking the train? **2** VTSEP **(a)** *(llevar de vuelta en coche)* George will drive you back to your hotel. **(b)** *(rechazar, repeler)* The soldiers did not have the strength to drive back another attack.

drive home VTSEP **(a)** *(clavar, meter)* Once you have driven the screws home... **(b)** *(hacer comprender)* I tried to drive it home to them that this was not an isolated incident.

drive off 1 VI *(partir en coche)* He drove off about an hour ago. **2** VTSEP **(a)** *(llevar en coche)* All three of them were driven off in an unmarked police car. **(b)** *(apartar)* The attackers were driven off when reinforcements arrived.

drive on 1 VI *(continuar el camino por carretera)* He decided to drive on rather than stop there for the night. **2** VTSEP *(incitar, animar)* Her friends drove her on to sue.

drive up VI *(llegar; un coche)* A car/He has just driven up.

drop back VI *(quedarse atrás)* He has dropped back and it looks as if he's given up the race.

drop behind 1 VI *(quedarse atrás)* You're dropping behind — do try to keep up. **2** VIC *(quedarse rezagado de)* That last lap exhausted her and now she's dropping behind the leaders.

drop in 1 VI *(pasarse por un sitio)* I'll drop in and see mother tomorrow. -Would you drop in at the supermarket on your way home? **2** VTSEP* *(depositar)* Drop this in (the night safe) for me, will you?

drop off 1 VI **(a)** *(caerse)* With all this heavy shopping to carry, I feel as if my arms are going to drop off. **(b)** *(quedarse dormido)* It was 4 am before she dropped off. -Why don't you go to bed instead of dropping off in the chair? **(c)** *(disminuir)* Church attendance has been dropping off for many years. **2** VTSEP *(dejar)* Drop these books off at the library. *(dejar; cuando se lleva a alguien en coche)* Where do you want to be dropped off?

drop out VI **(a)** *(caerse, salirse)* There's a hole in your pocket and the keys must have dropped out. **(b)** *Fam. (dejar; estudios)* He dropped out at the age of 14. -So many have dropped out that the course may be cancelled. **(c)** *(elegir vivir al margen de la sociedad)* In the sixties a lot of people dropped out (of society) and went off to places like India.

drum into VTSSC *(repetirle a alguien)* Drum it into the children that they mustn't take sweets from strangers.

drum up VTSEP *(conseguir, obtener)* How are you drumming up support for the campaign? We must drum up some more business.

dry off 1 VI *(secarse)* Don't touch the varnish while it's drying off. **2** VTSEP *(secar)* Come and dry yourself off in front of the fire.

dry out 1 VI **(a)** *(secarse)* Leave your wet things in the bathroom to dry out. **(b)** *(desintoxicarse; con referencia al alcohol)* I think she's somewhere drying out. **2** VTSEP *(resecar)* Soap can dry your skin out.

dry up 1 VI **(a)** *(secarse)* Streams and rivers are drying up because of this long heat wave. **(b)** *(quedarse en blanco)* She was haunted by the thought that she might dry up in the middle of her big speech in the second act. **(c)** *Pop. (cerrar el pico)* Why don't you dry up? **2** VTSEP *(limpiar)* Dry the bathroom floor up.

dwell (up)on VIC *(pensar sobre, dar vueltas sobre)* Get on with your life instead of dwelling on what might have been.

E

ease off/up VI *(bajar el ritmo, la velocidad)* He's been told to ease off if he doesn't want a heart attack. -Ease up — there's a 30 mile an hour limit here.

eat away VTSEP *(erosionar, consumir)* The action of the waves is eating the coastline away.

eat in VI *(comer en casa)* I'm tired of eating in all the time.

eat into VIC *(hacer mella en)* Long term unemployment eats into people's self-confidence. *(mermar)* It's silly to eat into your savings when you could get a bank loan.

eat out 1 VI *(comer fuera)* Let's eat out tonight. **2** VTSEP *(modismo)* The child is eating her heart out for a pony = «*La niña se muere de ganas por tener un pony.*»

eat up 1 VTSEP **(a)** *(comerse todo)* Eat up your spinach. **(b)** *Fig. (devorar)* Jealousy is eating him up. **2** VI *(comérselo todo)* Eat up, the taxi's waiting. -Eat up, there's lots more. (= es decir «*no te prives*»)

edge out 1 VI *(salir con cautela)* I opened the window and cautiously edged out. **2** VTSEP **(a)** *(ir con mucha cautela)* She edged her way out on to the ledge. **(b)** *(echar a alguien poco a poco)* There's a move to edge him out of the chairmanship.

egg on VTSEP *(animar)* It was sickening to hear the crowd egg the boxers on. -I wish I hadn't let you egg me on to accept.

end up VI *(terminar)* No one ever thought she would end up in prison. -How did the film end up? I ended up telling him in no uncertain terms what I thought.

enter into VIC **(a)** *(entrar en una actividad)* We entered into this contract with our eyes open. **(b)** *(tener que ver con)* Morality rarely enters into foreign policy.

enter (up)on VIC *(empezar, tomar)* She has entered on a new career.

even out 1 VI *(girar en torno a; para sumas, cantidades etc.)* Production figures are evening out at about 5 000 per week. **2** VTSEP *(repartir de forma ecuánime)* We have to even out the burden of caring for the handicapped.

even up VTSEP **(a)** *(igualar)* That last goal evened up the score. -If you pay for the meal, that will even things up. **(b)** *(redondear por arriba)* I hate these odd pennies — just even it up to a pound.

explain away VTSEP *(justificar de forma poco convincente)* He tried to explain away his absence from the last meeting. -Explain this away if you can.

eye up VTSEP *Fam. (mirar a)* I passed the time eyeing up all the men. -He eyed up every one of the women at the party.

F

face up to VIC **(a)** *(aceptar el hecho)* We'll have to face up to the fact that we're not getting any younger. **(b)** *(hacer frente a)* It might help if she faced up to her fears of rejection.

fade away VI *(apagarse, desaparecer, desvanecerse)* The sound of the procession faded away. -Old soldiers never die, they merely fade away.

fade in 1 VI *(subir/aparecer poco a poco; en una película)* The music faded in. **2** VTSEP *(hacer aparecer progresivamente, en fundido)* Fade in the crowd scenes.

fade out 1 VI *(desaparecer poco a poco; en una película)* The music fades out for the last few seconds. **2** VTSEP *(hacer desaparecer progresivamente, en fundido)* Fade out the crowd scenes.

fall about VI *(partirse de la risa)* Her scripts always make me fall about.

fall away VI **(a)** *(hacer cuesta)* Be careful — the ground falls away here. **(b)** *(disminuir)* Attendance at committee meetings has been falling away recently.

fall back VI *(retroceder)* The demonstrators fell back when they saw the water cannon.

fall back on VIC *(recurrir a algo en caso de urgencia)* I suppose we can always fall back on temporary staff.

fall behind VI **(a)** *(quedarse atrás)* He began well but now seems to be falling behind. **(b)** *(retrasarse en algo)* You mustn't fall behind with the payments.

fall down VI **(a)** *(caerse al suelo)* He fell down and bumped his head. **(b)** *(venirse abajo, desplomarse)* Why don't they demolish that old building instead of letting it fall down? **(c)** *(no mantenerse)* That's where their argument falls down. -If you fall down on this, she won't give you another chance.

fall for VIC **(a)** *(estar prendado de)* He has fallen for the girl next door. -I've really fallen for that Victorian chair in the antique shop. **(b)** *(tragarse, creerse)* You didn't fall for that old story, did you?

fall in with VIC **(a)** *(terminar por aceptar)* I fell in with the plans for a picnic because the children were so keen. **(b)** *(juntarse con)* The teenager next door has fallen in with a bad crowd.

fall off VI **(a)** *(caerse)* I was terrified of falling off and clung to the chimney for dear life. **(b)** *(disminuir)* Enrolment is falling off.

fall on VIC **(a)** *(recaer sobre)* If anything goes wrong you can be sure that the blame will not fall on him. **(b)** *(asaltar)* They fell on the meal as if they hadn't eaten for days.

fall out VI **(a)** *(caerse)* The window is open so be careful you don't fall out. **(b)** *(regañar)* My sister and I have fallen out.

fall over 1 VI *(caerse, no mantenerse)* The vase is top-heavy, that's why it keeps falling over. **2** VIC **(a)** *(tropezar con)* Move your suitcase before someone falls over it. **(b)** *(desvivirse)* He was falling over himself to buy the woman a drink.

fall through VI *(fracasar)* Their plans for a skiing holiday have fallen through.

farm out VTSEP **(a)** *(mandar hacer fuera)* If deadlines are to be met, then some of the work will have to be farmed out. **(b)** *(confiar, dejar)* Those two next door are always farming their kids out.

feed in VTSEP* *(meter; en un ordenador)* The keyboarders feed the data in.

feed up VTSEP *(atiborrar)* Mum always wants to feed us up when we come home for the weekend.

feel up VTSEP *Fam. (meter mano)* I slapped his face for feeling me up.

feel up to VIC *(sentirse con ganas de)* I don't feel up to cooking a big meal tonight — let's go out. -He suggested a long walk but she didn't feel up to it. -Do you feel up to a visit from my mother?

fetch up 1 VI *(encontrarse en, estar en)* We eventually fetched up in a tiny little village in the middle of nowhere. -The road was very icy and they fetched up in a ditch. **2** VTSEP *(devolver, vomitar)* He fetched up his dinner.

fiddle about/around VI **(a)** *(chapucear)* He fiddled about for ages and still couldn't get the car to go. **(b)** *(perder el tiempo)* Why don't you stop fiddling about and get down to some work?

fight back 1 VI **(a)** *(defenderse, devolver los golpes)* Everybody encounters a bully at some time — you must learn to fight back. **(b)** *(recuperarse)* He has been ill but is now fighting back. **2** VTSEP *(reprimir)* I fought back my anger and tried to answer calmly.

fight down VTSEP *(luchar contra)* You must fight down these fears.

fight off VTSEP *(rechazar)* Government troops have fought off a number of attacks. -His bodyguards had to fight off over-eager fans.

fight on VI *(seguir luchando)* She regards this as merely a setback and is determined to fight on.

fight out VTSEP *(arreglarlo; discutiendo o peleando)* You'll have to fight this one out. -I left them to fight it out.

figure on VIC *(contar con)* I didn't figure on your mother coming too. -He didn't figure on a woman for the position.

figure out VTSEP **(a)** *(comprender)* She can't figure you out at all. **(b)** *(llegar a comprender)* How did you figure it out that he was the culprit? -The dog figured out how to open the door. **(c)** *(calcular)* We figured out that they must be paying three times as much rent as we are.

fill in 1 VI *(hacer una sustitución)* This isn't her normal job — she's just filling in. -Who'll be filling in for you while you're on holiday? **2** VTSEP **(a)** *(terraplenar, rellenar)* Workmen are filling those potholes in at last. **(b)** *(rellenar)* I must have filled in twenty forms. **(c)** *(informar)* Will someone please fill us in on what's been happening? **(d)** *(pasar el tiempo)* Are you busy or just filling in time?

fill out 1 VI *(coger peso)* He's beginning to fill out at last after his long illness. **2** VTSEP *(rellenar)* Will you fill out this form please?

fill up 1 VI *(llenarse)* The room was filling up. **2** VTSEP **(a)** *(llenar un recipiente)* Fill her up (= *el depósito del coche).* -Let me fill your glass up. **(b)** *(rellenar un formulario)* There are one or two forms to be filled up first.

filter out 1 VI **(a)** *(abandonar lentamente)* Mourners filtered out of the church. **(b)** *(salir lentamente)* Information is beginning to filter out that... **2** VTSEP *(filtrar)* Filter out the impurities.

find out 1 VTSEP *(descubrir)* I could have found that out for myself. **2** VI *(descubrir algo que se mantenía en secreto)* Has your wife found out yet?

finish off 1 VTSEP **(a)** *(terminar)* Let me just finish this chapter off. -Finish off your lunch. -You can finish off the cream if you like. **(b)** *(agotar)* All that heavy digging has finished him off. **(c)** *(matar)* The men were finished off with a bullet through the skull. **2** VI *(terminar)* What did you have to finish off with?

finish up 1 VTSEP *(terminar)* Finish up your lunch. -Don't finish up the pie. **2** VI *(terminar; en un sitio o situación)* We finished up in the pub down the road. -He'll finish up in court. -Any more of this uncertainty and I'll finish up a nervous wreck.

fire away VI *Fam. (empezar, soltar; sobre todo cuando se trata de hablar o hacer preguntas)* Fire away — I'm all ears.

fish out VTSEP **(a)** *(sacar de)* They fished him out of the river. **(b)** *(sacar)* Just let me fish the keys out.

fish up VTSEP *(sacar)* She fished her purse up from the bottom of the bag.

fit in 1 VTSEP* **(a)** *(meter)* Could you fit this pair of shoes in the case? **(b)** *(encontrar un hueco de tiempo)* The hairdresser says she can fit me in tomorrow. **2** VI **(a)** *(caber)* There's not enough room — the books won't fit in. **(b)** *(concordar)* That doesn't fit in with what I was told. **(c)** *(ajustarse a)* How does that fit in with your plans? **(d)** *(encajar)* I hate parties like this — I never feel that I fit in.

fix on 1 VTSEP* *(fijar)* He fixed the handle on for me. **2** VIC *(fijar, decidir)* Have you fixed on a date yet?

fix up 1 VTSEP **(a)** *(montar, construir)* The marquee will be fixed up on their front lawn. **(b)** *(arreglar, hacer, fijar)* I've fixed up a blind date for you. **(c)** *(dar, proporcionar)* Our in-laws will fix us up with a bed. **(d)** *(arreglar; especialmente el aspecto)* They're busy fixing up the house. -If you're going out, don't you think you should fix yourself up a bit first? **2** VI *(tener previsto, tener hechos planes)* I'm sorry but I've already fixed up to go out.

fizzle out VI **(a)** *(apagarse; sentimientos)* People's enthusiasm is starting to fizzle out. **(b)** *(venirse abajo; planes, ideas)* All those big plans we had have just fizzled out.

flag down VTSEP *(parar)* It's impossible to flag a taxi down when it's raining. -I was cycling along when a policeman flagged me down.

flake out VI *Fam. (caer rendido)* Six late nights in succession — no wonder you flaked out. -I just want to flake out on the couch.

flare up VI **(a)** *(llamear)* The fire flared up, turning night into day. **(b)** *(estallar)* The argument flared up when she said something about favouritism. **(c)** *(encolerizarse)* He flares up at the least little thing.

flip over 1 VTSEP **(a)** *(dar la vuelta)* Do you want your egg flipped over? **(b)** *(hojear)* She was flipping over the pages of a magazine. **2** VI *(darse la vuelta)* The plane just seemed to flip over.

float (a)round VI **(a)** *(circular)* Rumours have been floating around about your resignation. **(b)** *(rondar un sitio)* I'm just floating around until my sister comes out of the hairdresser's.

flood in VI *(entrar como un torrente)* When she opened the door, water flooded in. -People are flooding in to see this film. -Light flooded in through the windows.

flood out VTSEP *generalmente en voz pasiva (verse obligado a marcharse a causa de inundaciones)* Thousands of people in Bangladesh have been flooded out.

fly in 1 VI *(llegar en avión)* The royal visitors will fly in tomorrow. **2** VTSEP *(llevar/transportar en avión)* The army will fly troops in if necessary.

fly off VI **(a)** *(irse por aire)* They flew off in a helicopter. **(b)** *(volarse)* His toupee flew off in the wind.

fly out 1 VI *(partir en avión)* The President flew out this morning. -Which airport are you flying out of? **2** VTSEP *(transportar/llevar por avión)* Troops are being flown out as quickly as possible. -The company is flying her out to be with her husband.

fly past 1 VIC *(sobrevolar)* The squadron will fly past the airfield at precisely two o'clock. **2** VI *(pasarse volando)* The weekend has just flown past.

fold away 1 VI *(plegarse)* Does this table fold away? **2** VTSEP *(doblar y recoger)* Fold your clothes away neatly. -She folded the tablecloth away.

follow on VI **(a)** *(seguir, continuar; una actividad)* You go ahead — we'll follow on. **(b)** *(seguir, continuar; una historia)* How did the story follow on? **(c)** *(resultar)* It follows on from this that...

follow out VTSEP *(realizar)* He followed out his plans.

follow through 1 VTSEP *(proseguir hasta el final)* She firmly intends to follow the idea through. **2** VI *(seguir el golpe)* The problem is that you're not following through after you hit the ball.

follow up 1 VTSEP **(a)** *(proseguir, ir tras de)* The police are following up a number of leads. -I want you to follow the matter up. **(b)** *(apoyar, completar)* He followed up his complaint to the shop with an angry letter to the manufacturer. **2** VI *(proseguir)* He followed up with a right to the jaw.

fool around VI **(a)** *(perder el tiempo)* He spent too much time just fooling around. **(b)** *(hacer el tonto)* Don't fool around with that glue or you'll get it all over you. **(c)** *Fam. (tener un rollo)* She thinks her husband is fooling around.

fork out *Fam.* **1** VTSEP *(proporcionar, de mala gana)* I suppose Daddy forked out the cash for the repairs to your new Porsche. **2** VI *(pagar, de mala gana)* We're all going to have to fork out.

freak out VI *Pop. (ponerse hecho una furia)* Mum will freak out when she sees that you've dyed your hair blue.

frighten away/off VTSEP *(ahuyentar)* We keep a couple of Dobermanns to frighten off potential burglars. -Don't look so grim or you'll frighten people away.

frown on VIC *(desaprobar)* They all frowned on my suggestion. -Her parents frowned on her marriage to a man so much younger.

G

gain on VIC *(alcanzar)* They're gaining on us.

gear up 1 VI *(prepararse)* The shops are already gearing up for Christmas. **2** VTSEP *(preparar)* His business is gearing up for expansion.

get about VI **(a)** *(salir de casa, desplazarse)* He doesn't get about much these days. **(b)** *(extenderse)* A rumour has got about that you're leaving.

get across 1 VI **(a)** *(atravesar)* There are no traffic lights there so I found it difficult to get across. **(b)** *(comunicarse, explicarse)* She can't get across to her audience. **2** VTSS **(a)** *(llevar al otro lado)* Because of flooding, they will be unable to get much needed supplies across the river. **(b)** *(hacer comprender)* Did you get it across to her just how important it was?

get along VI **(a)** *(partir, irse)* I must be getting along. **(b)** *(llevarse bien)* I wish I got along better with my neighbours. **(c)** How are you getting along in the new house? (es decir, «¿qué tal te va en...?»)

get around 1 VI **(a)** *(moverse; llevar una vida social sin problemas)* Handicapped people who find it hard to get around. -That young man really gets around! **(b)** *(extenderse)* I wonder how that story got around? **2** VIC *(evitar, esquivar)* There's no getting around it, you'll have to tell him what happened. -Can we get around this difficulty?

get at VIC **(a)** *(llegar a)* Their house is very easy to get at. **(b)** *(descubrir)* He intends to get at the truth. **(c)** *(insinuar)* Do you mind telling me what you're getting at? **(d)** *(lanzar indirectas, criticar)* His father is always getting at him for the length of his hair. **(e)** *Fam. (amenazar; y hacer cambiar de opinión)* The trial could not continue because a number of witnesses had been got at and refused to testify.

get away 1 vi **(a)** *(irse, marcharse)* I usually get away by six. -Will they manage to get away this year? **(b)** *(escapar)* The terrorists got away in a stolen car. **2** vtss *(quitar de las manos)* The policeman managed to get the gun away.

get away with vic **(a)** *(escaparse con)* The thieves got away with the old lady's life savings. **(b)** *(llevarse, salir parado con)* He got away with a small fine of £10. **(c)** *(modismo)* That child gets away with murder! (= «*A ese niño le tienen consentido todo*»).

get back 1 vi **(a)** *(volver)* When did you get back? -I must be getting back soon. **(b)** *(retroceder, alejarse retrocediendo)* Get back from the edge of the cliff! **2** vtsep **(a)** *(hacer volver)* The priest got the distraught woman back from the window ledge by promising that something would be done. **(b)** *(recibir de vuelta)* I'll get it back from him tomorrow. **(c)** *(devolver)* Get the file back to me as soon as you can.

get back at vic *(vengarse de)* I'll get back at you for that.

get back to vic **(a)** *(ponerse otra vez a)* I must get back to work soon. **(b)** *(volver a ocuparse de)* Can we get back to you on that point later?

get behind 1 vi *(retrasarse)* I've got so behind that I'm working late every night this week. **2** vic *(esconderse detrás de)* Get behind that tree.

get by 1 vi **(a)** *(pasar)* The car could not get by because of the roadworks. **(b)** *(arreglárselas)* He thinks he'll get by without studying. -It must be difficult getting by on so little money. -Do you think I'll get by in Greece without speaking the language? **2** vic **(a)** *(adelantar)* Can I get by you? **(b)** *(pasar inadvertido)* His latest book did not get by the censor.

get down 1 vi **(a)** *(bajarse; de un muro, un árbol etc)* Get down at once! **(b)** *(agacharse, esconderse)* Get down or she'll see us. **(c)** *(levantarse de la mesa)* May I get down? **2** vtsep **(a)** *(bajar)* Will you get my case down for me? **(b)** *(rebajar, hacer bajar)* The doctors have got his temperature down at last. **(c)** *(tomar nota, apuntar)* I'll get that down if you'll give me a moment. **3** vtss **(a)** *(deprimir)* This kind of weather gets everybody down. **(b)** *(tragar)* Her throat is so swollen she can't get anything down. -Get this soup down and you'll soon feel better.

get down to vic *(ponerse con/a)* When are you going to get down to your homework?

get in 1 vtsep **(a)** *(llamar, hacer que venga)* I was so worried about the baby that I got the doctor in. **(b)** *(*meter)* Just let me get the washing in before the rain starts. -Farmers are only now getting their crops in. **(c)** *(plantar)* You should get your bulbs in earlier than this. **(d)** *(lograr hacer)* She got some last-minute revision in the night before the exam. **(e)** *(meter baza)* She was talking so much I couldn't get a word in. **2** vtss **(a)** *(dar acceso a; especialmente a una universidad)* These excellent exam results will get you in anywhere. **(b)** *(asegurar la victoria de; en una elección)* It was the government's mistakes that got the opposition in. **3** vic *(entrar en, meterse en)* Get in the car! -The smoke from the camp fire got in their eyes.

4 vi **(a)** *(llegar)* When does the train get in? -He got in before I did. **(b)** *(entrar)* If they didn't have a key, how did they get in? **(c)** *(ser elegido)* She got in with a very small majority.

get in on vic *(participar en)* They'd all like to get in on the deal.

get into 1 vic **(a)** *(volver a)* She hasn't been able to get into any of her clothes since the baby was born. **(b)** *(pasarle a alguien; porque notamos un cambio repentino de humor)* I don't know what's got into her these days. **(c)** *(modismos)* There's no need to get into a panic (= «*No merece la pena asustarse así*»). You'll get into trouble for that (= «*Eso va a traerte problemas*»). They've got badly into debt (= «*Se endeudaron seriamente*»). **(d)** *(aprender; especialmente comportamientos, costumbres etc.)* She'll soon get into our ways. **(e)** *(meterse en; cuando algo nos despierta el interés)* Everyone says this is an excellent book, but I just can't get into it. **(f)** *(ser admitido en)* Only a small percentage of candidates get into university. *(entrar en)* The thieves got into the house through an open window. **2** vtssc **(a)** *(meter en)* Did you manage to get everything into the suitcase? -You got me into this mess, now get me out. **(b)** *(poner de)* She knows just what to do to get her father into a good mood. -Don't get her into one of her rages.

get in with vic **(a)** *(ponerse de buenas con alguien)* If you want to get in with him, tell him how much you enjoyed his singing. **(b)** *(frecuentar, ir con)* She's worried about her daughter getting in with a bad crowd.

get off 1 vi **(a)** *(bajarse, de un vehículo)* He got off at the traffic lights. **(b)** *(irse del trabajo)* I'd like to get off early tomorrow. **(c)** *(salir, salir bien)* He shouldn't have got off. -You got off lightly. *(es decir, bien parado)* **(d)** *(dormirse)* I couldn't get off last night. **2** vtss **(a)** *(mandar a)* It's time to get the children off to bed. -I must get this letter off in time to catch the last post. **(b)** *(quitar de)* Get your hands off that child. -Get those football boots off the chair. -You should have got that off your desk by now. **(c)** *(librar de una pena; aplicado a abogados)* He has a reputation for always getting his clients off. **(d)** *(coger libre)* Maybe I could get the afternoon off. **(e)** *(conseguirlo de)* I got it off the woman next door. **(f)** *(librar de, quitar de)* The burns were not very serious but they got him off work. **(g)** *(dormir a)* It always takes ages to get her off.

get off with vic **(a)** *(ligar con, tontear con)* Trust her to get off with the only decent looking chap here. **(b)** *(salirse con)* He got off with just a fine.

get on 1 vi **(a)** *(subir a; un medio de transporte)* Where did you get on? **(b)** *(progresar)* If he wants to get on, the best thing he can do is work hard. **(c)** *(envejecer)* My grandmother is getting on. **(d)** *(hacerse tarde)* Time is getting on. **(e)** *(llevarse bien)* We don't get on. **(f)** *(arreglárselas)* How is the old man going to get on without his dog? -How did you get on at the dentist's? (es decir, «*¿cómo te fue?*»). **2** vtsep* **(a)** *(poner/ponerse algo)* I can't get the lid on. -Once you get your coat on, will you start the car? **(b)** *(meter en, montar en)* You won't be able to get that on the bus, it's far too big. -I got her on (the train) with seconds to spare.

get on for vic *(acercarse, llegar casi a)* She must be getting on for 90, but she's very active. -It's getting on for four o'clock. -There were getting on for 500 guests at the wedding.

get on to VIC **(a)** *(descubrir, localizar)* How did you get on to me? **(b)** *(ponerse en contacto)* I'll get on to the bank about it. **(c)** *(llegar a un tema, sacar a colación)* I'd like to get on to the question of expenses.

get on with VIC **(a)** *(continuar, proseguir con)* Please get on with what you're supposed to be doing. -I would like to get on with my reading. **(b)** How are you getting on with the painting? (= «¿*Qué tal vas con...?*») **(c)** *(llevarse bien con)* I don't get on with my parents.

get out 1 VI **(a)** *(irse, marcharse)* I told her to go out. **(b)** *(salir libre)* When does he get out? **(c)** *(salir; con amigos o compañeros)* She doesn't get out much. -He ought to get out more. **(d)** *(difundirse)* How did the news get out? **2** VTSEP **(a)** *(sacar)* I got my purse out to pay the milkman. -Get your books out and turn to page 54. **(b)** *(liberar)* Our prime concern must be to get the hostages out. **(c)** *(decir, producir)* He couldn't get a word out when they told him his wife had had triplets. *(sacar, publicar)* We have to get this report out by Monday. **(d)** *(eliminar; en cricket)* John got their best batsman out for ten.

get out of 1 VIC **(a)** *(escaparse de)* He always gets out of the washing up. **(b)** *(perder; una costumbre)* I've got out of the habit of studying. -She has got out of the way of doing dishes without a dishwasher. **(c)** *(salir de)* Let's get out of here. -He got out of the country before the police came looking for him. -The children get out of school at about three o'clock. **2** VTSSC **(a)** *(sacar; sensaciones)* I don't see what pleasure he gets out of all this studying. -She really gets the most out of life, doesn't she? **(b)** *(sacar de)* Get the big pot out of the cupboard. **(c)** *(sacar, sonsacar)* The detective finally got the truth out of the suspect.

get over 1 VI *(atravesar)* You get over first. **(b)** *(comunicarse)* She cannot get over to her audience. **2** VIC **(a)** *(recuperarse por)* He hasn't got over the shock of his wife's death yet. -I'm getting over it gradually. **(b)** *(superar, salvar)* She gave an excellent speech once she got over her difficulties with the microphone. -You must get over these silly fears. **3** VTSS *(cruzar)* It's not easy getting fifty children over a busy road. **4** VTSEP *(explicar, aclarar)* You got your point over very well.

get over with VTSS *(terminar con)* Once I got my appointment with the dentist over with, I thoroughly enjoyed my day off. -Can we get this over with quickly?

get round 1 VI **(a)** *(llegar a casa de alguien)* The vet said she'll get round as soon as she can. **(b)** *(extenderse)* The news is getting round. **2** VIC **(a)** *(esquivar, librarse de)* There's no way getting round it — you'll have to own up. -How did they get round the export regulations? **(b)** *(convencer)* I can always get round my father. **3** VTSS *(convencer de)* You've got me round to your way of thinking.

get round to VIC *(ocuparse de, terminar con)* I'll get round to it eventually, I promise.

get through 1 VI **(a)** *(conseguir línea telefónica)* The lines must be down, I can't get through. **(b)** *(llegar, a pesar de las dificultades)* Will the message get through? The cars could not get through because the pass was blocked with snow. (c) *Am. (terminar)* The evening class does not usually get through until nine o'clock. (d) *(pasar un examen, aprobar)* Only three of the class didn't get through. 2 VIC (a) *(atravesar)* You will not be able to get through the roadblock. (b) *(aprobar)* I got through my exams second time around. (c) *(terminar, acabar)* Will you get through your homework in time to come to the match? (d) *(usar)* He gets through a dozen shirts a week. (e) *(hacer que transcurra; e tiempo)* Since she retired, she's been finding it difficult to get through the days. 4 VTSS (a) *(hacer que se apruebe un examen)* It was your essay that got you through. (b) *(llevar a su destino)* They got the food supplies through just in time. (c) *(hacer comprender)* I finally got it through to him that I wasn't interested.

get to VIC (a) *(ir a)* How do we get to their house from here? (b) *(empezar a)* You know, I've got to wondering if maybe he isn't right after all. (c) *(poner negro)* She really got to me with her sarcastic remarks. -You shouldn't let it get to you. (d) *(llegar a, conseguir)* Did you actually get to speak to the Prime Minister?

get together 1 VI *(quedar, verse)* When can we get together to discuss the project? -He's getting together with the bank manager tomorrow. 2 VTSEP *(recoger)* Get your things together.

get up 1 VI (a) *(levantarse)* It's time to get up. -He got up to address the audience. (b) *(levantarse, prepararse)* There's a storm getting up. 2 VTSEP (a) *(aumentar)* We'll get up speed when we reach the motorway. (b) *(organizar, preparar)* We've got up a petition to protest about the closure. 3 VTSS (a) *(despertar)* Will you get me up early tomorrow? (b) *(subir)* Help me get this up. (c) *(vestirse)* She's getting herself up as Cleopatra.

get up to 1 VTSEP (a) *(llegar a)* It took ages to get up to the top. (b) *(planear; alguna travesura)* Those children are always getting up to mischief. -I don't want you getting up to anything while I'm out. 2 VTSS *(subir a otra planta)* Get this up to the top bedroom for me.

give away VTSEP (a) *(regalar, dar)* I gave it away to someone who needed it more. (b) *(repartir)* A former pupil is giving the prizes away. (c) *(llevar al altar; en una boda)* Her uncle is to give her away. (d) *(denunciar)* Who gave us away? (e) *(modismo)* to give the game away *(irse de la lengua)*.

give in 1 VTSEP *(entregar)* Give your homework in. -I gave the wallet in to the police. 2 VI (a) *(ceder)* Oscar Wilde said that the only way to get rid of temptation was to give in to it. (b) *(rendirse)* I give in — tell me what the answer is.

give off VTSEP *(producir, despedir)* This fire gives off a lot of heat. -Something is giving off a bad smell.

give on to VIC *(dar a)* The windows give on to the main road, so it's a noisy flat.

give out 1 VTSEP (a) *(repartir)* They were giving out leaflets about abortion. (b) *(dar a conocer)* The Chancellor gave out the trade figures today. (c) *(producir)* The radiators are not giving out much heat. 2 VI (a) *(agotarse)* Supplies have given out. (b) *(estar al borde, en el límite)* My patience is giving out. **(b)** *(averiarse)* The radio has given out.

give over 1 VTSEP **(a)** *(consagrar, dedicar)* They gave the entire evening over to a discussion of the film. **(b)** *(poner a disposición de)* The vicar gave the hall over to the scouts. **2** VI *Fam. (parar)* Give over, will you!

give up 1 VTSEP **(a)** *(abandonar, dejar a un lado)* The climbers gave up hope of being found before night fall. *(parar, dejar algo)* Give it up as a bad job. **(b)** *(renunciar a)* She is giving up chocolate as part of her diet. -I've given up trying. **(c)** *(no esperar más)* We had almost given you up. **(d)** *(considerar, dar por)* to give someone up as dead/lost. **(e)** *(ceder, dejar)* I gave up my seat on the bus to a pregnant woman. **(f)** *(entregar)* The escaped prisoner gave himself up after two days. **(g)** *(dedicar)* I gave the entire week up to studying. **2** VI **(a)** *(entregarse)* Don't shoot — we give up. **(b)** *(rendirse)* OK, tell me the answer then — I give up.

give up on VIC *(dejar por imposible)* How can a mother give up on her daughter and say she's no good?

give way VI **(a)** *(dar paso a)* His mother gave way to grief when she heard what had happened. -Give way to oncoming traffic. **(b)** *(convertirse en, transformarse en)* My laughter gave way to tears. **(c)** *(ser sustituido)* Natural fibres have given way to synthetics.

gloss over VTSEP **(a)** *(pasar por alto)* She very kindly glossed over my mistakes. -I tend to gloss those things over. **(b)** *(ocultar)* He glosses over his past.

go about 1 VI **(a)** *(circular)* Policemen always go about in pairs. -There is a story going about that they've separated. -There seems to be a virus going about. -You can't go about saying things like that (= «*No puedes ir por ahí...*»). **(b)** *(salir con, ir con)* My son has been going about with her for a year now. **2** VIC **(a)** *(hacerlo, ocuparse de, meterse en)* What's the best way to go about buying a house? **(b)** *(ocuparse de)* Just go about your business as usual.

go after VIC *(ir a por)* Go after them! -We are going after the big prize. -She really goes after what she wants.

go ahead VI **(a)** *(modismo)* If you have something to say to me, just go ahead! (= «*adelante*»). *(seguir con)* They have decided to go ahead with the wedding. -He just went ahead and did it. **(b)** *(avanzar)* The project is going ahead quite satisfactorily. **(c)** *(ir delante)* You go ahead, we'll follow later.

go along VI **(a)** *(ir a lo largo de)* She met him as she was going along the road. **(b)** *(ir avanzando)* Please check your punctuation as you go along. **(c)** *(estar de acuerdo)* I cannot go along with you on that. -The specialist proposed therapy instead of surgery and his colleagues went along.

go back VI **(a)** *(volver)* Let's go back some day. **(b)** *(ser devuelto)* When do these library books go back? -The sheets you bought will have to go back because there is a flaw in them. **(c)** *(atrasarse; los relojes)* Don't forget that the clocks go back tomorrow. **(d)** *(remontarse)* The church has records going back to the 16th century.

go back on VIC *(dar marcha atrás; decisiones)* I cannot go back on my promise to her. -He never goes back on his decisions.

go by 1 VI **(a)** *(pasar)* As the parade was going by... Many years have gone by since we met! **(b)** *(pasar por alto)* Don't let this opportunity go by. **2** VIC **(a)**

(fiarse de) Don't go by my opinion — I hate that kind of film. -If you go by that clock, you'll miss the train. **(b)** *(seguir)* He never goes by the rules. -Go by your brother's example. **(c)** *(llevar: un nombre)* She has been going by her maiden name since the divorce.

go down VI **(a)** *(ponerse)* The sun is going down. **(b)** *(hundirse)* The ship went down with all hands. **(c)** *(bajar)* House prices may go down. -Flood waters are going down. **(d)** *(rendirse, ceder)* I won't go down without a fight. **(e)** *(ser aceptado)* My suggestion did not go down very well. -British television programmes always go down big in North America. -How did your suggestion go down? **(f)** *(entrar; para bebidas)* This wine goes down very nicely, don't you think? **(g)** *(bajar)* Some water will help the pill go down. **(h)** *(decaer)* My old neighbourhood has really gone down. -His family has gone down in the world since losing all their money. **(i)** *(bajar puntos, descender en la escala)* She went down in my estimation when I found out what really happened. **(j)** *(pasar a, dejar tras de sí)* How will Ronald Reagan go down in history? **(k)** *(coger; enfermedad)* Trust me to go down with flu on the day of the exams.

go for VIC **(a)** *(ir a por, atacar a)* What was I supposed to do when she went for me with a knife? -Go for him, boy! -Billiard players always go for the balls in a certain order. **(b)** *(luchar por, disputarse)* If you really want it, go for it! -With his next jump, he's going for the gold. **(c)** *(prendarse de)* I could go for you in a big way. -She's always gone for the Scandinavian type.

go in for VIC **(a)** *(participar en)* Are you going in for the four hundred metres? **(b)** *(ser aficionado a, estar atraído por)* He doesn't go in for team sports. -Why do scientists go in for all that jargon? -My parents don't go in for pop music. **(c)** *(dedicarse a)* They have decided to go in for catering.

go into VIC **(a)** *(entrar en)* Our special training programme is now going into its third year. -She has to go into hospital. **(b)** *(ponerse, coger)* He nearly went into hysterics at the thought of it. **(c)** *(dedicarse a)* She wants her daughter to go into teaching. **(d)** *(entrar en, abordar)* We won't go into that for the moment. **(e)** *(pasar a, empezar a)* My grandmother then went into a long and detailed description of her childhood. **(f)** *(empezar a ponerse)* Their son did not go into long trousers until he was fifteen.

go off 1 VI **(a)** *(irse)* She has gone off with the man next door. -He's gone off on some business of his own. **(b)** *(pasarse, pudrirse)* The milk has gone off. **(c)** *(empeorar)* Your work has gone off recently — is anything wrong? **(d)** *(sonar)* The alarm went off at the usual time. *(dispararse)* He said that the gun just went off his hand. **(e)** *(apagarse)* The lights went off all over the city last night. **(f)** *(salir, resultar)* How did the play go off? My presentation went off well/badly. **2** VIC *(dejarle de gustar a uno algo)* I've gone off him since I found out what a male chauvinist pig he is. -She says she has gone off Spain.

go on 1 VI **(a)** *(continuar)* Go on — what did he say then? -Just go on with what you were doing. -Do we have enough coffee to be going on with or should I buy some more? **(b)** *(modismo)* That will do to be going on with *(es decir, «para ir tirando»)*. **(c)** *(estar bien; ropa)* Your coat won't go on unless you wear a different sweater. **(d)** *(encenderse)* The street lights go on when it gets dark. **(e)** *Fam. (no parar de hablar)* Once he starts, he goes on and on.

(meterse con) My aunts keeps going on at me about getting a job.
(f) *(pasar)* What's going on? **(g)** *(pasar)* As time went on, I realized that...
2 VIC **(a)** *(empezar con)* Most people go on a diet at least once. -He goes on unemployment benefit next week. **(b)** *Fam. (estar colado por)* My sister is really gone on the boy next door. **(c)** *(basarse en)* I have nothing concrete to go on — I just don't trust him. **(d)** *(aproximarse a, estar cerca de)* She's two years old, going on three.

go out VI **(a)** *(salir)* They were just about to go out. **(b)** *(salir; socializar o actividades)* She doesn't go out much these days. -We're going out for dinner. **(c)** *(salir con)* She first went out with him six months ago. **(d)** *(ser eliminado)* I bet his team goes out in the first round. **(e)** *(apagarse)* Put some wood on the fire before it goes out. -The lights went out. **(f)** *(salir; correo)* Has that letter gone out? **(g)** *(modismo)* I went out like a light (= «caí frito»). **(h)** *(pasar de moda)* The stores are betting on the miniskirt not going out for another year. **(i)** *(bajar; la marea)* The tide has gone out.

go over 1 VI **(a)** *(ir a un lugar concreto)* I went over and tapped him on the shoulder. **(b)** *(pasarse a, cambiar de bando)* They've gone over to the Conservative Party. -He's thinking about going over to cigars. **(c)** *(ser aceptado)* My suggestion didn't go over at all well. **2** VIC **(a)** *(repasar)* We should go over the accounts. -Let's go over your speech a second time. **(b)** *(discutir, hablar de)* We must have gone over this point a dozen times already.

go round 1 VI **(a)** *(girar)* Everything is going round. **(b)** *(desviarse)* The policeman said we would have to go round. **(c)** *(visitar a alguien)* You ought to go round and see him. -She's gone round to her mother's. **(d)** *(dar de sí para todos)* There won't be enough to go round. **2** VIC **(a)** *(coger; un camino)* I went round the long way to be sure of not getting lost. **(b)** *(visitar)* We must have gone round every museum in town. -She went round the neighbourhood looking for her cat. **(c)** *(dar para)* Is the roast big enough to go round everyone?

go through 1 VI *(entrar en vigor)* The deal has gone through. -When does the divorce go through? **2** VIC **(a)** *(sufrir)* She has gone through a lot. **(b)** *(examinar, analizar)* The detective went through the witness's statement very carefully. **(c)** *(hojear, mirar)* I've gone through all the papers and I still can't find it. **(d)** *(repetir)* How often do you have to go through your lines before you know them by heart? **(e)** *(utilizar, gastar)* Children go through a lot of shoes. **(f)** *(tomar, consumir)* We've gone through six pints of milk in two days.

go through with VIC *(llevar a cabo, cumplir)* He decided at the last moment that he couldn't go through with the wedding. -Management went through with its threat to close the factory.

go together VI **(a)** *(casar)* Do these colours go together? **(b)** *(salir juntos)* We've been going together for a long time.

go towards VIC *(ir destinado a)* The proceeds from the fête are going towards a new village hall.

go under 1 VI **(a)** *(hundirse)* It's too late — he's gone under. **(b)** *(hundirse, venirse abajo)* His business is going under and there isn't much he can do about it. **2** VIC *(llevar; un nombre)* Since the divorce she's been going under her old name of Williams.

go up VI **(a)** *(subir)* Just go up — he's expecting you. **(b)** *(subir, ascender)* The patient's temperature had been going up. -House prices are going up again. **(c)** *(alzarse)* The curtain will go up at eight o'clock. **(d)** *(ser arrasado)* The building went up in flames. *Fig.* **(e)** *(desvanecerse, ser llevado por el viento)* His plans went up in smoke.

go with VIC **(a)** *(ir junto con, ir emparejado con)* Mathematical skills usually go with an ability to play chess. **(b)** *(ir bien con, pegar con)* Change your tie — it doesn't go with that shirt. **(c)** *(ir incluido en el precio de)* Do the carpets go with the house?

go without 1 VI *(prescindir de algo, quedarse sin algo)* Those are too dear — if you don't like any of the others, you'll just have to go without. 2 VIC *(prescindir de, dejar, olvidarse de, pasar de)* I went without breakfast so I wouldn't be late.

grow apart VI *(perder el contacto)* They have grown apart over the years.

grow in *(crecer de nuevo)* Your hair will grow in soon.

grow out of VIC **(a)** *(quedársele a uno algo pequeño)* He has grown out of those shoes we bought just a few months ago. **(b)** *(dejar de, despegarse de)* I've grown out of my friends. -When are you going to grow out of biting your nails?

grow up VI **(a)** *(crecer)* Children grow up so fast nowadays. **(b)** *(comportarse como un adulto)* I wish you would grow up! **(c)** *(surgir, desarrollarse)* A theory has grown up that...

guard against VIC *(protegerse de, guardarse de)* Take Vitamin C to guard against colds.

H

hammer home VTSEP **(a)** *(clavar bien)* Be sure to hammer all the nails home. **(b)** *(insistir en, machacar)* We hammered home the importance of wearing seat belts.

hammer out VTSEP **(a)** *(sacar a martillazos)* I'll have to hammer these dents out. **(b)** *(trazar, elaborar; con dificultades)* They have finally managed to hammer out an agreement on the withdrawal of troops.

hand back VTSEP *(devolver)* I'll hand it back to you as soon as I've finished.

hand down VTSEP **(a)** *(bajar algo que está en lo alto)* Hand that plate down to me. **(b)** *(pasar, en herencia)* She handed the necklace down to her granddaughter. **(c)** *(dictar; una sentencia)* The sentence will be handed down soon.

hand in VTSEP *(entregar; a una autoridad)* I want you to hand in your essays tomorrow.

hand out VTSEP **(a)** *(repartir)* I've offered to hand leaflets out. **(b)** *(repartir; sobre todo cuando se trata de consejos no deseados)* You can always rely on him to hand out advice.

hand over 1 VTSEP **(a)** *(traspasar)* She handed the papers over to the lawyer for safekeeping. -He will be handing over the reins of power very soon.

(b) *(entregar)* Hand over your wallet. **(c)** *(pasar con)* We now hand you over to our foreign affairs correspondent. **2** vi **(a)** *(entregar)* I know you have it, so hand it over! **(b)** *(dejar su lugar a)* I now hand over to the weatherman. -When will he be handing over to the new chairman?

hang about/around 1 vi *Fam.* **(a)** *(esperar)* I had to hang about for ages before he finally arrived. -Now hang about, that isn't what he said! **(b)** *(estar de moscón, merodear)* Don't hang about or we'll never finish. **2** vic *(visitar, frecuentar)* I don't want you hanging about amusement arcades.

hang back vi **(a)** *(quedarse atrás; por timidez)* There's always one child who hangs back when Santa Claus is handing out the presents. -If you have a contribution to make to the discussion, please don't hang back.
(b) *(abstenerse de)* I hung back from saying anything because...

hang down vi *(colgar, pender)* Her hair hung down in ringlets.

hang in vi *Pop.* *(resistir, mantenerse)* Hang in there, boys. - We'll get you out soon. -He'll just have to hang in until a better job comes along.

hang on 1 vi **(a)** *(agarrarse)* Hang on tight. **(b)** *(esperar)* Can you hang on for a couple of minutes? **2** vic **(a)** *(estar pendiente de)* The audience was hanging on the speaker's every word. **(b)** *(depender de)* The fate of the project hangs on the availability of supplies.

hang on to vic **(a)** *(colgarse de, agarrarse a)* He hung on to the cliff face.
(b) *(guardar, conservar)* I'd hang on to those documents if I were you.

hang out vi **(a)** *(salirse)* Your shirt tails are hanging out. **(b)** *Fam.* *(parar por un sitio)* I'm looking for Bill — any idea where he hangs out? **(c)** *Fam.* *(obstinarse en, metérsele en la cabeza)* I'm hanging out for a rise.

hang together vi *(casar, encajar, tener sentido)* The plot of the film doesn't hang together.

hang up 1 vi *(colgar; el auricular del teléfono)* Don't hang up until you've heard what she has to say. -Hang up immediately. **2** vtsep *(colgar)* Hang your coat up.

happen along vi *(pasar por casualidad)* Then, thank goodness, a policeman happened along.

hark back vi *(volver a sacar un tema)* He keeps harking back to the Blitz.

have around vtss **(a)** *(tener a mano)* It's always a good idea to have some candles around. **(b)** *(invitar a casa)* We must have them around for supper soon.

have back 1 vtsep *(recuperar, serle devuelto)* Can I have it back? -I'll have my book back please (= «¿Me devuelves el libro?»). **2** vtss *(invitar a casa a alguien porque a uno le toca hacerlo)* We're having them back next Saturday.

have in vtss **(a)** *(llamar, hacer que alguien venga)* We'll have to have the plumber in to fix that leak. **(b)** *(invitar a casa)* The old ladies across the street like having people in for tea. **(c)** *(modismo)* to have it in for someone (= «tenerla tomada con alguien»).

have off vtss **(a)** *(quitar, retirar)* The doctor had the plaster off in no time at all.
(b) *(quitarle a uno)* She's having the plaster off next week.

(c) *(follar)* Those two look as if they have it off every night.

have on 1 VTSEP *(llevar; ropa)* He looks totally different when he has something casual on. **2** VTSS **(a)** *Fam. (picar a alguien)* Didn't you realize I was having you on? **(b)** *(tener cosas que hacer)* She has a lot on this week. -I have something else on, I'm afraid. **(c)** *(tener información sobre)* He told the police they had nothing on him. - He'd been in hospital at the time. **(d)** *(instalar, colocar)* Once we have the roofrack on, we'll be all set.

have out VTSS **(a)** *(serle a uno sacado algo)* He's in hospital having his appendix out. **(b)** *(aclarar)* Let's have this out once and for all.

have up VTSS **(a)** *(llevar a juicio)* The two old tramps were had up for vagrancy. **(b)** *(montar, instalar)* They worked all night to have the exhibits up in time for the opening.

head for VIC **(a)** *(dirigirse a)* Where is he headed for? -Let's head for home. **(b)** *(ir de cabeza, llevarse)* She's heading for a disappointment if she thinks he's going to propose. -The country is heading for civil war.

head off VTSEP **(a)** *(distraer)* Head Mum off for a couple of minutes while I finish wrapping her present. **(b)** *(evitar)* to head off accusations of favouritism...

head up VTSEP *(presidir, dirigir)* How many committees does she head up?

hear of VIC *generalmente en forma negativa (permitir)* I won't hear of you going to a hotel when we've got a spare room.

hear out VTSEP *(escuchar, dejar hablar)* Please hear me out. -The committee heard her out before reaching a decision.

heat up 1 VI **(a)** *(calentarse)* The room will soon heat up. **(b)** *(animarse, encenderse)* The discussion heated up and turned into an argument. **2** VTSEP **(a)** *(calentar)* Heat up some milk. **(b)** *(reanimar)* A bowl of soup will heat you up.

hide out VI *(esconderse)* He's hiding out in some hotel to get away from his fans.

hit back 1 VI *(responder)* He has questioned my integrity and I firmly intend to hit back. **2** VTSEP **(a)** *(devolver con un golpe)* Hit the ball back. **(b)** *(devolver el golpe)* He hit her, so she hit him back.

hit off VTSEP **(a)** *(imitar)* He hits the prime minister off very well. **(b)** *(modismo)* We hit it off immediately (= «*Conectamos enseguida.*»)

hit on VIC *(dar con)* I've hit on a possible solution.

hit out VI **(a)** *(dar/lanzar golpes)* All of a sudden he started hitting out. **(b)** *(atacar)* All of the speakers at the conference hit out at the proposals.

hive off 1 VI *(pasarse a)* They're hiving off into the retail side of things. **2** VTSEP *(separar, desglosar)* My boss is furious that the company wants to hive off the research team.

hold against VTSSC *(reprochar)* Why do you hold my past against me? -I hold it against him that...

hold back 1 VI *(mantenerse callado)* I held back while the two of them discussed old times. -He held back for a time but finally spoke his mind. **2** VTSEP **(a)** *(contener)* Marshals held the fans back. -He held back his rage. **(b)** *(mantener en desventaja)* It's your poor performance in maths that is holding you back. **(c)** *(ocultar, reservarse)* She's holding something back, I know she is. -Don't hold anything back.

hold down VTSEP **(a)** *(mantener bajos)* The government must take action to hold down the interest rates. **(b)** *(sujetar en el suelo)* It took two of us to hold him down. **(c)** *(ocupar, tener; un cargo o empleo)* She is holding down a fairly high-powered job in the City. **(d)** *(mantener; un cargo o empleo)* Can he hold this job down?

hold forth VI *(disertar, soltar una perorata)* She held forth at great length on the benefits of fresh air.

hold in VTSEP *(contener)* For heaven's sake, hold your stomach in. -She shouldn't hold her emotions in.

hold off 1 VI *(no decidirse)* The rain seems to be holding off. **2** VTSEP *(mantener a distancia)* The remaining men managed to hold off the attack until reinforcements arrived.

hold out 1 VI **(a)** *(durar)* Our supplies will not hold out for long. **(b)** *(resistir, aguantar)* Can you hold out until the doctor gets here? **2** VTSEP **(a)** *(tender)* She held out her hand. **(b)** *(ofrecer; la esperanza, la posibilidad)* The doctor doesn't hold out much hope for a complete recovery.

hold out on VIC *(ocultar algo)* You've been holding out on me — I didn't know you played the saxophone.

hold to VIC *(mantener, ser fiel a)* He held to his decision.

hold up 1 VI **(a)** *(tenerse en pie)* The centuries-old house continues to hold up. **(b)** *(mantenerse calmada, no excitarse)* She held up magnificently under the strain. **2** VTSEP **(a)** *(alzar, levantar)* She held her face up to the sun. **(b)** *(mantener en pie)* What's holding the tent up? **(c)** *(retrasar)* Bad weather is holding the project up. **(d)** *(atracar)* Armed men held up another bank yesterday.

hold with VIC *(aprobar, encontrar algo del agrado de uno)* I don't hold with all these fancy names for children.

hole up VI *Fam.* *(esconderse)* The bank robbers decided to hole up for a while.

home in on VIC **(a)** *(dirigirse de forma automática por)* The missiles can home in on the heat of aircraft engines. **(b)** *(dar con, hallar)* She homed in on my one mistake.

hook up 1 VI **(a)** *(abrocharse)* The dress hooks up. **(b)** *(hacer una emisión conjunta)* We will be hooking up with European networks to bring you this very special programme. **2** VTSEP *(abrochar)* Hook me up.

hot up *Fam.* **1** VI *(encenderse, ponerse al rojo; discusiones, tonos etc)* The argument hotted up when... -Things are hotting up again on the labour relations front. **2** VTSEP *(acelerar)* They are hotting up the pace.

hunt down VTSEP **(a)** *(buscar, ir tras los pasos de)* They are being hunted down by state and federal police. **(b)** *(hallar, localizar)* He was finally hunted down.

hunt out VTSEP *(encontrar; tras revolver por todas partes)* I've hunted out those old family photographs you wanted to see.

hurry along 1 VI *(ir deprisa, acelerar)* Hurry along please, the museum is now closed. -You're hurrying along as if we were late. **2** VTSEP *(acelerar, dar un* *empujón)* I'm trying to hurry the project along but it's not easy. -You can't hurry these things along.

hurry up 1 VI *(darse prisa)* Hurry up or we'll be late. **2** VTSEP *(hacer que se dé prisa, hacer que vaya más rápido)* I'll go and hurry them up. Could you hurry things up a bit, please — this is my lunch hour.

I

ice over VI *(congelarse, helarse)* This river is too fast flowing to ice over.

ice up VI *(cubrirse de hielo)* The crash was attributed in part to the plane's wings having iced up. -I can't get the key in — the lock must have iced up.

improve on VIC *(mejorar)* I told him you can't improve on perfection. -She'll have to improve on that score with her next jump.

iron out VTSEP **(a)** *(quitar con la plancha)* I'll iron out these creases in your shirt for you. **(b)** *(resolver)* There are one or two little problems that must be ironed out. **(c)** *(eliminar)* Have you ironed out your differences?

J

jack in VTSEP *Pop.* **(a)** *(dejar, librarse de)* I'm going to jack this job in as soon as I can. **(b)** *(cortar; parar)* Jack it in!

jack up VTSEP **(a)** *(levantar con el gato)* He had to jack up the car to change the wheel. **(b)** *Fam. (subir)* They've jacked up the price of petrol again.

jam in(to) 1 VTSEP *(meter, colocar; en poco espacio)* Can you jam anything else in? **2** VI *(apretujarse, meterse en un sitio pequeño)* Hundreds of people jammed in to hear his speech.

jam on VTSEP **(a)** *(pisar a fondo)* I had to jam on my brakes or I would have hit him. **(b)** *(calarse, meterse hasta el fondo)* She jammed her hat on and marched out.

jam up VTSEP *(bloquear)* Sunday motorists in search of a good spot for a picnic have jammed up the roads.

jar on VIC *(poner de punta)* That constant banging is jarring on my nerves.

jazz up VTSEP *Fam. (animar)* It's very dull in here tonight — couldn't we jazz things up a bit? *(alegrar)* jazz up a plain dress with some costume jewellery.

jockey for VIC *(disputarse; un empleo, un cargo)* Everyone is jockeying for the position of chairperson.

jockey into VTSSC *(persuadir)* They jockeyed me into volunteering my services.

jog along VI *(seguir su ritmo)* The work is jogging along.

join in 1 VI *(participar)* I want everyone to join in. **2** VIC *(tomar parte)* I joined in the fun. -They all joined in the chorus.

join on 1 VI *(ir, ajustarse, corresponder)* Where does this bit join on. **2** VTSEP* *(unir, añadir, adosar)* They've joined on another carriage.

join up 1 VI **(a)** *(entrar en el ejército)* He joined up as soon as war was declared. **(b)** *(encontrarse)* The two groups will join up there. **2** VTSEP *(unir)* Join the ends up.

jot down VTSEP *(apuntar de forma rápida)* He jotted down a few notes for his speech. -Just jot it down.

jump at VIC *(lanzarse a por)* I jumped at the chance of a holiday in Spain. -When he offered her the position, she jumped at it.

jump down 1 VI *(saltar; hacia abajo)* There aren't any steps — you'll have to jump down. -He jumped down from the window. **2** VIC *(modismo)* to jump down someone's throat *(ponerse hecho una fiera con alguien)*.

jump on 1 VI *(montar)* There was a bus sitting at the traffic lights so he decided to jump on. **2** VIC *Fam.* **(a)** *(atacar, agredir)* The hooligans jumped on the old man at the corner of the street. **(b)** *(echarse encima de, meterse con, arremeter contra)* He jumps on me for the least little thing.

K

keel over VI **(a)** *(zozobrar, volcarse)* The lifeboat keeled over. **(b)** *(desamayarse, caerse)* The hat stand just keeled over.

keep at 1 VIC **(a)** *(trabajarse algo más)* If he wants to get into university, he'll have to keep at his maths. **(b)** *(importunar)* The pair of them kept at me, morning, noon and night. **2** VTSSC *(hacer trabajar en)* The boss kept us hard at it all morning.

keep away 1 VI **(a)** *(mantenerse alejado, apartarse)* I knew you had visitors, so I kept away. **(b)** *(ignorar, pasar de)* She can't keep away from chocolates. **2** VTSS *(mantener alejado)* Keep him away from me.

keep back 1 VI *(echarse atrás, retroceder)* A policeman was telling people to keep back. **2** VTSEP **(a)** *(contener, mantener fuera de)* The marshals at the rock concert had a job keeping the fans back from the stage. **(b)** *(contener)* I couldn't keep back my tears. **(c)** *(callarse, ocultar)* She's keeping something back from us. **(d)** *(suspender)* We do not like keeping children back but in this case feel we have no alternative. **(e)** *(retrasar)* Am I keeping you back?

keep down 1 VI *(agacharse)* Keep down or he'll see us. **2** VTSS **(a)** *(bajar)* The policemen surrounding the house were told to keep their heads down. -Please keep your voice down — some people are trying to concentrate. **(b)** *(no vomitar)* The doctor was worried that her patient couldn't keep anything down. **3** VTSEP **(a)** *(contener, reprimir)* It's a full-time job keeping the weeds down in this garden. **(b)** *(mantener bajo)* The government is not doing anything to keep inflation down. -He's trying hard to keep his weight down, but he's not having much success.

keep from 1 VTSSC **(a)** *(ocultar)* They kept the news from the old lady as long as possible. -What are you keeping from me? **(b)** *(impedir)* The climber hung on to his partner's hand to keep him from falling over the edge. **(c)** *(distraer de)* I mustn't keep you from your work. **(d)** *(proteger)* I'm trying to keep you from harm. **2** VIC *(evitar)* He was such a boring speaker that I couldn't keep from nodding off.

keep in with VIC *(tener buenas relaciones con)* If you want to keep in with him, just agree with everything he says.

keep off 1 VI *(mantenerse fuera)* That's my property. Keep off! **2** VIC **(a)** *(no* *acercarse a, no pisar)* Keep off the grass. **(b)** *(evitar)* They tactfully kept off the subject of divorce. -The doctor has ordered him to keep off the port and cigars. **3** VTSSC *(no acercarse a)* Mum told us to keep our hands off the cakes. **4** VTSS *(quitarse; una prenda)* Don't keep your coat off for long or you'll get cold.

keep on 1 VI **(a)** *(seguir)* If they keep on like this much longer, I'm going to call the police. -Are you sure you told her she had to keep on past the war memorial? **(b)** *(estar encima de)* The headmaster keeps on at his pupils about their behaviour at the bus stop. -It doesn't do any good to keep on about his drinking. **2** VTSEP **(a)** *(mantener; seguir dando empleo a)* Do you want to keep the cleaning woman on? **(b)** *(*no quitarse; una prenda)* Make sure your baby keeps her gloves on.

keep out 1 VI **(a)** *(no entrar)* Danger — keep out! **(b)** *(mantenerse fuera)* The poacher kept out of sight until the gamekeeper had finished his round. **(c)** *(mantenerse al margen)* I'm keeping out of this argument. **2** VTSEP **(a)** *(dejar fuera, no dejar entrar)* Lock the door to keep people out. **(b)** *(mantener fuera de)* Keep plastic bags out of the reach of children. **(c)** *(proteger de)* These boots are supposed to keep the rain out. **(d)** *(mantenerse al margen de)* I'll do my best to keep you out of this.

keep to 1 VIC **(a)** *(mantener)* People should keep to their promises. **(b)** *(guardar)* She's keeping to the house on doctor's orders. **(c)** *(mantenerse)* Keep to the right. *(respetar, seguir)* We must keep to the agenda and not go off at tangents all the time. **2** VTSSC **(a)** *(hacer mantener)* Be sure to keep her to her promise. **(b)** *(mantener)* We are endeavouring to keep delays to a mininum. **(b)** *(modismo)* to keep something to oneself (= «*guardarse algo para uno mismo*»).

keep up 1 VI **(a)** *(seguir, continuar)* If this snow keeps up much longer, the roads will be blocked. **(b)** *(seguir el ritmo)* She dictated so quickly that the secretary couldn't keep up. **(c)** *(mantener el contacto)* Do you keep up with them? **2** VTSEP **(a)** *(mantener, continuar)* We kept up a fairly regular exchange of letters until quite recently. -It seems impossible for him to keep this pace up. -Keep it up, you're doing fine. **(b)** *(mantener)* Her arthritis prevents her keeping up the garden the way she would like. **(c)** *(conservar, guardar, mantener)* Keep your spirits up. -He has lost so much weight he finds it difficult to keep his trousers up. **(d)** *(tener/mantener despierto)* Our dinner guests kept us up until three o'clock this morning.

kick about/around 1 VI *Fam.* *(andar rodando)* Don't leave the paper kicking about. -Find yourself something to do instead of kicking around. **2** VTSEP **(a)** *(dar patadas a)* They're not doing any harm kicking a ball around. **(b)** *(tratar a patadas)* You've kicked me around long enough. **(c)** *Fam.* *(poner sobre la mesa, discutir de)* We kicked the proposal around for a while but finally decided against it.

kick in VTSEP **(a)** *(tirar a patadas)* The soldiers kicked the door in. **(b)** *(machacar)* I'll kick his teeth in!

kick off 1 VI **(a)** *(hacer el saque; fútbol)* When do they kick off? **(b)** *Fam.* *(empezar)* Our speaker will now answer questions. Who's going to kick off? -Let's kick off with a situation report. **2** VTSEP* **(a)** *(quitarse con los pies)* It's always such a relief to kick your shoes off. **(b)** *(expulsar, echar)* They're going to kick him off the team for misconduct.

kick out 1 VI *(dar coces)* The mules kicked out whenever anyone approached. **2** VTSEP *Fam. (poner en la calle)* His wife has kicked him out and he's got nowhere to go.

kick up VTSEP *(montar, organizar; sentido negativo)* He'll kick up an awful fuss when he finds out.

knock about/around 1 VI = **kick about/around 1. 2** VTSS *Fam.* **(a)** *(maltratar, pegar)* He knocks her about regularly. **(b)** *(destrozar)* The car was knocked about a good bit but the driver is unharmed.

knock back VTSEP **(a)** *(pegarle a, dejar la botella dando tumbos; una bebida)* He's knocking the whisky back a bit, isn't he? **(b)** *Fam. (salirle por)* How much did that knock you back?

knock down VTSEP **(a)** *(demoler)* The council wants to knock those houses down. **(b)** *(atropellar)* The car that knocked her down was moving much too fast. **(c)** *(derribar)* The champion knocked his opponent down in the first round. **(d)** *(obligar a rebajar el precio)* We're trying to knock them down to something we can afford. **(e)** *(rebajar el precio)* She knocked it down a fair bit. **(f)** *(adjudicar; en una subasta)* Both paintings were knocked down to dealers.

knock off 1 VI *Fam. (terminar el trabajo)* I'll try to knock off early. **2** VTSEP **(a)** *(tirar)* The cat must have knocked it off. **(b)** *(*rebajar)* Could you knock a pound or two off? **(c)** *(hacer sin ningún esfuerzo y con rapidez)* She knocks those sketches off by the dozen. **(d)** *Pop. (mangar)* Those watches that he's trying to sell have probably been knocked off. **(e)** *Pop. (cargarse a alguien)* She's terrified he'll be knocked off for informing. **(f)** *Pop. (parar, cortar)* Knock it off you two!

knock out VTSEP **(a)** *(vaciar)* Knocking his pipe out, he said... **(b)** *(anestesiar)* Will they knock you out or just give you a local anaesthetic? *(dejar sin sentido)* The challenger knocked the champion out with a single punch. **(c)** *(eliminar)* That's knocked her out of Wimbledon already! **(d)** *Fam. (destrozar, dejar por los suelos)* Those children have knocked me out. **(e)** *(destrozar)* The government jets knocked out two rebel encampments. -The storm has knocked out power supplies to a great many homes. **(f)** *Fam. (hacer las delicias de)* His performance can hardly be described as knocking the critics out.

knock over VTSEP *(derribar, volcar, tirar)* He knocked several people over as he ran away. -A bus knocked her over. -It wasn't me that knocked the ornament over.

knock together 1 VI *(chocar uno contra el otro)* My knees were knocking together at the thought of the interview. **2** VTSEP *(construir sin mucho cuidado)* I've promised to knock a tree house together for the kids.

knock up 1 VI *(prepararse para el juego)* The players are allowed two minutes to knock up. **2** VTSEP **(a)** *Br. (despertar)* Will you knock me up at six o'clock? **(b)** *Am. Fam. (hacer una tripa)* He's knocked her up. **(c)** *(hacer, componer; con prisa)* If you don't mind leftovers, I'll knock up a quick meal for you.

know of VIC **(a)** *(saber)* Has Bill arrived yet? Not that I know of. **(b)** *(saber de)* Nothing is known of her whereabouts. -I don't know him; I know of him.

knuckle under VI *(ceder, rendirse a)* I won't knuckle under to threats.

L

lash down 1 VTSEP *(atar firmemente)* The lorry driver lashed the tarpaulin down. **2** VI *(llover con fuerza)* It's lashing down.

lash into VIC **(a)** *(atacar)* The two men lashed into each other. **(b)** *(meterse con)* I lashed into her for making such silly mistakes.

last out 1 VI **(a)** *(sobrevivir)* They can't last out for long in this weather unless they find shelter. **(b)** *(bastar, ser suficiente)* Will our water last out? **2** VTSEP **(a)** *(aguantar, resistir)* She is not expected to last out the night. **(b)** *(pasar)* We have enough coal to last out the winter.

laugh off VTSEP *(burlarse de)* He laughed off all warnings.

launch into VIC *(empezar)* He launched into a glowing description of the car he had just bought.

launch out VI **(a)** *(extenderse, expansionarse)* The company is going to launch out and add textiles to its product range. **(b)** *(modismo)* to launch out on one's own (= «*lanzarse uno por su cuenta*»).

lay about VIC *(atacar)* The old lady laid about him with her stick.

lay down VTSEP **(a)** *(dejar)* He laid his glass down on the table. **(b)** *(deponer)* The rebels have announced that they will lay down their arms. **(c)** *(renunciar a)* She laid down her life for her beliefs. **(d)** *(establecer, estipular)* It is laid down in the regulations. **(e)** *(modismo)* to lay down the law (= «*imponer/ establecer la ley*»).

lay in VTSEP *(recoger)* We have laid in enough canned goods to feed an army. -You had better lay some wood in.

lay off 1 VI *Fam. (cortar, dejarlo)* I've had as much criticism as I can take, so lay off. **2** VIC *Fam. (dejar en paz)* My sister doesn't want to go out with you, so lay off her. **3** VTSEP *(despedir)* The company will be laying 350 employees off within the next few weeks.

lay on VTSEP **(a)** *(suministrar)* Water and electricity are both laid on at the cottage. **(b)** *(poner en circulación)* Extra buses will be laid on if necessary. **(c)** *(ofrecer)* I'll lay on a meal for everyone.

lay out VTSEP **(a)** *(extender)* Lay the pattern out on the floor. **(b)** *(preparar, dejar preparado)* She always lays her clothes out the night before. **(c)** *(preparar; un cadáver para el entierro)* They laid Grandad out very nicely. **(d)** *(disponer, acondicionar)* I don't like the way the office has been laid out. **(e)** *(derribar, dejar fuera de combate)* He laid me out with one blow. **(f)** *(gastarse)* Your parents have laid out a considerable sum on your education.

lay up VTSEP **(a)** *(tener en cama)* This flu has laid her up. **(b)** *(atracar embarcaciones)* The severely damaged vessel will be laid up for repair.

lead on 1 VI *(ir delante)* Lead on! **2** VTSEP **(a)** *(engañar)* He led her on with promises of marriage. -You led me on to believe that... **(b)** *(llevar a alguien a, convencer a alguien)* It was those so-called friends of his that led him on to do it.

lead up VI **(a)** *(preceder)* In the years leading up to the Declaration of Independence... **(b)** *(llevar a)* Her opening remarks were plainly leading up to a full-scale attack on her critics. -What's this leading up to?

lean on VIC **(a)** *(contar con)* His mother leans on him for advice. **(b)** *(presionar)* The company is leaning on her to take early retirement.

leave behind VTSEP **(a)** *(dejar)* Drivers are advised to leave their cars behind and use public transport. -I think we should leave the children behind. **(b)** *(dejarse)* I came out in such a rush that I left my keys behind. **(c)** *(aventajar)* When it comes to maths, she leaves most of the others far behind.

leave off 1 VTSEP* *(no poner)* It was a beautiful day I left my coat off. -Who keeps leaving the lid off the coffee jar? -She wants to leave most of her relations off the guest list. **2** VIC *(dejar de)* He has left off seeing her. **3** VI *Fam.* *(parar, dejarlo; algo molesto)* Leave off, will you!

leave out VTSEP **(a)** *(olvidarse, excluir)* You've left out an entire line. -The old lady decided to leave her son-in-law out of her will. **(b)** *(no meter en)* Leave me out of this. **(c)** *(dejar a mano)* I'll leave out the instructions for the washing machine. -Do you want to leave the car out?

let down VTSEP **(a)** *(bajar, hacer descender)* They let a rope down to the men stranded on the beach. **(b)** *(engañar)* You must stop letting people down like this. **(c)** *(bajar, alargar)* She always lets down the hem on her daughter's dresses. **(d)** *(deshinchar)* The boys let his tyres down as a joke.

let in 1 VTSEP **(a)** *(*dejar entrar)* These shoes are letting water in. -Don't let him in. **(b)** *(poner al corriente)* They let me in on the secret. **2** VI *(calar, dejar entrar agua)* Are you boots letting in?

let in for VTSSC **(a)** *(ocasionar)* Your absence let us all in for a lot of extra work. **(b)** *(meterse en)* He didn't realize what he was letting himself in for.

let off VTSEP **(a)** *(explotar)* Animal rights activists have let off a number of bombs. **(b)** *(producir, despedir)* The fire was letting off a lot of smoke. **(c)** *(soltar, dejar en libertad)* He was let off because of lack of evidence. -The judge let him off with a fine. -The teacher lets us off early on Fridays. **(d)** *(dejar; a alguien cuando se le lleva en un vehículo)* I asked the taxi driver to let me off at the corner.

let on VI **(a)** *(desvelar, decir un secreto)* I'm pregnant but don't you let on. **(b)** *(simular, hacer creer, hacer que)* He likes to let on that he went to university.

let out VTSEP **(a)** *(dejar en libertad)* They're letting him out on parole soon. **(b)** *(acompañar a la puerta)* Don't bother seeing me to the door — I'll let myself out. **(c)** *(irse de la lengua)* Who let it out about the party? **(d)** *(emitir, soltar)* She let out a yelp of pain. **(e)** *(alquilar)* They let out rooms to students. **(f)** *(dar de sí, ensanchar)* I'm either going to have to go on a diet or let all my clothes out.

let up VI *(parar de una vez)* I wish this rain would let up. -Don't you ever let up?

lie back VI **(a)** *(recostartse)* You lie back and rest. **(b)** *(gandulear)* He just lay back and let the rest of us do the work.

lie in VI *(quedarse durmiendo hasta tarde)* Most people lie in on Sundays. -I wish I could have lain in this morning.

lie up VI (a) *(guardar cama)* The doctor says she's to lie up for a couple of days. (b) *(esconderse)* The police are convinced that the wanted men are lying up somewhere. (c) *(no dársele uso a algo)* That boat has been laying up for years.

light up 1 VI (a) *(iluminarse)* His face suddenly lit up. -The room seemed to light up when she came in. (b) *(encender un cigarrillo etc.)* He lit up and sighed with contentment. **2** VTSEP (a) *(iluminar)* The fireworks lit up the sky. (b) *(empezar a fumar)* They both lit up their pipes.

line up 1 VI *(hacer cola)* People are already beginning to line up outside the cinema. **2** VTSEP (a) *(poner en fila)* The headmaster lined everybody up in the playground. (b) *(arreglar, preparar)* I've lined a date up for you. -He's got something else lined up for tomorrow.

listen in VI *(escuchar, pegar el oído)* It's fascinating listening in on other people's conversations. -Do you mind if I listen in?

live down VTSEP *(permitir que algo se olvide)* We'll never live this scandal down. -He won't let her live it down that she made one stupid mistake.

live in/out *(residir en el/fuera del lugar en que se trabaja)* They have at least three maids living in. -I would rather live out than stay in a hall of residence.

live off VIC (a) *(vivir a base de, vivir de)* That child would live off ice-cream if he could. -She lived off what she earned as a cleaner. (b) *(vivir de, a expensas de)* His brother lives off him.

live on VI *(perdurar)* The memory of our sacrifice will live on.

live up to VIC (a) *(estar a la altura de)* Nothing ever lives up to expectations. (b) *(vivir de acuerdo con)* There's no point in trying to live up to my sister's reputation.

load down VTSEP *(estar cargado)* I'm loaded down with shopping.

load up 1 VI *(cargar)* There are a number of ships waiting to load up. **2** VTSEP *(cargar)* We loaded the car up with everything but the kitchen sink.

lock away VTSEP *(cerrar con llave)* Lock those papers away for the night. -The police said they could lock him away for ten years.

lock in VTSEP* *(encerrar)* She is locked in a cell with three other women. -You almost locked me in.

lock out VTSEP *(dejar en la calle)* They've gone to bed and locked me out. -The company has threatened to lock its employees out unless they return to work immediately.

lock up 1 VI *(echar la llave)* You go to bed — I'll lock up. **2** VTSEP (a) *(guardar bajo llave)* Lock up your valuables. (b) *(encerrar)* The dogs are locked up every night.

long for VIC *(esperar; con ansia)* I'm longing for the holidays.

look after VIC *(cuidar de)* We've been looking after our grandchildren for the weekend. -The car has been well looked after.

look at VIC (a) *(mirar)* Look at those punks! (b) *(examinar, echar un vistazo)* I'll need to get someone in to look at that damp patch. **(c)** *(ver; desde un punto de vista)* He doesn't look at it that way at all. **(d)** *(querer ver a alguien, ver a alguien con buenos ojos)* He sent her the most beautiful flowers for her birthday but she still won't look at him.

look back VI *(echar la vista atrás)* He stopped and looked back. -Looking back over the last five years, do you have any regrets?

look down on VIC *(despreciar)* He looks down on anyone who hasn't gone to university.

look for VIC *(buscar)* I'm really looking for something a bit bigger.

look forward to VIC *(esperar impacientemente, desear)* You must be looking forward to their visit.

look in VI *(pasarse por casa de alguien, hacer una visita breve)* I'll look in again tomorrow. -They looked in for a minute.

look into VIC *(examinar, estudiar, analizar)* The company has promised that it will look into my complaint.

look on 1 VI *(observar)* A crowd looked on as firemen fought the blaze. **2** VIC *(considerar)* They look on her as a daughter. *(tenerle algo a alguien)* I used to look on him with envy.

look on to VIC *(dar a)* Our house looks on to open fields.

look out 1 VI **(a)** *(mirar hacia afuera)* She opened the window and looked out. **(b)** *(tener cuidado)* Look out — you're very close to the edge. **2** VTSEP *(buscar)* Look out a scarf for me. -She has promised to look those letters out.

look out for VIC **(a)** *(estar al tanto de)* You could always ask the garage to look out for a second-hand car. **(b)** *Am. (ocuparse de, hacerse cargo de)* He promised his parents he would always look out for his younger brother. **(c)** *(tener cuidado con)* Look out for the bones in the fish.

look over VTSEP **(a)** *(ir a ver)* We're looking over a flat this evening. **(b)** *(repasar, examinar de arriba a abajo)* I'm sure I've been invited for the weekend just so his mother can look me over.

look to VIC *(contar con)* You must stop looking to other people to solve your problems.

look up 1 VI **(a)** *(alzar la vista)* She looked up when I entered the room. -Looking up from his book... **(b)** *(ir bien, hacer progresos)* His business must be looking up if he's bought a new car. **2** VTSEP **(a)** *(visitar)* You must look us up again. **(b)** *(buscar; en un libro)* Look it up in the encyclopaedia.

look up to VIC **(a)** *(mirar hacia arriba)* He's so tall I have to look up to him. **(b)** *(admirar)* Everyone looks up to her for her courage.

loosen up 1 VTSEP **(a)** *(relajar, distender)* Some massage will loosen you up. **(b)** *(relajar, hacer que algo sea menos estricto)* They've promised to loosen up the rules. **2** VI *(calentarse)* The athletes took a couple of minutes loosening up.

lose out VI *(salir perdiendo)* You're the one who'll lose out. -He lost out on a deal.

louse up VTSEP *Pop. (estropear)* You're always lousing things up for me.

M

make for VIC **(a)** *(dirigirse a)* Where are you making for? **(b)** *(contribuir a)* Handling a complaint in that way does not make for good customer relations.

make of VIC **(a)** *(pensar de, opinar de)* Well, what do you make of that? **(b)** *(dar importancia a)* You're making too much of this — I've known him since we were children. -The Press isn't making much of this.

make off VI *(largarse)* The boys made off at a run when they saw the policeman.

make off with VIC *(coger, robar)* Who's made off with the scissors again? Don't leave your bag lying around — someone might make off with it.

make out 1 VTSEP **(a)** *(escribir, firmar; un papel oficial)* Make the cheque out to me. **(b)** *(distinguir)* Can you make out who it is? **(c)** *(descifrar)* He can't make out his own handwriting. **(d)** *(comprender)* I can't make her out at all. **2** VI *(desenvolverse)* How is she making out in her new job? **3** VIC *(dar la idea, dar a entender)* The insurance company is making out that I was negligent.

make over VTSEP *(ceder, traspasar)* She has made her entire estate over to her granddaughter.

make up 1 VTSEP **(a)** *(maquillar)* I must go and make my face up. **(b)** *(finalizar, una discusión etc.)* Thank goodness they've made it up. **(c)** *(compensar)* He doesn't have to worry about making up any losses since he comes from a wealthy family. -Overtime will be necessary to make up the ground we lost because of the weather. -Sorry we had to cancel dinner, I promise I'll make it up to you. **(d)** *(inventarse)* She is making the whole thing up — it's not true. **(e)** *(poner, colocar)* Would you make these up into three separate packages? **(f)** *(componerse de)* The community is made up primarily of old people. **(g)** *(aumentar, recomponer)* For your birthday, I'll make your savings up to the price of a new bike. **2** VI **(a)** *(hacer las paces, reconciliarse)* Haven't you two made up yet? **(b)** *(recuperarse, ponerse a la altura de)* He's making up on the leaders.

make up for VIC **(a)** *(disculparse)* How can I make up for forgetting your birthday? **(b)** *(resarcirse)* He's certainly making up for lost time now.

make up to VIC *(alabar, dar coba)* Don't try making up to me. -They got the money by making up to the old man.

map out VTSEP **(a)** *(trazar)* Have you mapped out the route yet? **(b)** *(organizar)* I've mapped out a programme.

mark up VTSEP *(subir el precio de)* Most restaurants mark up wine by about ten per cent.

marry off VTSEP *(casarse con alguien por un acuerdo)* She's being married off to a man who's twenty years older than her.

measure up 1 VTSEP **(a)** *(medir)* After measuring up the timber... **(b)** *(sopesar)* She measured the situation up with one glance. **2** VI *(estar a la altura de)* I don't think you're going to measure up to the job.

meet up VI *(quedar, verse)* Let's meet up again soon.

meet with VIC **(a)** *(encontrar; obstáculos o facilidades)* The proposal has met with fierce opposition. -Rescue attempts have so far met with failure. -The suggestion met with acclaim. **(b)** *(tener cita con, ver a)* The senator is meeting with his advisors next week.

melt away VI **(a)** *(derretirse)* The ice has melted away. **(b)** *(desaparecer, desvanecerse)* The onlookers melted away after the initial excitement.

melt down VTSEP *(fundir)* The gold jewellery will have been melted down by now and will be impossible to identify.

mess about/around *Fam.* **1** VTSEP **(a)** *(enredar)* First we're going, then we're not going — I wish you would stop messing me about! **(b)** *(mezclar, desordenar)* They've messed the programmes around again. **2** VI **(a)** *(hacer el tonto)* Stop messing about! **(b)** *(entretenerse)* He's been messing about in the garden all day. **(c)** *(jugar con)* Don't mess around with something that doesn't belong to you.

mess up VTSEP **(a)** *(desordenar, ensuciar)* Don't mess the kitchen up. **(b)** *(estropear, fastidiar)* You've really messed your marriage up. -By changing his mind at the last minute he's messed things up for all of us.

miss out 1 VTSEP *(omitir, olvidarse de, saltarse a)* Have I missed anyone out? **2** VI **(a)** *(perderse algo)* You missed out on a great concert. **(b)** *(perder)* You missed out there.

mix up VTSEP **(a)** *(preparar; hacer un preparado)* Will you mix up some of my medicine for me? **(b)** *(hacer a alguien perderse)* Don't talk to me when I'm trying to count or you'll mix me up. **(c)** *(confundir con)* He mixes her up with her mother. **(d)** *(meterse en)* Everyone in that family is mixed up in something dishonest.

move along 1 VTSEP* *(hacer que alquien se vaya, echar a)* Policemen had to move the crowd along. **2** VI **(a)** *(echarse a un lado, apartarse)* Move along and let the lady sit down. **(b)** *(irse, marcharse)* I really ought to be moving along. -All the policeman said of course was «Move along, there's nothing to see.» **(c)** *(pasar a)* Moving along to my next question...

move in 1 VTSEP **(a)** *(mandar, enviar)* The government has decided to move troops in to quell the riots in the city. **(b)** *(instalar, acomodar)* The company can't move us in for another two weeks. **2** VI **(a)** *(avanzar sobre)* Troops are now moving in on the beleaguered capital. **(b)** *(mudarse a)* People are moving in next door.

move on 1 VTSEP *(hacer que alguien se marche)* The police moved us on. **2** VI *(pasar a)* Can we move on to the next item on the agenda?

move out 1 VTSEP **(a)** *(sacar)* You'll have to move the car out of the garage. *(sacar, echar)* They're being moved out of their homes to make way for a new road. **(b)** *(retirar)* The new government has promised to move its soldiers out. **2** VI **(a)** *(mudarse, irse)* The people next door have decided to move out. **(b)** *(retirarse)* Troops are already moving out.

move up 1 VTSEP **(a)** *(subir)* Move this section up. -His regiment was moved up to the front. **(b)** *(ascender)* They've moved him up to be assistant manager. **2** VI *(avanzar)* Troops are moving up to the combat zone.

muddle along/on VI *(arreglárselas)* They were muddling along quite happily and then management brought in a team of consultants to look at efficiency.

muddle up VTSEP *(mezclar, embrollar)* He's managed to muddle the dates up. *(hacer un lío)* You're muddling me up.

muscle in VI *Fam. (meterse en)* He's not keen on people muscling in on his territory. -I'm not going to let anyone muscle in.

N

narrow down 1 VI *(reducirse a, no ir más allá de)* The question narrows down to this... **2** VTSEP *(reducir a; después de hacer una selección)* We've narrowed down the candidates to four.

nod off VI *Fam. (echar una cabezada)* Grandpa was sitting nodding off in front of the television.

notch up VTSEP *Fam. (marcarse)* She has notched up yet another win.

O

open on to VIC *(dar a)* The back door opens on to a paved courtyard.

open out 1 VI *(abrirse)* The roses are beginning to open out. **2** VTSEP *(desplegar)* It's difficult to open out your newspaper on a crowded commuter train.

open up 1 VI **(a)** *(abrirse)* Another couple of warm days and the roses will have opened up. -New markets are opening up all the time. -There are some new shops opening up on the high street. **(b)** *(abrirse a; mostrar sus sentimientos)* He never opens up to anybody. **(c)** *(abrir)* Police: Open up! -The shopkeeper was just opening up when I passed. **2** VTSEP **(a)** *(abrir, conquistar)* The rain forest is being opened up for development. **(b)** *(abrir; locales)* When did you open the shop up this morning? **(c)** *(poner, fundar)* Opening up a restaurant in this part of town is a risky venture.

opt out VI *(salirse de)* I'm opting out of the committee because I have too many other commitments.

own up VI *(confesar, admitir)* I know it was you I saw, so you might as well own up. -He rarely owns up to his mistakes.

P

pack away VTSEP **(a)** *(guardar)* Maybe we packed our winter clothes away a little too soon. **(b)** *Fam. (zampar, tragar)* I've never seen anyone who can pack it away like you.

pack in 1 VTSEP **(a)** *(meter; en un cajón, maleta etc.)* You can't possibly pack anything more in. **(b)** *(atraer)* Her latest film is packing them in. **(c)** *Fam. (dejar, parar)* He's decided to pack his job in. -Go next door and tell them to pack that noise in. **(d)** *Fam. (dejar, plantar; a un novio o novia)* Are you going to pack him in or not? **2** VI **(a)** *(meterse, entrar, caber)* I don't know how all those people manage to pack in to one train. **(b)** *Fam. (averiarse)* The lawnmower's packed in on me.

pack off VTSEP *(mandar a)* I'll call you back once I've packed the kids off to school.

pack out VTSEP *(ocupar totalmente, llenar hasta la bandera)* The fans packed the hall out. -The pub was packed out so we went somewhere else.

pack up VI **(a)** *(hacer las maletas)* Pack up... we're not staying here another night. **(b)** *(prepararse; para salir del trabajo)* Are you packing up already? **(c)** *Fam. (averiarse)* The lawnmower has just packed up so I can't cut the grass.

palm off VTSEP *Fam.* **(a)** *(encasquetar, pasar el paquete)* They're palming the children off on us for the weekend. -Be careful he doesn't try to palm any rotten fruit off on you. **(b)** *(despachar)* The last time I complained, the company palmed me off with a standard letter.

pass away VI *Eufemismo (pasar a mejor vida)* The old lady passed away in her sleep.

pass by 1 VI **(a)** *(pasar)* Luckily a taxi was passing by just at that moment. **(b)** *(pasar; el tiempo)* Time is passing by. Are you going to meet the deadline? **2** VIC *(pasar delante de)* We pass by that house every morning. **3** VTSS *(modismo)* Do you ever feel that life passed you by? (= «¿Has tenido alguna vez la sensación de que la vida se te ha ido de las manos?»).

pass off 1 VI **(a)** *(desarrollarse)* The ceremony passed off without a hitch. **(b)** *(desaparecer, pasarse)* Is the nausea passing off? **2** VTSEP *(hacer pasar por)* He passed her off as a duchess.

pass on 1 VI **(a)** *Eufemismo (pasar a mejor vida)* When did your father pass on? **(b)** *(pasar a)* Why don't we pass on to the next item on the agenda and come back to this later? **2** VTSEP *(pasar, una información)* Don't pass this on, but... *(pasar a, entregar a)* I passed the file on to him yesterday.

pass out 1 VI *(desmayarse)* One look at the needle and she passed out. -I must have passed out. **2** VTSEP *(repartir)* He passed copies of the memo out to the people at the meeting.

pass over 1 VTSEP *(no tener en cuenta, ignorar)* They've passed me over for promotion again. **2** VI *Eufemismo (ir a la otra vida)* The clairvoyant began to talk about «our loved ones who have passed over».

pass up VTSEP *(dejar pasar)* Imagine passing up a job like that! -She has had to pass up the offer.

patch up VTSEP **(a)** *(arreglar por encima, de momento)* I've managed to patch the car up so that it gets us into town at least. **(b)** *(atender rápidamente)* The army doctor just patched him up and sent him back to the front. **(c)** *(modismo)* to patch things up (= «hacer las paces»).

pay back VTSEP **(a)** *(reembolsar, devolver)* Have you paid that money back yet? **(b)** *(vengarse)* I'll pay you back for this!

pay off VTSEP **(a)** *(despedir)* The company is going to pay half its labour force off at the end of the month. **(b)** *(terminar de pagar)* When we've paid the mortgage off... **(c)** *(sobornar)* The policeman admitted to having been paid off.

pay out VTSEP **(a)** *(gastarse)* He's had to pay out a lot on car repairs lately. **(b)** *(pagar)* The wages were paid out this morning. **(c)** *(soltar, dejar; para referirnos a una cuerda)* Pay out some more line.

pay up 1 VTSEP **(a)** *(pagar, una deuda)* Has she paid up what she owes you? **(b)** *(pagar del todo)* My subscription is paid up. **2** VI *(pagar)* I've asked him twice to pay up but I'm still waiting.

pick off VTSEP **(a)** *(*retirar, quitar)* Why spend all that time putting nail varnish on when you just pick it off a day later? **(b)** *(recoger)* Pick those papers off the floor. **(c)** *(*coger, tomar)* The birds have picked all the cherries off. **(c)** *(derribar; en el tiro)* The sniper picked them off one by one.

pick on VIC **(a)** *(elegir)* Who have you picked on for your bridesmaid? -Why pick on me to answer? **(b)** *Fam. (meterse con)* Stop picking on the boy, he's doing his best.

pick out VTSEP **(a)** *(escoger)* I've picked out one or two patterns you might like. **(b)** *(reconocer)* She picked the man out from an identity parade. -I picked you out immediately, you were the only one wearing a red coat. **(c)** *(retirar, dejar a un lado)* Pick out any badly bruised fruit. **(d)** *(realzar)* The panels on the door are picked out in a deeper shade of the colour used on the walls. **(e)** *(tocar de oído; un ritmo, una música)* He can pick out a few tunes but that's all.

pick up 1 VTSEP **(a)** *(recoger)* He picked up a book and started to read. -Will you pick my prescription up at the chesmist's? -When did he say he would pick us up? The bus stopped to pick up passengers. **(b)** *(dar con, encontrar)* They picked that wonderful old table up at an auction. **(c)** *Fam. (ligar)* He goes around picking up women. **(d)** *(coger; enfermedades)* She's constantly picking up colds. **(e)** *(coger; costumbres)* That child has picked up some very bad habits. **(f)** *(aprender)* I'll never pick this game up. **(g)** *(detener, arrestar)* He's been picked up for shoplifting. **(h)** *(proseguir)* To pick up my story... **(i)** *(descubrir, hallar)* The police have picked up a trail that might lead them to the wanted man. *(coger, sintonizar)* You can pick up a lot of foreign stations with a short-wave radio. **(j)** *(corregir)* Please pick me up if I make any mistakes. **2** VTSS *(subir la moral, reanimar)* A tonic will pick her up. -What would really pick me up would be... **3** VI **(a)** *(mejorar)* The weather is picking up. -He's been quite ill but he's picked up in the last day or two **(b)** *(retomar)* Let's pick up where we let off. **(c)** *(hacer amistad)* I don't like that crowd you've picked up with.

pile up 1 VI **(a)** *(acumularse, amontonarse)* The work tends to pile up at this time of year. **(b)** *(atascarse; la circulación)* One of the lanes has had to be closed and traffic is piling up. **2** VTSEP *(poner en un montón)* Pile the leaves up there. *Fam. (amasar, acumular)* They're piling up the money.

pin down VTSEP **(a)** *(inmovilizar)* They were pinned down by wreckage. -He has his opponent pinned down on the canvas. **(b)** *(hacer que alguien concrete)* I've tried to pin her down to a time. **(c)** *(definir)* It's just one of those feelings that are very difficult to pin down. **(d)** *(identificar)* I was sure I had seen him before but I couldn't pin him down.

pipe down VI *Fam.* **(a)** *(cerrar el pico)* I wish you two would pipe down while I'm trying to watch television. **(b)** *(cerrar el pico)* Just pipe down about it, OK? -She finally piped down when she realized he knew more about it than she did.

play about/around VI *(jugar con, no tomarse las cosas en serio)* It's about time he stopped playing about and settled down. -You shouldn't play around with people's feelings.

play along 1 VI *(colaborar)* If that's what you've decided then I'm quite happy to play along. **2** VTSS *(utilizar; a una persona)* He's just playing her along until he gets what he wants.

play back VTSEP *(poner otra vez; una grabación)* Play that last bit back.

play down VTSEP *(restar importancia)* She played down the extent of her injuries. -The government is trying to play down its involvement.

play off 1 VTSEP *(poner a... en contra de...)* She's playing Phil off against Tom. -You take pleasure in playing people off against each other, don't you? **2** VI *(jugar el partido de desempate)* The two teams will play off next week.

play on 1 VI *(seguir tocando)* The orchestra played on despite the bombardment. **2** VIC *(jugar con, sacar provecho de)* He's just playing on your kindness with all those hard luck stories.

play out VTSEP **(a)** *(representar)* That was quite a scene they played out for our benefit. **(b)** *generalmente en voz pasiva (estar agotado, destrozado)* He's played out as a world class boxer. -I feel quite played out. **(c)** *(acompañar; en música)* The organist played the congregation out.

play up 1 VI *Fam.* **(a)** *(hacer de las suyas)* The car is playing up again. **(b)** *(hacer la pelota)* He plays up to anyone who can further his career. **2** VTSS *(dar la lata)* The baby has been playing me up all day.

plough back VTSEP *(reinvertir)* All the profits are ploughed back into the company.

plug in 1 VTSEP *(enchufar)* Plug the iron in. **2** VI *(enchufar)* It would help if you plugged in first!

plug up VTSEP *(rellenar)* That gap will have to be plugged up.

plump for VIC *Fam. (preferir, decidirse por)* I see you plumped for a car instead of a holiday.

point out VTSEP **(a)** *(señalar)* Can you point him out? **(b)** *(señalar, indicar)* She pointed out the extra work that this would entail.

point up VTSEP *(destacar, resaltar)* Why point up the difficulties?

poke about/around 1 VI **(a)** *(echar un vistazo, rebuscar)* Poke about and see what you can find. -The dog was poking about in the bushes. **(b)** *(meterse uno donde no le llaman)* That social worker is always poking about. **2** VIC *(revolver, rebuscar)* I love poking about antique shops.

poke out 1 VI *(salirse, asomar)* The label on your coat is poking out. **2** VTSEP **(a)** *(sacar)* She opened the window and pocked her head out. **(b)** *(sacar; con algo puntiagudo)* Careful or you'll poke my eye out!

polish off VTSEP *Fam. (terminar con)* You polished that plate of pasta off in record time! -The sports commentators feel that Lendl will polish this opponent off too.

polish up VTSEP **(a)** *(sacar brillo)* The silver needs to be polished up. **(b)** *(mejorar)* I'm going to evening classes to polish up my maths.

pop off VI **(a)** *Fam. (palmarla)* Guess who popped off last night? **(b)** *(partir; de imprevisto)* They're popping off for the weekend.

pore over VIC *(sumergirse en)* He spends all his time poring over old manuscripts.

pour out 1 VI *(salir en grandes cantidades)* Smoke was pouring out of the windows. *(salir a borbotones)* Once she had composed herself, the words just poured out. **2** VTSEP **(a)** *(servir)* Will I pour out the tea? *(echar, verter)* Pour some sugar out into a bowl. **(b)** *(soltar; contar)* I hope you didn't mind me pouring my troubles out like that.

print out VTSEP *(imprimir)* The text is edited on screen and then printed out to be sent back to the author.

prop up VTSEP **(a)** *(reforzar, sostener)* The've had to prop the castle walls up. -The regime is being propped up by the military. **(b)** *(Para meterse con alguien)* You can usually find him propping up the bar at his local. **(c)** *(apoyarse)* He propped himself up against the gate.

pull away 1 VTSEP *(sacar tirando de)* They had to pull the distraught father away from the burnig car. **2** VI **(a)** *(arrancar)* The train slowly pulled away. **(b)** *(alejarse, retirarse)* The dog pulled away when I tried to pat it. -Why do you keep pulling away? **(c)** *(ganar distancia)* She's beginning to pull away.

pull down VTSEP **(a)** *(bajar)* Pull the blind down. **(b)** *(demoler)* How many more buildings are they going to pull down? **(c)** *(debilitar)* This cold is really pulling me down. **(d)** *Am. Fam. (ganar; dinero)* Considering his qualifications, he doesn't pull down much of a salary.

pull in 1 VTSEP **(a)** *(atraer)* The play is pulling people in by the coach-load. **(b)** *(detener)* The police pulled him in for questioning. **2** VI **(a)** *(detenerse)* Pull in here. **(b)** *(meterse en)* We'll pull in to the next garage we see. **(c)** *(llegar; trenes o autobuses)* The express pulled in two hours late.

pull off VTSEP **(a)** *(*quitar, quitarse)* When I had pulled the paper off... -He pulled off his clothes. **(b)** *(lograr)* I never thought we would pull it off. -He has pulled off a remarkable achievement.

pull out 1 VTSEP **(a)** *(sacar tirando de)* I'm stuck in this mud, you'll have to pull me out. **(b)** *(sacar)* He's having a tooth pulled out tomorrow. **(c)** *(retirar)* The president has promised that all troops will be pulled out by the end of the year. **2** VI **(a)** *(salir; generalmente cuando se pasa al otro carril para adelantar)* Look in your mirror before you pull out. **(b)** *(salir, partir; en tren o autocar)* When do we pull out? **(c)** *(retirarse)* Troops have begun to pull out.

pull over 1 VTSEP **(a)** *(*ponerse, tirando de)* He pulled his sweater over his head. **(b)** *(tirar)* Be careful or you'll pull the filing cabinet over on top of you. **2** VI *(apartarse)* The policeman asked us to pull over. *(echarse a un lado)* She's pulling over to let the other runners past.

pull through 1 VTSS *(sostener, mantener)* He says it was his faith that pulled him through. **2** VI *(sanar, curarse)* I think we can confidently say that she will pull through.

pull together 1 VI *(colaborar)* We must pull together on this. **2** VTSS *(calmarse, recomponerse)* Come on, pull yourself together, there's a lot to be done.

pull up 1 VTSEP **(a)** *(acercar, traer)* He pulled up a chair and joined us. **(b)** *(subir)* Pull the blind up. **(c)** *(regañar, reprender)* She pulled him up about his bad language. -The police pulled him up for not having his lights on. **2** VI **(a)** *(pararse)* Why are you pulling up? -The horse pulled up lame. **(b)** *(acortar distancia, acercarse)* He is beginning to pull up, but I think he's left it too late.

push ahead VI **(a)** *(avanzar)* Research on this is pushing ahead in various countries. **(b)** *(seguir adelante; a pesar de las dificultades)* I think we should push ahead nonetheless.

push along 1 VTSEP *(empujar)* As she pushed the pram along... **2** VI *Fam.* *(largarse)* I suppose I should be pushing along soon.

push around VTSEP *Fam.* *(tratar a patadas)* I'm not going to let him push us around like this.

push for VIC *(luchar por)* The company is pushing for more government funding.

push off 1 VTSEP *(*quitar, empujando)* Push the lid off. **2** VI *Fam.* **(a)** *(marcharse)* Everyone's pushing off at five o'clock. -I wish you would push off and let me finish what I'm doing. **(b)** *(soltar amarras)* We pushed off in the early hours of the morning.

push on 1 VI *(seguir)* We decided to push on. **2** VTSEP **(a)** *(ponerse algo haciendo esfuerzos)* I had to push it on to make it fit. **(b)** *(animar)* Both runners are being pushed on by the crowd.

push through 1 VIC *(abrirse camino a través de)* We'll have to push through the crowd. **2** VTSEP* *(imponer, hacer aceptar)* The government is pushing this bill through.

push up VTSEP **(a)** *(levantar, empujando)* You have to push up the garage door. **(b)** *(elevar)* Excessive wage increases are pushing up inflation.

put about VTSEP *(hacer correr, un rumor)* Who put that rumour about? -It's being put about that...

put across VTSEP **(a)** *(exponer sus ideas)* He didn't put that across very well. -She's a politician who certainly knows how to put herself across *(es decir, imponerse)* **(b)** *(modismo)* to put one across somebody (= «*tomar el pelo a alguien*»).

put away VTSEP **(a)** *(guardar)* Put your wallet away, I'm paying for this. -Could someone put the car away for the night? **(b)** *(apartar, ahorrar)* She puts something away every month for the proverbial rainy day. **(c)** *(tragar, engullir)* This family puts away so much meat that I'm the butcher's favourite customer. **(d)** *(pimplarse)* He's down at the pub every night putting it away. -You're putting it away a bit, aren't you? **(e)** *(encerrar)* That maniac should be put away somewhere.

put back VTSEP **(a)** *(volver a poner)* Put that back where you found it. **(b)** *(retrasar)* The meeting's been put back till next month. **(c)** *(atrasar la hora)* Isn't this the week we put the clocks back?

put down VTSEP **(a)** *(dejar, poner)* Put that down before you drop it. **(b)** *(dejar, cuando se lleva a alguien en coche)* If you put me down at the next corner, I can walk the rest of the way. **(c)** *(aterrizar)* The pilot had to put the plane down on the motorway. **(d)** *(rebajar, disminuir)* We will put this uprising down with the utmost firmness. **(e)** *Fam.* *(criticar, hablar mal de)* He's always putting her down. -Why do you keep putting yourself down?

(f) *(matar; a un animal)* The cat's in a great deal of pain. - I think we should have put her down. **(g)** *(pagar, entregar)* How much do you have to put down as a deposit? **(h)** *(anotar)* Have you put all the details down? **(i)** *(atribuir)* She puts it down to laziness.

put forward VTSEP **(a)** *(proponer)* Somebody put forward the rather good idea that... -They've put him forward for a knighthood. **(b)** *(adelantar; una cita etc.)* The meeting has been put forward to noon today. **(c)** *(adelantar el reloj)* Did you put your watch forward?

put in 1 VTSEP **(a)** *(*meter; en una maleta, armario etc.)* Have you put everything in? **(b)** *(instalar)* We're finally having a telephone put in. **(c)** *(trabajar)* I put in a lot of overtime last month. -Don't you think you should put in a bit of piano practice? **2** VTSS *(apuntar a, inscribir)* We're putting him in for the 500 and 1000 metres. **3** VI *(presentar su candidatura)* Has he put in for that job we saw advertised?

put off 1 VTSEP **(a)** *(*dejar; cuando alguien lleva a uno en coche)* Could you put me off at the High Street? **(b)** *(*hacer bajarse)* The bus conductor put the boys off because of their behaviour. **(c)** *(retrasar)* Let's put lunch off to another time. **(d)** *(aplazar una cita con alguien)* You can't keep putting him off like this. - Just tell him you don't want to go out with him. **(e)** *(apagar, desconectar)* Put the TV off. **2** VTSS **(a)** *(quitar el gusto por)* Their stories have put me off foreign travel. -That programme on slaughter houses put him off meat for a week. **(b)** *(molestar)* You would think that all those people standing round watching would put her off.

put on 1 VTSEP **(a)** *(*ponerse; ropa etc.)* Put your coat on. -She put on her glasses. **(b)** *(adoptar, simular)* The boss can put on a show of being fierce. -She puts on a posh accent sometimes. -He's just putting it on. (*es decir, está simulando*) **(c)** *(poner; espectáculos)* They're not putting Hamlet on again? -Why can't they put on something decent on TV for a change? **(d)** *(engordar)* He's put on a few inches round the waist. **(e)** *(encender, conectar)* Put the radio on. **2** VTSS *(adelantar la hora)* We had to put our watches on several times when we flew to Australia.

put on to VTSSC *(indicar)* I can put you on to an excellent restaurant. *(poner sobre la pista de)* What put the police on to him as the culprit?

put out 1 VTSEP **(a)** *(sacar)* Don't forget to put the milk bottles out. **(b)** *(sacar, poner)* Have you put the side plates out as well? **(c)** *(tender)* She put her hand out. **(d)** *(publicar)* We'll be putting out a new edition very soon. **(e)** *(apagar)* Put the light out. **(f)** *(dormir; a un paciente)* The drug will put you out very quickly. **2** VTSS **(a)** *(enfadar)* Everyone was put out by the two hour delay. **(b)** *(molestar)* Would one more guest put you out? -I don't want to put anyone out. **(c)** *(dislocar)* Don't lift that table or you'll put your back out again.

put through 1 VTSEP **(a)** *(*hacer aceptar)* A bill has been put through Parliament that... **(b)** *(poner con; al teléfono)* Will you put me through to the book department, please? **2** VTSSC *(causar a)* You've put your mother through a great deal of anxiety with your behaviour.

put up VTSEP **(a)** *(levantar)* Put up your hand if you know the answer. **(b)** *(construir)* A new block of flats is being put up just behind their house.

(c) *(colgar)* I want to put up a few more pictures in this room. **(d)** *(subir)* Car manufacturers are putting their prices up again. **(e)** *(alojar)* Could you put us up while we're in town? **(f)** *(poner)* A lot of people have put their houses up for sale. **(g)** *(presentar, ofrecer)* They put up a lot of resistance. -She put up a good fight but had to concede defeat in the end.

put up with VIC *(soportar, aguantar)* Why do you put up with that kind of behaviour? -It's a lot to have to put up with.

Q

quieten down 1 VI **(a)** *(calmarse)* If you don't quieten down I'm going to get very cross. -Business always quietens down after Christmas. **2** VTSEP *(calmar)* It took me ages to quieten the class down. -The nurse tried to quieten the child down, but he kept crying for his mother.

R

rain off *(Am. = rain out)* VTSEP *generalmente en voz pasiva (anular a causa de la lluvia)* The match was rained off.

rattle through VIC **(a)** *(circular haciendo ruido)* The two old cars rattled through the streets. **(b)** *(hacer o decir a toda velocidad)* She tends to rattle through her work. -The speaker fairly rattled through his speech.

read out VTSEP *(leer en voz alta)* He read out the names of the injured.

read up on VIC *(leer sobre, empaparse de)* The play might have meant more to you if you'd read up a bit on the events it depicted.

rein in 1 VTSEP **(a)** *(refrenar)* The girl reined her pony in and turned back towards the stables. **(b)** *(reprimir)* He tried very hard to rein his anger in. *(restringir)* The council wants to rein in its spending on sports facilities. **2** VI **(a)** *(refrenar)* They reined in so they could talk. **(b)** *(ahorrar)* We'll have to rein in this month.

rest up VI *(reposar)* The doctor has told him to rest up.

ring back VI *Br. (volver a llamar por teléfono)* Could you ring back in half an hour?

ring in VI *Br. (llamar por teléfono)* You ought to have rung in to say you were ill and couldn't come to work.

ring off VI *Br. (colgar el teléfono)* I must ring off now, there's someone at the door.

ring out VI *(resonar)* Her voice rang out. -The church bells were ringing out.

ring up VTSEP *Br. (llamar a alguien por teléfono)* Why not ring her up and ask?

rip off VTSEP **(a)** *(*arrancar)* As soon as they got their hands on the presents, the children ripped the paper off. **(b)** *Pop. (sangrar, clavar)* Let's choose another restaurant. -I was ripped off the last time I was at this one.

rip up VTSEP *(partir en trozos)* Just rip this letter up and forget the whole business.

root for VIC *(apoyar, decantarse por)* Which side are you rooting for? -The candidate I root for invariably loses.

rough out VTSEP **(a)** *(erizar)* Don't rough up my hair. **(b)** *(atacar, pegar)* He was roughed up by some soccer fans. -They roughed her up a bit, but she's all right.

round down VTSEP *(redondear; hacia abajo)* The price will be rounded down.

round off VTSEP **(a)** *(redondear)* Round off the edges. **(b)** *(terminar)* We rounded the meal off with coffee and liqueurs. -She rounded off her presentation by saying...

round on VIC *(volverse hacia alguien; en actitud de ataque)* Rounding on his tormentors, he shouted...

round up VTSEP **(a)** *(reunir)* About this time of year the cattle are rounded up. -Round everyone up for the meeting, will you? **(b)** *(redondear; hacia arriba)* Just round the bill up to £50.

rub down VTSEP *(secar)* The groom will rub your horse down. -He rubbed himself down with a towel.

rub in VTSEP **(a)** *(frotar con)* Rub the cream in well. **(b)** *Fam. (restregarle algo a alguien)* She kept rubbing in his unpunctuality. -I know I was wrong - Don't keep rubbing it in!

rub off 1 VTSEP* *(borrar)* Rub those dirty marks off the wall. -The teacher rubbed the equations off the blackboard. **2** VI **(a)** *(salir; manchas)* The stain won't rub off. **(b)** *Fig. (pegársele a alguien)* I hope his attitude to authority doesn't rub off on you.

rub out VTSEP **(a)** *(quitar restregando)* Try rubbing the stain out with soap and water. **(b)** *(borrar)* Don't rub out your calculations. **(c)** *Pop. (liquidar, eliminar a alguien)* The gang decided to rub the witness out before she could talk to the police.

run about 1 VIC *(correr de un... a otro)* I refuse to run about the shops looking for presents for people I don't like. **2** VI **(a)** *(correr de un lado a otro)* The children were running about on the beach. **(b)** *(estar ocupado)* She's been running about all day preparing for her mother-in-law's visit.

run across VIC *(encontrarse con)* If you should run across John give him my regards. -I've run across a word I don't know.

run away with VIC **(a)** *(escaparse con)* I know it sounds ridiculous, but his wife has run away with the milkman! **(b)** *(escaparse llevándose algo)* The man in the butcher's has run away with the week's takings. **(c)** *(metérsele en la cabe-za; una actividad o una idea)* Jogging five times a week is what I call letting your enthusiasm run away with you. -If I'm not careful, she'll run away with the idea that I'm very easy-going. **(d)** *(llevarse, costar)* Repairs to the house have run away with most of our savings.

run back 1 VI **(a)** *(volver corriendo)* I ran back to the car. **(b)** *(volver con su pareja)* He'll come running back once he's had his fling. **2** VTSS *(llevar de vuelta en coche)* Don't worry about the last bus. - I'll run you back.

run down 1 VI **(a)** *(bajar las escaleras)* Run down and see who's at the door. **(b)** *(debilitarse)* The government is accused of letting the industry run down. **(c)** *(pararse; un reloj)* Don't wind the clock until it has completely run down. **(d)** *(descargarse)* You've let the battery run down. **2** VTSEP **(a)** *(atropellar)* She was run down by a bus. **(b)** *(hablar mal de)* You shouldn't run everyone down so. **(c)** *(descargar)* Remember to switch off the lights or they'll run the battery down. **(d)** *(disminuir la producción de)* The factory is being deliberately run down. **(e)** *(dar con)* The police finally run him down in Hove.

run in 1 VI *(entrar corriendo)* She came running in to tell us. **2** VTSEP **(a)** *Br.* *(rodar, hacer funcionar)* It will be another couple of weeks before we've run the new machine in. **(b)** *Fam. (parar)* The police ran him in for drunk driving.

run into VIC **(a)** *(chocar con)* He ran into an old lady as he raced for his train. **(b)** *(encontrarse con)* Guess who I ran into last week. **(c)** *(ascender a)* The cost will run into millions.

run off 1 VI **(a)** *(salir corriendo)* He ran off when he saw me coming. **(b)** *(irse, escaparse)* I haven't seen next door's dog for ages. - I hope he's run off. **2** VTSEP **(a)** *(sacar)* Will you run off six copies of this? **(b)** *(escribir a prisa)* She runs these magazine articles off in her spare time. **(c)** *(perder corriendo; peso)* He's a bit overweight and wants to run off a few pounds.

run out 1 VI *(acabarse)* Your time is running out. **2** VTSEP *(eliminar; en el cricket)* He was run out for ten.

run out òf VIC *(acabársele)* I have run out of patience with you. *(quedarse sin)* We're running out of butter. -With two miles to go we ran out of petrol.

run over 1 VI **(a)** *(acercarse a)* I won't be a minute, I'm just running over to the shops. **(b)** *(ocupar espacio de)* Television broadcasts of sports events often run over into the next programme. **(c)** *(salirse, desbordarse)* The sink is running over. **2** VIC *(dar un ligero repaso, examinar rápidamente)* The doctor will want to run over you case history. -Let's run over the arrangements one last time. **3** VTSS *(llevar en coche)* I'm running Mum over to Grandad's. - Do you want to come? **4** VTSEP *(atropellar, un vehículo)* He ran an old lady over.

run through 1 VIC **(a)** *(usar)* I hate to think how many clean shirts he runs through in a week. **(b)** *(repasar)* Would you like me to run through your speech with you? **2** VTSEP *(atravesar)* The coachman ran the highwayman through.

run up 1 VI **(a)** *(subir corriendo)* Run up and fetch my purse for me. **(b)** *(acudir)* People ran up to see if they could help. **2** VTSEP **(a)** *(despachar, hacer deprisa)* The dressmaker said she could run the suit up for me in a couple of days. **(b)** *(acumular)* You've run up a lot of bills this month. **(c)** *(izar; banderas)* They run the flag up on special occasions.

rush at VI **(a)** *(atacar, lanzarse a)* He rushed at the burglar. **(b)** *(hacer a lo loco)* It's not the kind of job that can be rushed at. - Take your time.

rush through 1 VTSEP **(a)** *(enviar urgentemente)* The necessary equipment has been rushed through to the rescue workers. **(b)** *(despachar rápidamente)* Could you rush my order through? **2** VTSSC **(a)** *(hacer pasar a toda marcha)* They rushed us through Customs. **(b)** *(hacer a alguien que termine algo rápidamente)* You rushed me through lunch and now you're rushing me through dinner. - What's the hurry?

rustle up VTSEP *Fam. (preparar un plato o una bebida a toda velocidad)* Could you rustle up a meal for me?

S

save up 1 VI *(ahorrar)* If you want a new motorbike you'll have to start saving up, won't you? **2** VTSEP **(a)** *(ahorrar, guardar)* You should save up part of your pocket money for Christmas presents. **(b)** *(apartar, guardar)* One of the children's programmes on TV has asked viewers to save up silver paper.

score off 1 VTSEP* *(tachar, eliminar)* Score his name off the guest list. **2** VIC *(marcarse un tanto a costa de)* The speaker scored off the government when he reminded them of their campaign promises.

score out VTSEP *(eliminar, borrar)* Score any mistakes out neatly.

scrape along VI *(arreglárselas; financieramente)* She's scraping along until her next pay cheque.

scrape by VI *(andar justo)* I don't mind scraping by, as long as I pass the exam. - He's just been scraping by since he lost his job.

scrape together/up VTSEP *(juntar, con dificultad)* I'll scrape the money together for you somehow.

scream out 1 VI *(pegar un grito)* The pain made him scream out. **2** VTSEP *(gritar)* The sergeant major screamed out his orders.

screw up VTSEP **(a)** *(arrugar, hacer una pelota)* She screwed the letter up and threw it in the fire. **(b)** *(fruncir, arrugar)* Don't screw your face up like that. **(c)** *(fastidiar, destrozar)* This rush job has screwed up my plans for the weekend. -You screwed the whole thing up. - Next time let me do the talking. **(d)** *(destrozar los nervios)* He claims it was his parents that screwed him up. -She's all screwed up that girl.

see about VIC *(ocuparse de)* You'll have to see about those cracks in the ceiling. **(b)** *(ver, considerar)* I'll see about it. *(irónico)* So they're going to win, are they? Well, we'll see about that.

see across VTSS *(esperar hasta que alguien cruce)* She saw me across the road.

see in 1 VI *(ver lo de dentro)* They always keep the curtains drawn so people can't see in. **2** VTSEP *(acompañar a alguien que entra)* Always see guests in.

see off VTSEP *(despedir, en la estación, aeropuerto etc.)* Who's coming to see you off?

see out 1 VI *(ver lo de fuera)* Another passenger changed seats with the little boy so he could see out. **2** VTSEP **(a)** *(acompañar a la puerta)* My husband will see you out, doctor. **(b)** *(aguantar, resistir)* I don't think my boots will see the winter out.

see over/round VIC *(visitar)* Would you like to see over our new house?

see through 1 VIC *(no dejarse engañar por, ver que no es cierto)* Why do you persist with these stories? Everyone can see through them. **2** VTSS *(apoyar, ayudar)* Friends and neighbours are seeing them through this bad time. -A couple of hundred gallons of oil should see us through the winter.

see to VIC *(ocuparse de)* Let your husband see to the baby. - You relax for a bit.

see up VTSEP *(acompañar a una planta superior)* Do you know where his room is or do you want me to see you up?

seize up VI **(a)** *(atascarse)* If you don't put some oil in soon the engine will seize up. **(b)** *(anquilosarse)* My knee always seizes up at the most inconvenient times.

seize (up)on VIC *(aprovechar, tomar)* It seemed like an excellent idea and we seized on it immediately.

sell off VTSEP *(hacer liquidación, saldar)* The shoe shop is closing down soon and has started to sell off its stock.

sell out 1 VTSEP **(a)** *generalmente en voz pasiva (no tener existencias)* How can a supermarket be sold out of butter? **(b)** *(vender, traicionar)* The rebel leaders were accused of selling their supporters out. **2** VI **(a)** *(terminar las existencias)* All of the shops I tried had sold out. **(b)** *(liquidar)* They're selling out since they want to retire. **(c)** *(traicionar)* We will negotiate but we will never sell out.

sell up 1 VTSEP *generalmente en voz pasiva (verse forzado a vender)* Something has to be done to prevent farmers being sold up and losing their livelihood. **2** VI *(vender, hacer liquidación)* Since she can no longer run the business on her own, she has decided to sell up.

send away VTSEP *(mandar)* A boy of seven is too young to be sent away to school.

send away for VIC *(soliticar por correo)* Send away for your free gift now. -You should send away for an application form.

send down VTSEP **(a)** *(mandar; hacia abajo)* The people upstairs sent a lovely cake down for us. **(b)** *(bajar)* The rumours have sent share prices down. **(c)** *Br. Fam. (meter en chirona)* The judge sent her down for two years. **(d)** *Br. (expulsar de la universidad)* All of the students involved in the incident were sent down for a term.

send for VIC *(llamar, hacer venir)* I think we should send for the doctor.

send in VTSEP **(a)** *(mandar, enviar)* A lot of viewers have sent in comments on the programme we aired last week. **(b)** *(hacer entrar)* Send Mr Martin in as soon as he arrives please.

send off VTSEP **(a)** *(mandar por correo)* Have you sent that letter off yet? **(b)** *(*expulsar; en fútbol)* He was sent off for spitting at the referee.

send on VTSEP **(a)** *(hacer llegar)* Would you send on any letters that come for me? **(b)** *(enviar; con anterioridad a algo)* We've decided to send our luggage on so we don't have as much to carry.

send out VTSEP **(a)** *(expulsar, echar)* The teacher sent him out of the classroom for talking. **(b)** *(mandar)* I've forgotten to buy milk but I'll send one of the kids out for it. **(c)** *(emitir)* The satellite has stopped sending out signals. **(d)** *(enviar por correo)* Those invitations should have been sent out a week ago.

send out for 1 VIC *(pedir que le traigan algo a uno)* Do you want to send out for a sandwich? **2** VTSS *(pedir a alguien que traiga algo)* Send the office junior out for coffee.

send up VTSEP **(a)** *(lanzar al cielo, al espacio)* The crew sent up a distress rocket. **(b)** *(subir, ascender)* News of the takeover bid sent up the company's share prices. **(c)** *(ridiculizar)* Politicians are very easy to send up. -Don't you know when you're being sent up? **(d)** *Am. Fam. (meter en chirona)* He was sent up for armed robbery.

serve out VTSEP **(a)** *(repartir, servir)* The soup kitchen needs volunteers to serve food out. **(b)** *(completar, terminar)* Dad had only just served out his apprenticeship when the war started.

set about VIC **(a)** *(ponerse a)* She set about the washing up. **(b)** *(empezar a)* Be sure to take expert advice before you set about rewiring the house. **(c)** *(atacar, arremeter; física o verbalmente)* The old lady set about the boys with her stick. -Mum set about me for leaving my room in such a mess.

set against VTSSC **(a)** *(poner en contra de)* Something must have set him against the idea. -It was her friends who set her against me. **(b)** *(desgravar)* Some expenses can be set against taxes. **(c)** *(analizar a la luz de)* We must set the government's promises against its performance in the past.

set apart VTSEP *(diferenciar, distinguir)* What sets her apart from all the other children in my class is...

set aside VTSEP **(a)** *(apartar, dejar a un lado)* Could you set aside what you're working on and do this instead? -I've decided to set aside some money every week. -Setting that particular aspect of the issue aside... **(b)** *(anular)* The Supreme Court has set aside the decision.

set back VTSEP **(a)** *(retirar)* They set the frontage back a few feet. -The cottage is set back quite a bit from the road. **(b)** *(atrasar)* The strike has set the company back at least a month in its deliveries. **(c)** *Fam. (salirle a uno por, costarle)* That new car must have set him back a bit. -Will it set me back more than a thousand?

set down VTSEP **(a)** *(poner, dejar)* You can set those cases down in the hall. **(b)** *(dejar; cuando se lleva a alguien en un medio de transporte)* The bus stopped to set down one or two passengers. **(c)** *(fijar; legalmente)* Permissible levels of pollution are set down in the regulations. **(d)** *(anotar)* The policeman set down the details in his notebook.

set forth VTSEP *(presentar)* Would you like to set forth your suggestions to the committee? -This document sets forth a detailed description of...

set in VI **(a)** *(declararse)* The doctors are worried that gangrene might set in. **(b)** *(llegar)* Winter seems to be setting in early this year.

set off 1 VTSEP **(a)** *(hacer estallar)* Terrorists have set off yet another bomb in a crowded street. **(b)** *(arrancar, encender)* What set the argument off? **(c)** *(hacer llorar; tanto de alegría como de tristeza)* That last joke of his set us all off. -If you say any more you'll only set her off again. -He's so allergic to pollen that even a vase of cut flowers sets him off. **(d)** *(realzar)* Those velvet curtains really set the room off. **(e)** *(obtener compensación)* Can I set these expenses off against my tax liability? **2** VI *(partir, salir de viaje)* We'll have to set off at dawn.

set on 1 VTSSC *(echar, lanzar; algo a modo de ataque)* If you don't get off my land immediately, I'll set the dogs on you. **2** VIC *(atacar)* Travellers were often set on by highwaymen.

set out 1 VTSEP **(a)** *(presentar, disponer)* The desserts were set out on a trolley in an eye-catching display. **(b)** *(fijar, señalar)* This document sets out the steps that must be taken. **2** VI **(a)** *(partir, salir de viaje)* They set out late last night. **(b)** *(empezar)* I didn't realize when I set out just how long the job was going to take me. **(c)** *(modismo)* to set out to do something (= «*proponerse hacer algo*»).

set to 1 VI *(ponerse manos a la obra)* Isn't it about time that we set to and cleaned out the garage? **2** VIC *(empezar)* When are the builders going to set to work?

set up 1 VI **(a)** *(establecerse)* They've decided to set up in business for themselves. -She's setting up as a hairdresser. **(b)** *(hacerse pasar por)* He sets himself up as a poet. **2** VTSEP **(a)** *(instalar, montar)* Marquees will be set up on the front lawn. **(b)** *(fijar, una cita)* I'd like to set up an appointment with the doctor. **(c)** *(colocar, acomodar)* He's set her up in a flat of her own. **(d)** *(formar, organizar)* A task force will be set up to investigate the matter. **(e)** *(causar, provocar)* These pills won't set up a reaction, will they? **(f)** *Fam. (dársela a alguien)* There's no point in claiming you were set up, no-one will believe you.

settle down 1 VI **(a)** *(colocarse, instalarse)* I had just settled down with a book when the phone rang. **(b)** *(calmarse)* Now settle down, children. **(c)** *(concentrarse en)* He must settle down to his homework. **(d)** *(asentarse)* When are you going to settle down and get married? **2** VTSEP **(a)** *(poner, colocar, acomodar)* Just let me settle the baby down for the night. **(b)** *(calmar)* I couldn't settle my class down at all today.

settle for VIC *(aceptar algo en lugar de otra cosa)* We haven't got any brandy, I'm afraid. - Will you settle for Scotch? -Is that a fixed price for the house or would the seller settle for less?

settle in 1 VI *(adaptarse, hacerse a)* How are you setting in in the new house? - He'll soon settle in at the job. **2** VTSEP* *(integrar, acomodar)* I'm just going to settle the new secretary in and then I'm having a holiday. -Do you want us to come over and help settle you in?

settle on VIC *(fijar; después de pensárselo)* Have you settled on a date for the wedding yet?

settle up VI **(a)** *(pagar la cuenta)* Can I leave you to settle up? **(b)** *(hacer cuentas)* He said he would settle up with us later.

shake off VTSEP* **(a)** *(quitarse algo de encima sacudiéndolo)* Shake the snow off your coat before you come in. **(b)** *(quitarse de encima)* I can't seem to shake this cold off. **(c)** *(librarse de)* She shook the detective off by going into the ladies and leaving by a back door.

shake up VTSEP **(a)** *(agitar)* Shake it up a bit, all the solids are at the bottom. - Don't shake the champagne up. **(b)** *(sacudir; cojines, almohadas etc.)* Let me shake your pillows up for you. **(c)** *(conmocionar)* The news of the accident shook her up. -I was badly shaken up for my narrow escape. **(d)** *(estimular)* This committee needs shaking up a bit. -This will shake their ideas up.

shell out VTSEP *Fam. (soltar, apoquinar)* I'm not going to shell out any more on that motorbike of his. -How much do we each have to shell out for petrol?

shoot down VTSEP **(a)** *(derribar)* He was shot down over France. The guerrillas claim to have shot down three planes in the last week. **(b)** *Fam. (hacer trizas, pisotear)* She shot his argument down. -If he doesn't like your proposal he'll shoot it down.

shoot out 1 VI *(surgir, emerger, salir de pronto)* Bulbs are shooting out all over the garden. **2** VTSEP *(tender rápidamente)* She shot out her hand and grabbed him before he could fall.

shoot up 1 VI **(a)** *(dispararse, subir rápidamente)* House prices have shot up in the last year. **(b)** *(levantarse, alzarse)* Hands were shooting up all over the room to ask questions. **(c)** *(chutarse)* A government poster showing kids shooting up. **2** VTSEP *(destruir mediante bombardeos)* The runways are so badly shot up that they are unuseable.

shop around VI *(comparar precios)* It pays to shop around.

shout down VTSEP *(desaprobar, rechazar)* Union members shouted down management's proposal. -Don't shout her down. - Listen to what she has to say.

show off 1 VI *(fardar)* He was flexing his muscles and generally showing off. **2** VTSEP **(a)** *(presumir de)* I think I'll go for a drive round town and show the new car off. **(b)** *(destacar)* Wearing white always shows off a tan.

show up 1 VI **(a)** *(verse)* The dirt really shows up on a pale carpet. **(b)** *Fam. (presentarse, aparecer)* He showed up wearing a new suit. -She's always showing up late. **2** VTSEP **(a)** *(demostrar, hacer ver)* The loss of export markets shows up the company's failure to modernize. **(b)** *Fam. (poner en evidencia)* I don't want you showing me up in front of people, so don't tell any of your crude jokes. **(c)** *(acompañar; a una planta superior)* The porter will show you up to your room.

shrug off VTSEP *(hacer caso omiso de)* He shrugs off all criticism.

shut away VTSEP *(encerrar)* He's been shut away in prison for the last year. -Ever since her husband's death, she has shut herself away.

shut down VTSEP y VI = **close down**

shut in VTSEP* *(encerrar)* Shut the dog in.

shut off 1 VTSEP **(a)** *(apagar)* Shall I shut the television off? **(b)** *(aislar)* Don't they feel shut off living in the depths of the countryside? **2** VI *(desconectarse)* I want a kettle that shuts off automatically.

shut out VTSEP **(a)** *(dejar fuera)* The door's locked. - They've shut us out. -Close the door and shut the noise out. **(b)** *Fig. (mantener aparte)* People want to help. - Why do you insist on shutting them out? **(c)** *(ocultar, tapar)* We're going to plant some trees to shut out the view of the railway line.

shut up 1 VTSEP **(a)** *(encerrar)* Shut the cat up somewhere. - You know Mrs Williams is allergic. **(b)** *(cerrar)* They're away shutting up their cottage for the winter. **(c)** *Fam. (callar, tranquilizar)* Shut those kids up. I'm trying to concentrate. **2** VI *Fam. (cerrar la boca)* Don't tell me to shut up!

shy away VI *(alejarse, echarse atrás)* She shied away when he tried to put his arm around her.

shy away from VIC *(evitar; por temor)* He has shied away from driving ever since the accident.

sift out VTSEP **(a)** *(tamizar)* Sift out any impurities. **(b)** *(eliminar, hacer una criba)* We have sifted out the most obviously unsuitable candidates.

sign away VTSEP *(renunciar a; mediante la firma)* Read the small print to be sure you're not signing away any of your rights.

sign for VIC *(firmar la recepción de)* There's a registered letter for you. Will you sign for it please?

sign in 1 VI *(firmar la entrada)* It's a rule of the club that all visitors must sign in. **2** VTSEP *(meter a alguien, conseguir que alguien entre)* I'm a member, so I can sign you in.

sign off VI **(a)** *(finalizar la emisión)* They usually sign off for the day at midnight. -He always signs off with that catch phrase. **(b)** *Fam. (expresión utilizada al final de una carta = te/le dejo)* I think I'll sign off now and go to bed.

sign on VI *Br. (apuntarse, fichar)* How long do you have to be out of work before you can sign on? -I have to sign on every Monday.

sign up 1 VTSEP *(enrolar)* The committee wants to sign up more volunteers to help with the fund drive. **2** VI **(a)** *(meterse al ejército)* My uncle tried to sign up when he was only 15. **(b)** *(apuntarse; a un curso)* She has signed up for a class in car maintenance.

simmer down VI *(calmarse)* I'll tell you what he said once I've simmered down.

single out VTSEP *(elegir, seleccionar)* Why single her out for praise? - We all contributed to the success of the project.

sink in VI **(a)** *(filtrarse, ser absorbido)* Pour the syrup over the cake and allow it to sink in. **(b)** *(ser entendido)* His remark didn't sink in until she was halfway down the stairs.

sit about/around VI *(esperar de brazos cruzados)* We had to sit about in the airport lounge for two hours.

sit back VI **(a)** *(sentarse cómodamente)* Now sit back and watch the next episode of our thriller. **(b)** *(quedarse de brazos cruzados)* We can't just sit back if we think something's wrong next door.

sit down 1 VI *(sentarse)* You'd better sit down. - I've got some bad news. **2** VTSS *(sentar)* The doctor sat her down and explained the operation.

sit in VI **(a)** *(ocupar un edificio; en acto de protesta)* Students used to sit in regularly in the sixties. **(b)** *(sustituir)* The chairwoman is ill and has asked me to sit in for her at the meeting.

sit on VIC **(a)** *(ser miembro de)* How many people sit on the congress? **(b)** *(mantener en secreto)* Reporters were asked to sit on the news until the hostages were safely out of the country. **(c)** *(guardarse; una información etc.)* The company decided to sit on the consultant's recommendations. **(d)** *Fam. (cortar a alguien; no dejarle que hable)* I'm sorry I had to sit on you like that but you were about to be indiscreet.

sit out VTSEP **(a)** *(quedarse sentado en un baile)* I'd rather sit this one out. **(b)** *(resistir hasta el final)* We sat the concert out to the bitter end but it didn't get any better.

sit up 1 VI **(a)** *(sentarse recto)* She was sitting up in bed when I arrived. -Sit up straight for goodness sake and don't slouch! **(b)** *(incorporarse)* Sit up! - I've brought you breakfast in bed. **(c)** *(quedarse despierto)* We sat up until midnight waiting for them to arrive. **2** VTSS *(sentar, incorporar)* The nurse sat the old man up.

size up VTSEP *Fam. (juzgar)* She looked round the room, sizing everyone up.

skim off VTSEP* *(sacar la crema; también en sentido Fig.)* He always skims off the best applicants for his department.

slap on VTSEP* *Fam.* **(a)** *(poner de cualquier forma)* Just slap some paint on and that will hide the marks. **(b)** *(añadir)* I bet the government slaps some more on the cost of a pint in the next budget.

sleep around VI *Fam. (acostarse hoy con uno mañana con otro)* Aids has stopped people sleeping around.

sleep in VI **(a)** *Fam. (quedarse en la cama hasta tarde)* I always sleep in on Sunday. **(b)** *(vivir interno en el lugar donde se trabaja)* She has two maids sleeping in.

sleep off VTSEP *(dormir; una borrachera etc.)* He's upstairs sleeping his hangover off.

sleep on **1** VI *(seguir durmiendo)* Let her sleep on for as long as she likes. **2** VIC *(consultarlo con la almohada)* You don't have to make your mind up now. Sleep on it and then call me.

sleep together VI *(acostarse con alguien)* When did you start to sleep together?

sleep with VIC = *(acostarse con alguien)* She's been sleeping with him for a year.

slip away VI *(marcharse/pasar sin que alguien se dé cuenta)* She slipped away from the party. -The time just slips away when I'm with him.

slip by **1** VI *(pasar rápido)* The time has slipped by. **2** VIC *(pasársele a uno algo)* How did that mistake manage to slip by you?

slip in **1** VI *(entrar sin llamar la atención)* He slipped in to the room. **2** VTSEP *(hacer, soltar)* She slipped in a remark about...

slip off **1** VI *(marcharse sin llamar la atención)* We didn't see you go. - When did you slip off? **2** VTSEP *(quitarse rápidamente)* She slipped off her coat.

slip on VTSEP *(ponerse)* She slipped a dress on and ran to answer the door.

slip out VI **(a)** *(salir; generalmente cuando se hace sin llamar la atención)* We slipped out halfway through the concert. **(b)** *(escapársele un comentario a alguien)* She's very apologetic about giving the secret away. -It just slipped out when she was talking to him.

slip up VI *Fam. (meter la pata)* Slip up one more time and you're fired.

slow down/up **1** VI *(reducir velocidad)* Slow down! There's a speed limit here. - Slow down. - I can't understand what you're saying. **2** VTSEP *(hacer ir más despacio)* Can't you walk any faster? You're slowing everyone down.

smooth down VTSEP **(a)** *(alisar)* The duck smoothed down her ruffled feathers. **(b)** *(calmar, tranquilizar)* He's really very upset. Give me a few minutes to smooth him down.

smooth out VTSEP **(a)** *(eliminar, arrugas, dobleces etc.)* She smoothed out the creases from the tablecloth. **(b)** *(resolver)* We have a little problem we hope you can help us smooth out.

smooth over VTSEP *(restar importancia, suavizar)* The chairman smoothed over the dispute with a light remark.

snap out VTSEP *(decir bruscamente)* The sergeant snapped out an order.

snap out of VIC *(salir de; estados de ánimo)* You must snap out of this depression.

snap up VTSEP *Fam. (tirarse a, caer sobre; objetos a la venta a muy buen precio)* The towels are so cheap people are snapping them up.

snarl up VTSEP *(bloquear)* Because of the accident, traffic is all snarled up on the motorway.

snow under VTSSC *Fam. generalmente en voz pasiva (abrumar, inundar)* We have been snowed under with requests for a repeat of the programme about bird migration.

soldier on VI *(perseverar, proseguir)* I know you're very tired, but if you could soldier on till the project is finished, I'd be very grateful.

sort out VTSEP **(a)** *(colocar)* I've sorted out all those tools that you had just thrown in the drawer. **(b)** *(retirar, quitar)* The women on the production line sort out the flawed goods with incredible speed. **(c)** *(resolver)* Maybe he needs some psychiatric help to sort out his problems. **(d)** *Pop. (decir cuatro cosas a alguien, darle lo que se merece)* It's about time someone sorted him out.

sound off VI *(quejarse de)* She is always sounding off about rude shop assistants.

sound out VTSEP *(preguntar la opinión a alguien)* I want to recommend you for the job but I thought I should sound you out first and see if you'd be interested.

spell out VTSEP **(a)** *(deletrear)* It's rather an unusual name, so I'll spell it out for you. **(b)** *(explicar algo de forma muy clara)* The chairman spelled out what a strike would mean for the company's future. -Do I have to spell it out for you?

spin out VTSEP **(a)** *(estirar, hacer que algo dure)* Can you spin the housekeeping money out until the end of the month? **(b)** *(prolongar)* I'd like to spin my leave out for another couple of days.

splash down VI *(amerizar; naves espaciales)* The capsule splashed down at 13.00 hours just off Haiti.

splash out VI *Fam. (ser generoso, gastar sin duelo)* Let's splash out for once and stay in the best hotels.

split up 1 VTSEP *(repartir)* We're going to split the money up among our children. **2** VI *(separarse; una pareja)* I hear they're splitting up.

spring up VI *(surgir, salir)* Weeds are springing up all over the garden after the rain. -The company sprang up almost overnight.

square up VI **(a)** *(hacer cuentas)* Can we square up later? -I'll square up with you when I get paid if that's all right. **(b)** *(llegar casi a las manos)* The two men were so angry with each other they began to square up. **(c)** *(hacer frente)* It was wonderful the way you squared up to that bully.

stamp out VTSEP *(aplastar)* The military government has vowed to stamp out unrest.

stand by 1 VI **(a)** *(quedarse al margen)* People just stood by and watched the policeman being beaten up. **(b)** *(estar a la espera)* Viewers were told to stand by for further developments. **2** VIC *(mantener, respetar)* The government has promised to stand by its election promises.

stand down VI *(retirarse)* He will stand down as chairman of the football club at the end of the year.

stand for VIC **(a)** *(presentarse a)* I have decided to stand for the chairmanship of the committee. -She is standing for election. **(b)** *(significar)* In a recipe, «tsp» stands for teaspoonful. **(c)** *(tolerar)* I won't stand for that kind of behaviour.

stand in VI *(reemplazar)* Mr Wilson has very kindly agreed to stand in at short notice for our scheduled speaker.

stand out VI **(a)** *(sobresalir, destacarse)* He is so tall that he stands out in a crowd. -What makes her stand out is... **(b)** *(resistir)* We are standing out against management's attempts to break our strike.

stand up 1 VI **(a)** *(levantarse)* Everyone stood up when the president entered the room. **(b)** *(tener valor, tenerse en pie; una afirmación, teoría etc.)* The prosecution hasn't got enough evidence for the charge to stand up. **2** VTSEP *(dar un plantón)* Poor old Tom, that's the second time this month she's stood him up.

stand up for VIC *(luchar por, defender)* My parents stood up for me when I was in trouble. -Stand up for what you believe in.

stand up to VIC *(hacer frente a)* I admired the way she stood up to that aggressive drunk.

start off 1 VI *(salir)* The runners will be starting off in the coolness of the early morning. *(empezar)* To put your audience at ease, start off with a joke or two. **2** VTSEP **(a)** *(empezar)* Start your presentation off with a brief history of the problem. **(b)** *(hacer que alguien/algo empiece)* There's the baby crying again. - What started her off this time?

start up 1 VI **(a)** *(arrancar)* She heard a car starting up next door. **(b)** *(abrir; un negocio)* There's a new dry cleaner's starting up on the corner. **2** VTSEP **(a)** *(arrancar)* Start the engines up. **(b)** *(abrir)* They're starting up another restaurant.

stay off 1 VI **(a)** *(quedarse en casa y no ir al trabajo a la escuela)* He's decided to stay off and see if he can cure this cold. **(b)** *(esperar, no decidirse; el mal tiempo)* Do you think the rain will stay off until the washing's dry? **2** VIC *(no ir a)* Can I stay off school today?

stay out VI **(a)** *(no volver a casa)* What do you mean by staying out until this time of night? **(b)** *(continuar la huelga)* The women have decided to stay out until their demands are met.

step in VI *(intervenir)* The government should step in and order the strikers back to work.

step up VTSEP *(acelerar, aumentar)* Research into this disease must be stepped up. -The company is stepping up production of the vaccine.

stick around VI *Fam. (estar localizable)* Stick around, we may need you.

stick out 1 VI **(a)** *(sobresalir, salirse)* The label on your dress is sticking out. -His ears stick out. **(b)** *(hacerse notar)* She sticks out because of the way she dresses. **2** VTSEP *(sacar por)* Stick your head out the window and see if they're coming.

stick to VIC **(a)** *(pegarse a, estar pegado a)* The cloth is sticking to the table. **(b)** *(seguir, mantener; un plan, una decisión etc.)* She's sticking to her plans despite her parents' opposition. -It's a very tough programme of work. - Do you think you'll stick to it? **(c)** *(contentarse con, ceñirse a)* If red wine gives you a headache, stick to white.

stop by VI *(pasarse por un sitio)* Stop by at the post office on your way home. - We'll stop by and see you next week.

stop off VI *(hacer un alto)* They're stopping off at Bali for a couple of days on their way back.

stop over VI *(hacer escala)* We stopped over at Manchester on the flight to Toronto.

straighten out 1 VTSEP **(a)** *(estirar, alisar)* She straightened out the crumpled bedclothes. **(b)** *(aclarar)* We need to straighten out a few things out in this relationship. **2** VI *(hacerse recto, enderezarse; un camino etc.)* After twisting and turning for a couple of hundred yards, the path finally straightened out.

straighten up 1 VTSEP **(a)** *(poner recto)* He cannot pass a picture on the wall without straightening it up. **(b)** *(poner en orden)* Straight your room up a bit. It's very untidy. **2** VI *(estirarse, erguirse)* She straightened up and rubbed her back.

strike back VI *(responder)* The government struck back at its critics with a strong defence of its actions.

strike off VTSEP* *(tachar)* Your name has been struck off (the list).

strike out 1 VTSEP *(tachar)* Strike out whichever does not apply. **2** VI **(a)** *(golpear)* He struck out at his opponent. **(b)** *(ir en dirección hacia)* We are all tired, let's strike out for home. **(c)** *(independizarse, vivir su vida)* I'm striking out on my own.

strike up 1 VTSEP **(a)** *(empezar a tocar)* The orchestra struck up a waltz. **(b)** *(hacer)* They struck up a friendship at school. **2** VI *(empezar a tocar)* The band struck up.

string along VTSEP *Fam. (dársela a alguien)* That garage is just stringing you along. - The car can't possibly be repaired. -He just strung her along till he'd taken all her money and then he vanished.

string up VTSEP *Fam (colgar)* They should string child abusers up from the nearest lamp post.

strip down VTSEP *(desmontar de arriba a abajo)* The garage can't find the fault without stripping the engine down.

strip off 1 VTSEP *(hacer caer)* The wind stripped all the leaves off the trees. *(quitarse)* He stripped off all his clothes and jumped into water. *(quitar)* We'll have to strip off about six layers of paint from this door. **2** VI *(desvestirse)* Strip off and let the doctor examine you.

sum up 1 VTSEP **(a)** *(resumir)* The chairman summed up the committee's discussions. **(b)** *(evaluar, analizar; en el momento)* Summing up the situation, he... **2** VI *(recapitular)* When summing up, the judge warned the jury against...

summon up VTSEP *(armarse de; cuando se trata de valor, fuerza etc.)* I summoned up all my courage and asked to speak to the manager.

swallow up VTSEP *(tragar)* I watched them walk down the road and they were soon swallowed up by the mist. -The sea swallowed them up.

swear in VTSEP *(tomar juramento)* When the witness had been sworn in... -The new president was sworn in today.

swear out VTSEP **(a)** *(sudar, una enfermedad etc.)* Have a sauna and sweat your cold out. **(b)** *(soportar)* You were found guilty and now you're just going to have to sweat your sentence out.

switch back VI *(volver a)* We tried electricity but we've decided to switch back to gas.

switch off/on 1 VTSEP *(apagar/encender un mecanismo eléctrico)* Switch the radio off/on. **2** VI *(encenderse/apagarse)* Where does the power switch off/on?

switch over VI *(cambiar de canal o de emisora; radio o televisión)* Shall I switch over? The news is on the other side.

switch round VTSEP *(cambiar de sitio)* Someone switched the drinks around and the Duchess got the poison by mistake.

T

tail away/off VI *(perderse, difuminarse)* The noise of the lorry tailed away in the distance. *(descender de volumen poco a poco)* Her voice tailed off as she realized that no one was listening.

tail back VI *(estar un coche pegado a otro)* The traffic tailed back all the way to the intersection.

take aback VTSS *(sorprender, coger por sorpresa)* He quite took me aback with his insolence. -The enemy was completely taken aback by the speed of our attack.

take after VI *(parecerse a, salir a; los hijos respecto a sus padres)* Don't blame me, it's her father she takes after.

take apart VTSEP **(a)** *(desmontar)* The radio hasn't worked since he took it apart. **(b)** *Fam. (derrotar; en deporte)* Who would have expected the Wimbledon title-holder to be taken apart by a completely unknown player?

take around VTSEP* *(guiar, enseñar sitios)* Would you like someone to take you around?

take away 1 VI *(restar, quitar)* Having to go home by public transport takes away from the pleasure of going out. **2** VTSEP **(a)** *(restar)* What do you get if you take 28 away from 70? **(b)** *(llevar)* They took the man next door away in an ambulance last night. **(c)** *(comprar para llevar; alimentos)* How about some curry to take away?

take back 1 VTSEP **(a)** *(devolver, volver a poner en su sitio)* Take these library books back, will you? **(b)** *(recoger)* When is Tony coming to take those records you borrowed? **(c)** *(retirar, algo que se ha dicho anteriormente)* Now that I know her better, I take back all that I said about her. **(d)** *(aceptar de nuevo)* Will the shop take it back if it doesn't fit? -She's a fool to take him back. **2** VTSS *(transportar en el tiempo, recordar a alguien algo)* These old songs take me back to when I was a teenager.

take down VTSEP **(a)** *(descolgar, bajar, quitar)* It's time we took the curtains down for a wash. -Take all your posters down. **(b)** *(desmontar, retirar)* When are the workmen going to take down the scaffolding? -The shops still haven't taken down their Christmas decorations. **(c)** *(apuntar, tomar nota)* The reporter took down very little of what was said at the meeting.

take home VTSEP *(ganar; salario neto)* How much does she take home every week?

take in VTSEP **(a)** *(llevar)* Take your coat in to the cleaner's tomorrow. **(b)** *(alojar, dar cobijo)* They take in all the stray cats in the neighbourhood. -Taking in lodgers is not my idea of fun. **(c)** *(meter, acortar; prendas de vestir)* Could you take this skirt in? **(d)** *(recordar, memorizar)* He reeled off so many facts and figures that I couldn't take them all in. **(e)** *(incluir)* The Prime Minister's tour will take in a number of urban renewal projects. **(f)** *Am. (ir a ver)* Do you want to take in a movie? -Let's take a few of the sights first. **(g)** *(tomar el pelo, engañar)* He took the old lady in by telling her he had known her son. -Don't be taken in by appearances. (= «*No te dejes engañar por las apariencias.*»)

take off 1 VI **(a)** *(despegar)* We took off an hour late. **(b)** *Fam. (dispararse)* The company's sales really took off last month. **(c)** *Fam. (partir, salir)* They're taking off for France next week. *(salir del trabajo)* He's taking off early tonight. **2** VTSEP **(a)** (*quitarse)* Take your hat off. *(retirar)* The policeman was taken off the murder enquiry because he knew the people involved. **(b)** *(amputar)* They had to take her leg off below her knee. **(c)** *(rebajar)* The saleswoman took a pound off because of this stain. -He needs to take a few pounds off. *(es decir, necesita perder peso)*. **(d)** *(coger libre)* Why don't you take the rest of the day off? **(e)** *(imitar a)* He takes the president off extremely well.

take on 1 VI *Fam. (ponerse; estado de ánimo)* Don't take on so, he's not badly hurt. **2** VTSEP **(a)** *(echarse sobre la espalda; trabajo, responsabilidades)* When I married you I didn't realize I'd be taking on your whole family too. -She's exhausted with all the extra work she's been taking on recently. **(b)** *(contratar)* That new electronics firm took on 200 people this week. **(c)** *(enfrentarse a)* Why did you agree to take him on? - He's twice your size. -It was a mistake to take on the best snooker player in the club. **(d)** *(adoptar, tomar; una actitud o un rumbo)* His face took a cunning look. -Life has taken on a whole new meaning since I met you. **(e)** *(tomar, aceptar; medios de transporte)* The train made an unscheduled stop to take on passengers.

take out VTSEP (**a**) *(sacar)* If you want to work in the garage, you'll have to take the car out. -How much do you think we need to take out of our account? *(sacar, eliminar)* I'm having two teeth taken out tomorrow. -Washing won't take that stain out, the dress will have to be dry cleaned. (**b**) *(sacar, invitar)* He took her out to dinner at a very fancy restaurant. (**c**) *(sacar; certificados etc.)* Have you taken out insurance on the new car? -How about taking out a subscription to this computer magazine? (**d**) *(descargar)* Why should he take his anger out on us? (**e**) *(modismo: fatigar)* Kids take a lot out of you. -That really took it out of me. (**f**) *Fam. (destruir, arrasar)* Our men took out three enemy encampments.

take over 1 VI (**a**) *(tomar posesión; de un cargo o de las riendas de algo)* The new chairman will take over next week. (**b**) *(invadir todo)* We ought to do something about the garden, the weeds are taking over. **2** VTSEP (**a**) *(hacerse cargo de)* She will be taking over the running of the hotel. (**b**) *(*mostrar, enseñar)* A guide will take you over (the house).

take round VTSEP (**a**) *(llevar)* Take this cake round to your grandmother's for me. (**b**) *(*acompañar, mostrar)* The supervisor was asked to take the trade delegates round (the factory).

take to VIC (**a**) *(sentir inclinación por alguien)* I've never really taken to the people next door. (**b**) *(coger la costumbre de)* He has taken to treating me like an enemy. (**c**) *(huir a)* The outlaws took to the hills.

take up 1 VI *(coger, seguir)* To take up where I let off... **2** VTSEP (**a**) *(levantar)* During their search, the policemen even took up the floorboards. *(coger, alzar)* She took up the newspaper and pretended to read. (**b**) *(subir)* Take this tray up to your mother. (**c**) *(acortar)* These curtains need to be taken up a couple of inches. (**d**) *(tomar, ocupar)* I've taken up too much of your time. -The bed is so large it just about takes up the entire room. (**e**) *(tratar, discutir sobre)* I think you should take the question of training up with the personnel manager. (**f**) *(empezar; una actividad)* He must be mad taking up jogging at his age! (**g**) *(aceptar)* I'm going to take up that offer of a weekend in the country. (**h**) *(captar, coger)* Her sister took up the thread of the conversation.

take up on VTSS (**a**) *(tomar la palabra)* The Leader of the Opposition took the Prime Minister up on that last point. (**b**) *(aceptar; un ofrecimiento etc.)* If they don't take me up on this offer it's their loss, not mine. *(hacer cumplir, una promesa)* Have you taken him up on his promise of...? -I'll take you up on that sometime. (= «¡*Te tomo la palabra!*»).

take upon VTSSC *(hacerse cargo de)* You took that task upon yourself. -Why did she take it upon herself to call the police?

take up with VIC *(juntarse con; sobre todo con malas compañías)* I'm afraid he has taken up with a bad lot.

talk at VIC *(dirigirse a; de forma muy formal)* He tends to talk at people rather than to them.

talk away 1 VI *(hablar sin parar)* The old lady was talking away about her youth. **2** VTSEP *(pasarse charlando)* We talked half the night away.

talk back VI *(contestar; generalmente cuando se habla de niños respondones)* Don't talk back to your father!

talk down VTSEP *(dirigir el aterrizaje desde la torre de control)* The fog was so thick at the airport that several planes had to be talked down.

talk down to VIC *(hablar en tono condescendiente, como a un niño)* I wish she wouldn't talk down to me, I'm not stupid.

talk over VTSEP *(discutir algo)* They've decided to talk things over and see if they can reach some kind of agreement.

talk round 1 VTSS *(convencer)* Dad won't let me go to that pop concert. - Could you try talking him round? **2** VIC *(dar vueltas en torno a)* They seemed nervous about tackling the problem directly and just talked round it.

tamper with VIC *(manipular, hurgar)* After the car accident, he claimed that the brakes had been tampered with.

tangle up VTSEP **(a)** *(enredar, enmarañar)* The kitten tangled all the wool up. **(b)** *generalmente en voz pasiva (enredarse)* He got tangled up in the barbed wire when he tried to climb the fence. **(c)** *(meterse)* I'm sure she's tangled up in something dishonest.

tangle with VIC *Fam. (pelearse)* He tangled with a drunk about some stupid football game.

tear apart VTSEP **(a)** *(destruir, arrasar)* The country is being torn apart by civil war. **(b)** *(poner patas arriba)* The police tore the place apart looking for drugs.

tear away 1 VTSEP *(arrancar)* I tore away the wrapping paper. **2** VTSS *(separarse, despegarse)* If you can tear yourself away from that television for a minute...

tear into VIC *(arremeter contra)* The lion tore into the flesh of the deer it had killed. -The boss tore into me for being late for the meeting.

tear off VTSEP* *(arrancar, quitar, desprender)* She tore the label off the suitcase.

tear up VTSEP **(a)** *(romper en pedazos)* His letter made her so angry she tore it up and threw it in the fire. **(b)** *Fig. (romper, anular)* The football player threatened to tear up his contract if the club didn't pay him more.

tell off VTSS *(regañar)* I told him off for his impudence.

tell on VIC **(a)** *(repercutir de forma negativa)* The strain of waiting for news is telling on her. **(b)** *(delatar)* Mum knows about the practical joke we were planning. - Someone must have told on us.

thaw out VI **(a)** *(descongelarse)* Leave the meat to thaw out. *Fig.* **(b)** *(entrar en calor)* Have a cup of tea and thaw out. -He's pretty unsociable, but he does thaw out sometimes.

thin out 1 VI **(a)** *(perder pelo)* He's thinning out on top. **(b)** *(menguar)* Audiences are thinning out. -His hair is thinning out. **2** VTSEP *(entresacar)* Thin the plants out in the autumn.

think about VIC **(a)** *(pensar en)* It's strange that you should have phoned just when I was thinking about you. **(b)** *(pensar)* I'm thinking about going to the cinema tonight. - Do you want to come?

think back VI *(recordar; la acción de esforzarse en recordar)* The policemen asked him to think back and try to remember what had happened. -Thinking back, I don't believe we did send them a Christmas card.

think of VIC **(a)** *(pensar en, tener en consideración a)* It's about time she started thinking of herself instead of other people all the time. **(b)** *(acordarse de)* I can't think of his telephone number at the moment. **(c)** *(imaginarse algo)* Just think of it, a holiday in the Caribbean! **(d)** *(opinar de)* What do you think of the latest fashions? -I don't think much of their new house. (es decir, «*no me gusta demasiado*»). **(e)** *(ocurrírsele algo)* We wouldn't think of our daughter hitchhike across Europe on her own. -Who thought of coming to this restaurant? -I've though of a solution to the problem.

think out/through VTSEP *(reflexionar sobre)* Have you thought out the effect that this proposal will have on our employees? -Let's think things through.

think over VTSEP *(pensarse algo)* I told him I would think his offer over.

think up VTSEP *(ocurrírsele)* They've thought up a brilliant idea.

throw away VTSEP **(a)** *(tirar)* Throw those old papers away. **(b)** *(desperdiciar)* She threw away her chance of a place at university. -You're just throwing your money away buying all those records.

throw back VTSEP **(a)** *(devolver)* The fish was so small that the angler threw it back. **(b)** *(reclinar)* She threw her head back.

throw in VTSEP *(dejar; en un precio o condiciones mejores por una compra que se ha hecho)* The man in the furniture shop said that if we took the bed, he would throw in the mattress for thirty pounds.

throw off VTSEP **(a)** *(quitarse a toda prisa)* He threw off his outer clothes and jumped into the river. **(b)** *(librarse de, quitarse de encima)* I can't seem to throw off the virus.

throw out VTSEP **(a)** *(tirar)* Don't throw those photographs out. **(b)** *(rechazar, una propuesta)* After discussion, the committee threw the proposal out. **(c)** *(echar; por mal comportamiento)* The manager of the cinema threatened to throw the boys out if they didn't behave themselves.

throw together VTSEP **(a)** *Fam.* *(hacer de cualquier forma)* It's not very well made, it looks a bit thrown together. **(b)** *(meter; sin gran cuidado)* He threw some clothes together in a suitcase and raced to the airport. **(c)** *(unir, juntar; a personas)* Fate threw the two of them together. -On such a small cruise ship, everyone is thrown together, like it or not.

throw up 1 VI *Fam.* *(vomitar, devolver)* No wonder you threw up, mixing your drinks like that. **2** VTSEP *(dejar pasar, desperdiciar, desaprovechar)* Imagine throwing up a chance to go to the United States.

tick off VTSEP **(a)** *(marcar, señalar)* Will you tick people's names off as they come in to vote? **(b)** *Fam.* *(regañar)* The teacher ticked him off for being late.

tick over VI *(marchar, funcionar)* The restaurant is ticking over quite well.

tide over VTSS *(sacar del apuro)* Could you lend me five pounds to tide me over until the end of the week?

tie down VTSEP *(atar)* Children tie you down. -I don't want to be tied down to any specific date.

tie in VI *(casar, corresponderse con, encajar)* How does the suspect's story tie in with his wife's?

tie up 1 VI *(casar, encajar; una serie de cosas)* His debts, the robbery, and now a new car, ... it all ties up. **2** VTSEP **(a)** *(inmovilizar, un capital)* His money is tied up until he is twenty-five. -My capital is tied up in stocks and shares. **(b)** *(estar ocupado; a causa del trabajo)* She'll be tied up all this afternoon.

tighten up VTSEP **(a)** *(apretar, ajustar)* He bent to tighten up his shoelaces. **(b)** *(someter a controles más estrictos)* They're tightening up the rules on tax shelters. -The company has decided that security must be tightened up.

tip off VTSEP *Fam. (dar un/el soplo)* Someone must have tipped him off that the police were on their way. -The reporter was tipped off about an interesting story.

tone down VTSEP **(a)** *(dulcificar, suavizar)* We toned our original colour scheme down. **(b)** *Fig. (moderar, suavizar, bajar el tono)* The reporter was told to tone his article down or the paper would be sued.

top up VTSEP *(llenar)* He kept topping my glass up. *(volver a servir; una bebida)* Can I top you up?

touch down VI *(aterrizar)* Concorde touched down exactly on schedule.

touch up VTSEP **(a)** *(retocar)* This bit of the window frame needs to be touched up. -She's just gone to touch up her make-up. **(b)** *Fam. (meter mano)* If you don't stop touching me up I'll slap your face.

touch (up)on VIC *(tener en cuenta, mencionar)* His speech didn't even touch on the pollution problem.

toughen up VTSEP *(curtir, hacer más duro)* He's one of those parents who send their sons to boarding school to toughen them up.

trail away/off VI *(apagarse)* His voice trailed away with embarrassment.

trot out VTSEP *Fam. (venir otra vez con, volver a contar)* Don't trot out the same old excuses. -He's not going to trot that speech out again, is he?

try for VIC *(intentar obtener)* She is trying for a place at music school. -He's trying for the record.

try on VTSEP *(probarse)* I've been trying dresses on all morning.

try out VTSEP *(tener a prueba)* The football club is trying him out in goal. *(probar)* You can have the car for a day or two to try it out.

turn against 1 VIC *(ponerse en contra de)* Why have you turned against me? **2** VTSSC *(poner en contra de)* She claims that her ex-husband is turning their children against her.

turn back 1 VI *(dar marcha atrás, volver sobre sus pasos)* We turned back because the path had become too faint to follow. **2** VTSEP **(a)** *(impedir la entrada de)* The refugees were turned back at the border. **(b)** *(echar hacia* *atrás)* She reluctantly turned back the bedclothes and got up. **(c)** *(retrasar; un reloj)* We turned our watches back an hour.

turn down VTSEP **(a)** *(bajarse)* Since the rain had stopped, he turned his coat collar down. **(b)** *(reducir, bajar; la temperatura, el volumen)* Turn the gas down a bit. -Please turn the radio down, it's far too loud. **(c)** *(rechazar)* I've been turned down for that job I applied for. -She turned down his offer of a weekend in Paris.

turn in 1 VI *Fam. (irse a la cama)* It's late. - Why don't we turn in? **2** VTSEP **(a)** *(denunciar a la policía)* His former wife turned him in. **(b)** *(devolver)* At the end of the war, lots of soldiers kept their handguns as souvenirs instead of turning them in. -Hundreds of weapons were turned in during the amnesty.

turn off 1 VI *(girar; un vehículo)* You turn off at the second street on the left. **2** VTSEP **(a)** *(apagar, desconectar)* Be sure to turn the stove off. *(cerrar)* Who didn't turn the tap off? **(b)** *Fam. (dar asco)* People who pick their noses in public turn me off.

turn on 1 VTSEP **(a)** *(encender; cualquier aparato)* Turn the gas on for me. **(b)** *(excitar; a menudo con un sentido sexual)* Rock music turns her on. -He is turned on by her. **2** VIC **(a)** *(atacar/arremeter, repentinamente)* One of the dogs turned on her. -He turned on me when I suggested that he retire. **(b)** *(depender de)* The company's success turns on the skills of its employees.

turn out 1 VI **(a)** *(estar presente)* Not many people turned out for his funeral. **(b)** *(resultar)* It's one of those silly stories where the heroine turns out to be a lost heiress. **(c)** *(salir; referido al resultado)* How did the cake turn out? - Everything will turn out fine. **2** VTSEP **(a)** *(apagar)* It's time you turned the light out and went to sleep. **(b)** *(vaciar)* I turned out my handbag to look for my keys. **(c)** *(producir)* We're turning out 100 computers a day. **(d)** *(echar, expulsar)* The old man was turned out of his cottage.

turn over 1 VI *(darse la vuelta)* He turned over in bed. *(volcarse)* The lifeboat turned over and sank in seconds. **2** VTSEP **(a)** *(entregar)* The suspect was turned over to the police. -They have turned the running of the restaurant over to their son-in-law. **(b)** *generalmente sin separarse (ganar alrededor de, obtener unas ganancias de aproximadamente)* He must be turning over a good thousand a week.

turn round 1 VI **(a)** *(dar media vuelta)* He turned round and looked at her. **(b)** *Fam. (se utiliza para indicar que la acción que sigue ocurre de improviso)* -He just turned round and punched the other chap. -One day she'll just turn round and leave you. **2** VIC *(girar, tomar)* Turn round the next corner. **3** VTSEP **(a)** *(dar la vuelta; a una situación)* The company was headed for bankruptcy, but the new management team turned it round. **(b)** *(realizar, llevar a cabo)* How quickly can you turn this order round? **(c)** *(dar la vuelta a)* She turned the chair round and sat down.

turn up 1 VI **(a)** *Fam. (presentarse, llegar)* He always turns up late. -She turned up at the party with her new boyfriend. **(b)** *(aparecer; ser encontrado)* If you're sure that you lost it indoors, then it's bound to turn up one day. **(c)** *(producirse, tener lugar)* Things always have a habit of turning up when you least expect them to. **2** VTSEP **(a)** *(subirse)* He turned his collar up in the wind. **(b)** *(subir)* Turn the television up, will you, I can hardly hear. -Turn the heat up a bit.

U

urge on VTSEP *(animar, empujar a)* The marathon runner said he managed to finish the race only because the crowd urged him on. -Her family is urging her on to go to university.

use up VTSEP **(a)** *(terminar)* Use up the last of the milk before it turns sour. **(b)** *(agotar, gastar)* The children used up all their energy playing.

V

venture on VIC *(aventurarse a)* He refused to venture on any criticism of the book until he had read it.

verge on VIC *(estar al borde de)* I was verging on tears. -The sailors were told that their behaviour verged on mutiny.

vote down VTSEP *(rechazar; mediante el voto)* The amendment to the law was voted down.

vote in VTSEP *(elegir)* The other members of the committee voted her in as chairwoman.

vote on VIC *(someter a votación)* Union members will be asked to vote on management's latest offer. -It was voted on last night.

W

wade in VI *Fam. (meterse)* When the fight started, everybody waded in. -Our discussion wasn't really anything to do with her, but she waded in anyway.

wade into VIC *Fam.* **(a)** *(ponerse a)* He got up early and waded into the job of cleaning the windows. **(b)** *(ponerse furioso con alguien)* I'm sorry, I shouldn't have waded into you for something so minor.

wait behind VI *(quedarse esperando)* She volunteered to wait behind until the doctor came.

wait in VI *(quedarse; en un local)* I was late because I had to wait in for the telephone engineer.

wait on 1 VI *(seguir esperando)* He waited on in the hope that she would eventually arrive. **2** VIC *(servir)* The waitress who was waiting on them seemed to have vanished.

wait up VI *(esperar despierto)* Don't wait up, I'll be very late.

wake up 1 VI *(despertarse)* She woke up when the church bells started ringing. **(b)** *Fig. (querer abrir los ojos)* His mother never did wake up to the fact that he was a thief. **2** VTSEP **(a)** *(despertar)* Don't wake me up too early tomorrow. **(b)** *Fig. (despabilar, dar un meneo)* This country needs waking up.

walk into VIC **(a)** *(entrar)* She walked into the room. **(b)** *(caer, meterse)* The suspect walked right into the trap the police had set for him. **(c)** *(chocar con, darse con)* I almost walked into a lamp post.

walk off 1 VTSEP *(bajar; moverse para facilitar la digestión)* Let's go out and walk our Christmas dinner off. **2** VI *(irse, marcharse)* He walked off and left us standing there.

walk off with VIC *Fam.* **(a)** *(llevarse)* She walked off with all the first prizes for her flowers. **(b)** *(llevarse, robado)* The bank manager has walked off with a million pounds. **(c)** *(coger; algo que no nos pertenece)* Who keeps walking off with the scissors?

walk out VI **(a)** *(salir)* She walked out of the room. **(b)** *(abandonar)* You can't just walk out on your wife and children!

walk over VIC *(vencer, derribar)* The champion walked all over another opponent today.

walk through VIC *(pasar sin dificultad)* You'll walk through the job interview.

walk up VI **(a)** *(subir a pie)* The lift was out of order, so we had to walk up. **(b)** *(acercarse)* A complete stranger walked up and started talking to me.

warm up 1 VI **(a)** *(subir la temperatura)* I hope it starts warming up now that spring is here. **(b)** *(calentarse)* Tennis players get a couple of minutes to warm up before the match. **2** VTSEP **(a)** *(calentar)* Warm up some soup for yourself. **(b)** *(poner en ambiente)* The star of the show doesn't appear until the other acts have warmed the audience up. **(c)** *(animar, avivar)* Can't we do anything to warm this dinner party up?

warn off VTSEP* *(aconsejar lo contrario)* I was going to buy it but someone warned me off.

wash down VTSEP *(ayudar a tragar)* Have a glass of wine to wash your meal down.

wash off 1 VI *(desaparecer, en el lavado)* Do you think these stains will wash off? **2** VTSEP* *(quitarse algo lavándolo)* Just let me wash the oil off my hands.

wash out VTSEP **(a)** *(enjuagar)* Wash your mouth out please. **(b)** *generalmente en voz pasiva (anular a causa de la lluvia)* The women's tennis final has been washed out.

wash over VIC *(no afectar)* His mother's death seems to have washed over him. -Anything I say just washes over her.

wash up 1 VI **(a)** *Br.* *(fregar los cacharros)* Whose turn is it to wash up? **(b)** *Am.* *(lavarse)* Don't serve supper until I've washed up. **2** VTSEP **(a)** *Br.* *(fregar, cacharros)* Why I am always left with the greasy pots to wash up? **(b)** *Fam. generalmente en voz pasiva (estar acabado)* He's washed up as a boxer. **(c)** *(arrastrar a la orilla; el mar)* A body was found washed up on the beach.

watch out VI *(prestar atención, tener cuidado)* Watch out for bones when you're eating the fish. -Watch out - you nearly broke the window.

water down VTSEP **(a)** *(regar)* Water this down with a drop of soda, will you? *Fig.* **(b)** *(suavizar)* The drama critic accused the editor of watering his review down.

wave down VTSEP *(echar el alto)* He didn't see the policeman waving him down.

wave on VTSEP *(hacer un gesto para que se continúe)* The border guard waved them on without looking at their passports.

wear away VTSEP *(erosionar)* The sea is wearing the coastline away.

wear down VTSEP **(a)** *(gastar)* I've worn the heels of my shoes down. **(b)** *(agotar)* She is worn down by looking after all those children.

wear off VI *(desaparecer)* The effect of the anaesthetic is wearing off.

wear out 1 VTSEP **(a)** *(utilizar)* That's the second pair of shoes he's worn out in six months. **(b)** *(agotar)* She's wearing herself out with the preparations for her daughter's wedding. **2** VI *(desgastarse)* The carpet is wearing out.

weed out VTSEP *Fig. (eliminar)* We have weeded out the least promising candidates.

weigh down VTSEP **(a)** *(sobrecargar)* Don't weigh me down with anything more to carry. *Fig.* **(b)** *(apesadumbrar)* They are both weighed down with grief.

weigh in VI **(a)** *(pesarse)* The champion weighed in at just under the limit. -Have you weighed in yet? **(b)** *(intervenir, meterse en la conversación)* I wish she wouldn't keep weighing in with comments that are totally irrelevant.

weigh up VTSEP *(hacerse una idea)* He boasts that he can weigh people up with a single glance. -Weighing up the situation, she...

while away VTSEP *(pasar el rato)* How did you while away all those hours you had to spend in the airport lounge?

whip away VTSEP *Fam. (retirar, quitar; de forma brusca)* The waiter whipped our plates away before we'd finished eating.

whip out *Fam.* **1** VTSEP *(sacar de forma brusca)* He whipped out his wallet. **2** VI *(acercarse corriendo)* I'm just whipping out to the car for my briefcase.

whip round *Fam.* VI **(a)** *(acercarse a)* Whip round to the chemist's for me. **(b)** *(hacer una colecta)* We whipped round to get a retirement present for him.

whip up VTSEP **(a)** *(conmover)* Such speeches are intended to whip an audience up. **(b)** *(atraer, conseguir)* What can we do to whip up support for the campaign? **(c)** *(batir)* Whip up some cream. -Make an omelette by whipping up some eggs. **(d)** *Fam. (hacer a toda prisa, en un tris tras)* I whipped a meal for them.

whisk away VTSEP **(a)** *(ahuyentar con la mano)* Whisk the wasps away from the jam. **(b)** *Fam. (salir disparado)* The president was whisked away by helicopter.

whittle away VTSEP *(hacer brecha en)* She is whittling away her opponent's lead. -Support for the government is being whittled away by its evident failure to control inflation.

whittle down VTSEP *(conseguir reducir)* We've whittled the number of candidates down.

win back VTSEP *(volver a ganar)* He won back all the money he had lost the previous week.

win out/through VI *(salirse con la suya)* He finally won out over his parents' objections. -We won through in the end.

win over/round VTSEP **(a)** *(convencer)* They're trying to win me over to the idea of a holiday abroad. **(b)** *(conquistar, seducir)* She is charming and has quite won us over.

wind down **1** VTSEP *(reducir progresivamente)* The company has decided to wind down its operations in that part of the world. **2** VI *(llegar a su fin, dar los últimos coletazos)* We went home since the party was winding down.

wind up **1** VTSEP **(a)** *(dar cuerda)* The clock needs to be wound up. **(b)** *(terminar, poner fin)* We wound up our holiday with a weekend in Paris. **(c)** *Fam.* *(tomar el pelo a)* He really wound her up with those remarks about her dress. -Don't you know when you're being wound up? **2** VI = **end up**

winkle out VTSEP *Fam. (sacar, sonsacar)* I finally winkled the information out of him. -It's no good trying to winkle any money out of me.

wipe off VTSEP* *(borrar)* The teacher wiped the equation off the board. -Wipe that grin off your face!

wipe out VTSEP **(a)** *(borrar)* She has completely wiped out the memory of the crash. -The power failure wiped out three weeks' keyboarding. **(b)** *(dilapidar)* His gambling debts wiped out his entire fortune. **(c)** *(agotar)* I feel wiped out. **(d)** *(destruir, deshacer)* Enemy fire wiped out the village. -Whole families have been wiped out by the disease.

work in VTSEP **(a)** *(mencionar)* I think we should work something in about the help we received from other people. **(b)** *(añadir, incorporar)* Work the other ingredients in.

work off VTSEP *(dejarse; el mal humor, la energía)* She worked her anger off on the squash court.

work on VIC **(a)** *(trabajar en)* He is working on a new project. **(b)** *(basarse en)* We'll have to work on what we have. **(c)** *(convencer)* I've tried working on him but without much success.

work out **1** VI **(a)** *(ascender)* How much do you make that work out to? **(b)** *(funcionar, ir bien)* That relationship will never work out. **(c)** *(hacer ejercicio)* She's been working out all morning. **2** VTSEP **(a)** *(resolver)* Once you've worked out the problem... -They'll have to work things out between themselves, I'm not getting involved. **(b)** *(concebir, idear)* He's worked out a plan.

work up VTSEP **(a)** *(experimentar, sentimientos)* I can't work up any enthusiasm for this project. **(b)** *(ilusionar)* She was getting all worked up at the prospect of a holiday.

work up to VIC *(prepararse para, tomar fuerza para)* He's working up to proposing marriage to her. *(preparar, idear)* It was easy to see what she was working up to.

wriggle out of VIC *(quitarse de encima, librarse de)* Why did you let them wriggle out of doing their homework? -You can't wriggle out of this one.

write away for VIC *(escribir solicitando algo)* If you want to know more, write away for our free brochure.

write in VI *(mandar cartas)* A great many viewers have written in with their comments about last week's programme.

write off 1 VTSEP **(a)** *(anular)* His debts have been written off. **(b)** *(criticar duramente)* The critics wrote the play off. **(c)** *(dejar hecho trizas; coches etc.)* She wrote her father's car off. **2** VI *(solicitar por correo)* I've written off for tickets.

write out VTSEP **(a)** *(redactar)* Have you written out your essay? **(b)** *(firmar)* Just write me out a cheque. **(c)** *(completar, preparar)* The shop assistant wrote out the receipt. **(d)** *(eliminar un papel en una obra de teatro)* Her part has been written out.

write up VTSEP *(preparar, escribir)* He's writing up a report on his business trip.

Z

zap up VTSEP *Fam. (retocar; para mejor)* The prose style could do with a bit of zapping up. -They've certainly zapped up the colour scheme.

zero in on VIC **(a)** *(ir derecho a)* The missile zeroes in on its target from a range of... **(b)** *(poner el dedo en)* They immediately zeroed in on the one weak point in the argument.

zip up 1 VTSEP *(cerrar con cremallera)* She zipped her skirt up. -Zip me up, will you? **2** VI *(cerrarse con cremallera)* The dress zips up at the back.

ÍNDICE

- Los códigos en este índice de verbos remiten a los modelos que aparecen explicados en las páginas 8 a 10.
- El código P9 indica que el verbo es irregular (ver págs. 13 a 18).
- Los verbos terminados en -ate y en -ize se conjugan siempre según el modelo P4, por ello no aparecen.
- Por lo que se refiere a los verbos que empiezan por de-, dis-, is-, out-, over-, re- y un- téngase sólo en cuenta el segundo elemento.
- (Am.) indica que la ortografía del verbo en cuestión en inglés americano aparece indicada en el verbo modelo P5.

Este ejemplar se terminó de imprimir en Abril de 2016,
En COMERCIALIZADORA DE IMPRESOS OM S.A. de C.V.
Insurgentes Sur 1889 Piso 12 Col. Florida
Alvaro Obregon, México, D.F.